90°
80°
FLORIDA
GULF OF MEXICO
25°
Grand Bahama I.
Great Abaco I.
New Providence I.
BAHAMA ISLANDS
Eleuthera I.
Nassau
Andros Islands
Cat I.
Rum
Long I.
Exuma I.
Acklin I.
Straits of Florida
Habana
Channel of Yucatan
CUBA
GREATER
Zapata pen.
Isle of Pines
YUCATAN
20°
Isla Cozumel
Little Cayman
Grand Cayman
Cayman Brac
Santiago de Cuba
JAMAICA
Kingston
Swan Is.
Islas de la Bahia
CARIBBEAN
15°
HONDURAS
NICARAGUA
Old Providence
St. Andrew
10°
COSTA RICA
Panama Canal
PANAMA
COLOMBI
PACIFIC OCEAN
90°
80°

THE WEST INDIES

*Area enclosed by dotted line comprises
the West Indies as a faunal region*

70°

60°

25°

Scale of Miles

| 0 | 50 | 100 | 200 | 300 | 400 |

ador I.
(ling)

Mayaguana I.

Caicos Is.

Turks Is.

Great Inagua

20°

Tortue I.

ANTILLES

St. Thomas

Anegada

Anguilla

St. Martin I.
St. Bartholomew

HAITI

DOMINICAN
REPUBLIC

San Juan

Barbuda

au
Prince

Mona

PUERTO
RICO

St. Croix

Saba

St. Eustatius
St. Christopher
(St. Kitts)

Nevis

Antigua

Montserrat

Santo Domingo

Désirade

HISPANIOLA

Guadeloupe

Marie Galante

LESSER
ANTILLES

Dominica

15°

Martinique

St. Lucia

SEA

Barbados

St. Vincent

Grenadines

Carriacou

Aruba

Curaçao

Bonaire

Grenada I.

Isla
Margarita

Tobago

Trinidad

10°

VENEZUELA

70°

60°

THE PETERSON FIELD GUIDE SERIES®

Edited by Roger Tory Peterson

DR = Dominican Republic 3/28/97 to
4/5/97

THE PETERSON FIELD GUIDE SERIES®

A Field Guide to Birds of the West Indies

JAMES BOND

Illustrated by

DON R. ECKELBERRY
ARTHUR B. SINGER
EARL L. POOLE

Fifth Edition

*Sponsored by the National Audubon Society,
the National Wildlife Federation,
and the Roger Tory Peterson Institute*

HOUGHTON MIFFLIN COMPANY

Boston   New York

1993

To my many friends
in the West Indies in
appreciation of their
hospitality and
assistance

For information about permission to reproduce selections from
this book, write to Permissions, Houghton Mifflin Company,
215 Park Avenue South, New York, New York 10003

PETERSON FIELD GUIDES and PETERSON FIELD GUIDE SERIES
are registered trademarks of Houghton Mifflin Company.

Library of Congress Cataloging-in-Publication Data is available.

ISBN 0-395-67701-7(cl)

ISBN 0-395-67669-X (pa)

Fifth American Edition
1993 Impression
Printed in Hong Kong
VB 10 9 8 7 6

Contents

Contents

List of Plates

Coloured illustrations of over half of the species known from the West Indies are included in the various published guides to birds of eastern North America.

Preface

The primary purpose of this book is to enable the reader to identify in the field the various birds that inhabit the West Indies. I also hope that it will serve as a stimulus to further research, in particular on the life-histories of the endemic species, which have been inadequately studied, although the Antilles are in other respects better known ornithologically than any other tropical region.

The avifauna of the West Indies is fundamentally and predominantly "tropical North American", derived for the most part from Central America. Many of the native birds will be more or less familiar to the visiting ornithologist from the north. The northern element is so well represented here that the reader is advised to have on hand one of the standard field guides to North American birds to supplement this book, for such a work will contain coloured plates depicting over half of the species found in the West Indies! *A Field Guide to the Birds* by Roger Peterson, and *Birds of North America* by Robbins, Bruun, Zim and Singer are the most useful for this region, with many illustrations of immature plumages as well as summer and winter plumages of adults.

Area covered: The West Indies are considered to include the Bahama Islands, Greater Antilles, the Cayman and Swan Islands, Old Providence and St. Andrew in the south-west Caribbean, and the Lesser Antilles south to Barbados and Grenada (see inset map). This area comprises two fairly distinct "provinces", the Greater Antillean (including the Bahamas and extending east to the Virgin Islands) and the Lesser Antillean.

A Guide to the Birds of Trinidad and Tobago by Richard ffrench should be acquired by the visitor to these islands. Trinidad and Tobago, politically part of the West Indies, have a South American or neotropical fauna. The number of indigenous genera of land birds would be approximately doubled if these two islands were regarded as part of the West Indies. There is an Antillean element among the birds of Bonaire, Curaçao and Aruba, but many are of South American derivation. For those interested in the birds of the latter islands, I recommend the well-illustrated *Birds of the Netherlands Antilles* by K. H. Voous, the revised English version published in 1983.

My survey of the avifauna of the West Indies began in 1926 and has since continued intermittently. The longest periods were spent in Cuba

Fig. 1 Diagram of a Bird

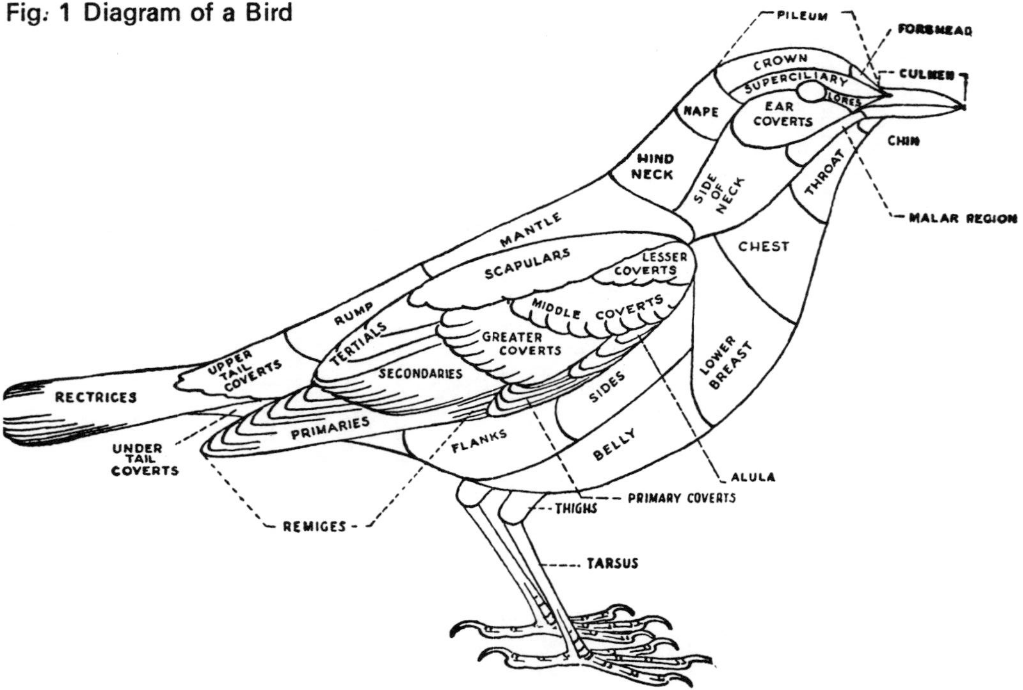

and Hispaniola, the largest and least known of the Antilles. Virtually the entire area was explored fairly thoroughly with the exception of some of the more southern Bahamas. Of the native West Indian species of birds and those known to have been successfully introduced prior to 1930 I encountered approximately 98 per cent in life.

In late years I visited many extralimital islands in the Caribbean primarily to determine the extent of the Antillean element in their avifauna. Included among these were Cozumel (Mexico), the Turneffe Cays (Belize), Bay Islands (Honduras), the Dutch "Leeward Islands", Venezuelan Islands from Los Roques to Los Testigos, Trinidad and Tobago. None of these islands could properly be included in the Antillean Subregion, a conclusion also reached by workers in other fields of natural history.

Technical names: Scientific nomenclature follows closely that of my *Check-list of Birds of the West Indies* (ed. 4, 1956, and supplements), Peters' volumes of the *Check-list of Birds of the World*, and Hellmayr's volumes of the *Catalogue of Birds of the Americas*. No novel treatment is presented, for this would be out of place in a popular book of this kind. Some taxonomists prefer to stress differences rather than similarities between various species or groups of species, and physiological rather than morphological characteristics in their treatment of closely related, allopatric insular forms. This would result in the addition of many more species than I have recognised. Generic sequence follows for the most part that adopted by the *A.O.U. Check-list of North American Birds* (1957).

English names: A number of English names differ from those used in my previous books (*Birds of the West Indies*—1936; *Field Guide to the Birds of the West Indies*—1947) in order to conform more closely with those employed in Mexico and Central America, as well as in current North American bird guides. In a few instances I have felt it necessary to coin a new name for the sake of euphony or appropriateness, but only for an endemic West Indian species. Where a name of any other bird differs from that applied elsewhere the scientific name will indicate its identity.

Local names: Knowledge of vernacular West Indian names of birds should be helpful, particularly in locating the rare or local species. In this book the English names appear first, followed by the Spanish and French. The inhabitants of the Dutch islands of the Lesser Antilles speak English, which accounts for the absence of Dutch names. Actually, the number of local names of birds in the West Indies is infinite, and many readers of this book will come across some on the islands that are not listed, although those widespread in use are included. Any woodsman, or "maître-bois" as he is called on a French-speaking island, knows most of the resident birds, and there are names that have been in use for centuries. However, it is well to bear in mind that a West Indian when asked the name of a bird he does not know is apt to conjure up one that he thinks is suitable. The North American migrants have for the most part no specific local names in the West Indies.

Illustrations: The paintings by Mr. Eckelberry and Mr. Singer depict many of the more remarkable and exotic birds of the West Indies, whereas the line-cuts by Dr. Earl L. Poole represent other native species and a few North American migrants. Where the sexes differ markedly adult males have been selected unless otherwise stated. The aforementioned *Birds of North America* and *Birds of the West Indies* include coloured illustrations of nearly three hundred species described in the main text of this book, and black-and-white drawings of the majority of the remainder.

Description: As aids to identification, the plates and line-cuts are of paramount importance. These were prepared from specimens kindly loaned to the artists by the American Museum of Natural History and the Academy of Natural Sciences of Philadelphia. The written descriptions are brief and cover specific diagnostic features. Subspecies are virtually ignored, although striking geographical variations in colour and size within a species are of course mentioned. Thus when describing the Mangrove Cuckoo, specimens of all the seven West Indian races were before me and the remarks on plumage are sufficiently general to cover the lot. A description of a particular species does not necessarily apply to an extralimital form. I have used this method because of its simplicity and because subspecific characters are usually trivial and often involved. The reader who is interested in ascertaining what subspecies he encounters is referred to my Check-list already mentioned. Descriptions point out marked differences in the adult sexes, but immature plumages are discussed briefly if at all. When adults are known, it is usually possible to recognise individuals in immature plumages by their structural features, if not by colour; but some of the North American migrants, in particular among the wood-warblers, are often impossible to identify in the field when in first winter plumage.

All species known to occur in the West Indies, apart from recent introductions, are included in this book, and all are described with the exception of some of the vagrants or rare visitants.

Voice: Song and call-notes of birds are difficult to describe, but they are important to learn, for in tropical forest and shrubbery more birds are apt to be heard than seen. Since most of the North American migrants

rs and Petrels

ed Grebe

hat of Least Grebe.
ke that of preceding species.
ghout the West Indies. Also North, Central and South

ERS & PETRELS *Procellariidae*

arwaters are essentially oceanic, passing all their time a
ng the breeding season. Even when nesting, they are no
near land by day, although at night their peculiar wailing
ard in the vicinity of their burrows. Their food consist:
fish and squids.

hearwater
inieri

imleco; Wedrego;
otin; Rié; Cahen.
–12″. This shear-
brownish black
parts mostly white;
e entirely sooty.
surface of the sea
ides. Fig. 4.
pulled out of its
not apt to be seen
ticularly numerous
Grenadines.
s in burrows or in
ne white egg is
rly spring.
the Bahamas,

Fig. 4 Audubon's Shearwa

---

black throat-patch and
band on bill. The upper-
parts are dark greyish
brown, the underparts mostly white. The *pale bill with
rounded culmen* is diagnostic.
Fig. 3.
Voice: A rapid, cuckoo-like
cow-cow-cow, etc., slowing
up at end. Also, more
subdued murmurings.

---

are not vociferous while in the West Indies, descriptions of their voices
are given in only a few instances. Most birds have a varied repertoire of
songs and call-notes, and many such sounds heard by the reader will
differ from those that I have attempted to describe in this book. Since
syllabic renderings of bird voices are even at best unsatisfactory, the
reader is urged to acquire George Reynard's series of records entitled
Caribbean Bird Songs, currently being produced by the Cornell Laboratory
of Ornithology.

Habitat: Paragraphs on habitat should be particularly valuable in locating
the rarer native species. Although most West Indian land birds (virtually
all those of Jamaica and Puerto Rico) may be found along or near the
roadsides, there are a few that may be encountered only after rather
lengthy trips on foot, by horse, or by boat. Two interesting excursions
of this kind are to Santo Tomás in the Zapata Swamp of Cuba, and to
the Morne La Selle ridge in south-eastern Haiti. At the former locality,
reached by boat from Batabanó, may be seen a peculiar rail, wren and
sparrow, in addition to many water-fowl widespread in range. On the
high mountains of the Massif de la Selle, best reached by horse from
Kenscoff or Furcy, one may see Hispaniolan Trogons, White-winged
Crossbills and Antillean Siskins among the pines, La Selle Thrushes,
White-winged and Ground Warblers, and Chat-Tanagers among the
bracken and shrubbery. Black-capped Petrels breed in winter on the steep
cliffs; but one may now go to both these places by car.

Most of the commoner species are widespread, occurring in both
mountains and lowlands. Apart from Hispaniola, birds that are primarily
montane are apt to occur at elevations well below a thousand feet, particularly during the winter months.

Nidification: Brief accounts of the nests and eggs of West Indian birds
are given. Since nests of a particular species often vary greatly in different
localities, the materials used in their construction are rarely mentioned.
Unless the colour or markings of spotted eggs are unusual, such eggs are
described merely as "spotted". Figures indicating clutch-size pertain to
normal sets so far as known.

There is no well-marked breeding season for many of the commoner
West Indian birds, such as hummingbirds, bananaquits and grassquits, but
for the rarer land birds the height of this season is in spring, from April
until June. The season is somewhat later in mountainous districts than
in the lowlands.

Range: Although the ranges of native West Indian birds, apart from
widespread forms, are presented more or less in detail, those of North

American migrants are admittedly sketchy. For example, a North American species widespread east of the Rocky Mountains may be said to inhabit merely "eastern North America". The North American book that should be used in conjunction with the present one will have more detailed information on the breeding ranges of those species that are winter residents or transients in the West Indies. Note that a few of these have been recorded throughout the year on the islands, but with the exception of certain waders, none is likely to be seen between mid-May and mid-July. Recent minor changes in dates of occurrence of migratory species and new island records of little import are omitted. Most of these have been published in the latest supplements to my Check-list.

Interior excursions: The following suggestions are submitted for those willing to undertake trips to more remote districts or to primitive "out-islands". For lowland use a hammock is a necessity, being cool, clean and comfortable. This should be covered with mosquito netting. In the mountains, blankets or sleeping-bags are called for, since it becomes chilly and damp at night at high altitudes even in summer. In any inhabited district staple foods, including vegetables and fruit, can be procured, but it is advisable to carry some extra provisions. I have never found it necessary to boil water for drinking purposes in the West Indies, but in some lowland districts it may be wise to do so.

Natives on all the islands are extremely pleasant and hospitable, and one should accept and reciprocate as far as possible the many courtesies that are offered to strangers. Some country people can be helpful in locating rare birds or other animals.

Conservation: In conclusion, I wish to stress the fact that a number of West Indian birds are very rare and in danger of extinction. This is particularly true of the Lesser Antilles. A continued open season on pigeons may eventually result in the extermination of the four splendid parrots on these islands, for though they are protected by law I have noticed that most native hunters will shoot any large, edible bird or other animal that they encounter. Were it not for the protection afforded by the Luquillo National Forest Preserve in Puerto Rico, the parrot of that island would by now have become extinct. I therefore suggest that the island authorities create game sanctuaries under the supervision of wardens, where no shooting of any kind is permitted, for I am convinced that sanctuaries are the only means of preserving some of the more remarkable West Indian birds and mammals for posterity.

The Academy of
Natural Sciences
of Philadelphia

GREBES *Podicipedidae*

Grebes comprise a small, cosmopolit
When seen from afar they somewh;
tinguished by their pointed bills an
they infrequently take to wing, pref;
under water they propel themselves
consists of small fish, crustaceans, aq
species are native to the West Indie;

Least Grebe *Podiceps domin*

Local names: Diver; Hell Diver; Diving Dapper; Tigua; Zaramagullón; Zaramagullón Chico; Plongeon; Petit Plongeon.
Description: 9–10″. Readily identified in all plumages by its *small size*. The *slender bill*, black in the adult, also serves to distinguish this species from the Pied-billed Grebe, which it somewhat resembles in colour, for the white wing-patch c in the field; iris light orange or y
Voice: A chattering; also a repe;
Habitat: Prefers fresh-water pon;
Nidification: Nest a mass of deca; located where the water is shall merely attached to its surroundi; ture. Eggs (usually less than 6) d but soon become nest-stained.
Range: Greater Antilles, and the (unrecorded from Grand Baham; America to South America.

Pied-billed Grebe *Podily*

Local names: Diver; Hell Diver; lón; Zaramagullón Grande; P
Description: 13–15″. When not
B.W.I.

Fig. 3 Pied-bil

Habitat: Like
Nidification: L
Range: Throu
America.

SHEARWA

Petrels and she
sea, except dur
likely to be see;
cries may be h;
mainly of flyin;

Audubon's S
Puffinus lherr

Local names: ;
Pampero; Diab
Description: 1;
water is dark
above, the unde;
rare dark pha
Flies close to th;
and frequently ;
Habitat: Unless
nesting burrow,
except at sea. Pa;
in vicinity of the
Nidification: Ne;
rock crevices.
laid, usually in e
Range: Nests

Virgin Islands, Lesser Antilles and at Old Providence Island; also on extra-limital islets. Among the Antilles, occurs west to Navassa Island and the northern coast of Cuba. Widely distributed in the tropical Atlantic, Pacific and Indian oceans.

Black-capped Petrel   *Pterodroma hasitata*

Fig. 5 Black-capped Petrel

Local names: Blue Mountain Duck; Dry Land Booby; Diablotín; Diablotin; Chathuant.
Description: 14–16″. Upperparts mostly dusky to black, the crown black in sharp contrast with white of neck, forehead and underparts; *upper tail-coverts white.* In dark "phase" entirely dusky, apart from white at base of tail. Fig. 5.
Habitat: Most apt to be seen far out at sea.
Nidification: In burrows or crevices on mountain cliffs; colonies in south-western Hispaniola and eastern Cuba (Monte La Bruja) *in winter.* One white egg is laid.
Range: Cuba, Hispaniola: formerly (?) Jamaica (dark "phase" only; perhaps a distinct species), Guadeloupe, Dominica, and Martinique.

STORM PETRELS   *Hydrobatidae*

These small oceanic birds are usually seen far from land. They sometimes follow a steamer in search of galley refuse or marine life killed by the ship's propeller. They subsist mainly on shrimp-like crustacea and other minute organisms obtained near the surface of the sea.

Leach's Petrel   *Oceanodroma leucorhoa*

Local names: Pamperito; Golondrina de Mar; Lavapiés.
Description: 7.4–9″. Larger and paler than Wilson's Petrel, and has a forked tail. The tarsi are much shorter (about .9″). From a distance it may be distinguished by its erratic flight, resembling that of a butterfly. Fig. 6.
Habitat: Well out at sea.
Range: Breeds on islands in Northern Hemisphere. Occasionally seen among the West Indies (Nov.–June).

Fig. 6 Leach's Petrel

Wilson's Petrel *Oceanites oceanicus*

Local names: Similar to those of Leach's Petrel.
Description: 7–7.5″. A small, sooty coloured little sea bird with *conspicuously white upper tail-coverts* and a patch of white on the flanks. Tail not forked as in preceding species. Tarsi very long (about 1.35″). Flight more direct than that of Leach's Petrel.
Habitat: Well out at sea.
Range: Breeds on islands in Southern Hemisphere. Occasionally seen among the West Indies (May 9–July 1).

TROPICBIRDS *Phaethontidae*

In the West Indies, tropicbirds are most frequently observed among the Virgin Islands and Lesser Antilles. When in full adult plumage, the elongated central tail feathers or, when lacking these, the pointed appearance of the tail, pigeon-like flight or buoyancy when floating on the water, should readily distinguish them from gulls or terns.

Tropicbirds feed mainly on squids and flying fish, which they obtain by plunging into the sea after the manner of boobies. Near shore they pick up crabs. They are often molested by frigatebirds and forced to disgorge their prey.

Two of the three species of this family inhabit the West Indies. The lovely Red-tailed Tropicbird (*P. rubricaudus*) is confined to the Pacific and Indian oceans.

Red-billed Tropicbird   *Phaethon aethereus*

Fig. 7 Red-billed Tropicbird

Local names: Truphit; Trophic; White Bird; Boatswain Bird; Paille-en-queue; Paille-en-cul; Flèche-en-cul; Fétu.

Description: 16–32″. Somewhat stockier than the Yellow-billed Tropicbird. Mainly white; a black streak through eye; upperparts barred with black; in flight shows black band on outer edge of wing, but *no black on inner portion of wing.* A barred-backed, red-billed bird is this species. Fig. 7.

Voice: A shrill, tern-like *careek* or *kek.*

Habitat: Shows a preference for small islands. Most numerous among the northern Lesser Antilles and the Grenadines.

Nidification: The single, variously spotted egg is laid on a ledge of a cliff or cave by the sea.

Range: In the West Indies, chiefly confined to the Lesser Antilles, Virgin Islands and islets east of Puerto Rico; rare vagrant elsewhere. A widespread oceanic species.

White-tailed Tropicbird *Phaethon lepturus*

Local names: "Chitee-churo"; Trophic; Truphit; White Bird; Boatswain Bird; Long-tail; Contramaestre (Cuba); Rabijunco (Cuba; D.R.); Chirre (P.R.); Gaviota Caracolera (P.R.); Paille-en-queue; Paille-en-cul; Flèche-en-cul; Fétu; Cibérou.

Description: 16–32″. Plumage mainly white, in flight shows black on outer part of wing, and *a black band on inner portion of wing*; a black streak through the eye. The bill is coral-red in the adult, yellow in immature; elongated rectrices more or less buffy. Young have the upperparts barred with black, but have less black on wings. Fig. 8.

Fig. 8 White-tailed Tropicbird

Voice: A shrill, harsh *kak-kak* or *creek-creek*, occasionally heard around ships at sea in the evening after dusk, for the birds are evidently attracted to lights.

Habitat: More apt to be seen about the larger islands than the Red-billed Tropicbird.

Nidification: Like that of Red-billed Tropicbird.

Range: Virtually throughout the West Indies, but rarely seen in the western Caribbean and Gulf of Mexico. A widespread oceanic species.

PELICANS *Pelecanidae*

Of the eight species of these well-known water birds only two are American; both of these are known from the West Indies. The Brown Pelican, the smallest of its family, is indigenous to the islands, but the American White Pelican, primarily a fresh-water bird, is merely a rare or sporadic winter visitor.

Pelicans feed on fish, which the brown species obtains by plunging into the sea, the white by scooping in shallow water. They are remarkably buoyant, due to their thin, hollow bones and the air reservoirs that permeate and envelop their bodies.

American White Pelican *Pelecanus erythrorhynchos*

Local name: Alcatraz Blanco.
Description: 54–70″. A large, *white* pelican; all but innermost remiges black, appearing as a broad, black band in flight; bill and feet yellow in winter. Occurs on lagoons or lakes, usually in flocks.
Range: Western North America. Casual in the West Indies; recorded from the Bahamas, Cuba, Isle of Pines, Grand Cayman, Jamaica and Puerto Rico (Nov. 5–May 20, June 26).

Brown Pelican *Pelecanus occidentalis*

Local names: Pelican; Alcatraz; Grand Gosier; Pélican.
Description: 44–55″. Readily identified by its large size and characteristic features. Unlike other sea birds the neck is not extended in flight, the head being drawn back on to the shoulders. Coloration largely dark brown, the upperparts mostly silvery grey; upper part of head and stripe down neck white, the neck entirely white during postnuptial moult. Young have the head, neck and upperparts brownish, the underparts mostly white. Fig. 9.

Either solitary or associated in small flocks, when usually seen

Fig. 9 Brown Pelican

flying in oblique single file close to the surface of the sea. In normal flight a few wing-beats are followed by a glide, but both Brown and White Pelicans occasionally soar high in the air.

Habitat: Coastal areas.

Nidification: In colonies. The roughly built nests are situated on the ground or in bushes or low trees, usually on small islands. Eggs (2–3) white when freshly laid, but soon become nest-stained.

Range: Virtually throughout the West Indies. Also North, Central and South America, including the Galápagos Islands.

BOOBIES & GANNETS   *Sulidae*

This family comprises nine species of which three are gannets (*Morus*) and the remainder boobies (*Sula*). Of the latter genus, which is chiefly confined to the Tropics, three species inhabit the West Indies. The Northern Gannet (*Morus bassanus*) is not uncommon in the Gulf Stream off the east coast of Florida north of West Palm Beach; it has been recorded from Cuba, but the record is questionable.

Boobies, unlike pelicans, wander well out to sea and, except when nesting, are not so apt to congregate in flocks. They fly with head and neck outstretched close to the surface of the water, alternately flapping and scaling. They obtain their food, mainly flying fish, by plunging into the sea.

Blue-faced Booby   *Sula dactylatra*

Local names: White Booby; Whistling Booby; Fou Blanc.

Description: 32–36″. Largely white, but remiges and their coverts dark chocolate-brown, appearing as *a broad black band on rear edge of wing* when bird is in flight (gannets have broad *black wing-tips*); *tail also dark chocolate-brown*, not white as that of Red-footed Booby or Northern Gannet. Immature birds are dark greyish brown above, the back streaked with whitish; underparts mostly white.

Habitat: Open sea and coastal waters.

Nidification: Nests on ground. Eggs (1–2) bluish, covered with a white, chalky deposit. Colonies comparatively small.

Range: Breeds in the Bahamas (Santo Domingo Cay), Pedro and Serranilla Cays, Virgin Islands (Cockroach Cay), Dog Island and the Grenadines (Battowia Bullet, All-awash Islet and Kick-'em-Jenny); also on extralimital islands in Gulf of Mexico and on islands in southern Caribbean Sea. Occasional among outer Florida Keys and off northern coast of Cuba. A widespread oceanic species.

Brown Booby   *Sula leucogaster*

Local names: Booby; Pájaro Bobo; Pájaro Bobo Prieto; Boba Prieta; Bubí Chaleco; Fou Noir; Fou Brun.
Description: 28–30″. The commonest West Indian booby. Breast, abdomen and under-wing-coverts white; rest of plumage dark chocolate-brown; bill and feet yellowish. The immature is entirely dusky brown, paler below; bill blackish. Fig. 10.

Fig. 10 Brown Booby

Habitat: Open sea and coastal waters.
Nidification: Like that of Blue-faced Booby, but colonies usually large.
Range: Virtually throughout the West Indies, nesting on many islets. Also breeds on extralimital islands in the Caribbean Sea. A widespread oceanic species.

Red-footed Booby   *Sula sula*

Local names: Booby; White Booby; Pájaro Bobo; Pájaro Bobo Blanco; Boba Blanca; Bubí Blanco; Fou Blanc.
Description: 27–29″. Resembles the Blue-faced Booby, but smaller; dark area on inner part of wing narrower and paler; *tail white and feet red.* The immature is dull brown, later becoming paler on head and underparts and acquiring a white rump and tail, some individuals attaining full development in this plumage. Fig. 11.

Fig. 11 Red-footed
Booby

Habitat: Open sea and coastal waters.
Nidification: In colonies. Unlike other West Indian boobies, builds a rough nest of sticks in a bush or low tree. Eggs like those of other species, but rarely more than one is laid.
Range: The Antilles and extralimital islands in the Caribbean Sea. Nesting colonies on Little Swan Island, Little Cayman, Navassa, Mona and on some of the Grenadines (e.g. Battowia and Kick-'em-Jenny). A widespread oceanic species.

CORMORANTS   *Phalacrocoracidae*

Cormorants comprise a rather large family of some thirty species and are widely distributed throughout the world. They are for the most part large, long-winged and long-necked water birds. In flight they scale less frequently than do the boobies and pelicans and do not plunge into the sea for fish but pursue their prey under water.

Double-crested Cormorant   *Phalacrocorax auritus*

Local names: Cormorant; Cormoril; Corúa; Corúa de Mar.
Description: 29–35″. Mainly *glossy black*, the feathers of the mantle, scapulars and wing-coverts with silvery centres; a tuft of black, or black and white, feathers on each side of the head in breeding plumage; naked

skin of face and throat orange. The immature is more or less whitish
below.
Habitat: Mainly coastal waters.
Nidification: In colonies. In the West Indies the nests are situated in trees,
usually mangroves. Eggs (2–4) usually pale greenish blue, more or less covered with a white chalky deposit.
Range: Northernmost Bahamas, Cuba and the Isle of Pines: vagrant elsewhere in the West Indies east to Guadeloupe. Widespread in North America.

Olivaceous Cormorant   *Phalacrocorax olivaceus*

Local names: Cormorant; Cormoril; Corúa; Corúa de Agua Dulce.
Description: 25–27″. Closely resembles the preceding species, but
smaller (wing under 11.5″) and
slimmer, with a *relatively longer
tail*. In breeding season, *throat patch
often bordered with white* and white
tufts of feathers on sides of head. The
disproportionately *long tail* is the
best field mark. Fig. 12.
Habitat: Interior lakes and rivers,
including Zapata Swamp; also
coastal lagoons and estuaries.
Nidification: Like that of Double-
crested Cormorant.
Range: Breeds in Cuba, Isle of
Pines, Great Inagua, San Salvador
and Cat Island; casual on other

Fig. 12 Olivaceous Cormorant

islands (e.g. Jamaica, Puerto Rico and Dominica). Also southern North
America to South America.

DARTERS   *Anhingidae*

Darters are a small family of only four species, one occurring in the New
World, one in Africa and Madagascar, one in southern Asia south to
Celebes, and one in Australia and New Guinea. They are closely related to
cormorants, from which they are distinguished by their very long, thin
necks, and pointed, rather than hooked, bills.

Anhinga *Anhinga anhinga*

Local names: Marbella, Corua Real.

Description: 34–36″. Male mostly glossy black; back and wings marked with silvery white, appearing as long streaks on scapulars; some whitish feathers on head and neck in nuptial plumage; a pale band across tip of tail; lower mandible yellow; gular sac orange. The female has the head, neck and underparts brownish, more or less mottled on the neck with buffy. The immature is brown above and the underparts are pale brownish white. Fig. 13.

Fig. 13 Anhinga

Habitat: Borders of rivers or lakes, where often seen perched on a tree or stub sunning itself with wings outstretched. When swimming often submerges with only the head and neck visible.

Nidification: Nesting habits like those of the cormorants. Eggs (3–5) bluish white, covered with a chalky deposit.

Range: Cuba and the Isle of Pines. Widespread in tropical and sub-tropical America; casual on Andros, Little Cayman; reported from Haiti.

FRIGATEBIRDS *Fregatidae*

The five species of this tropical family are the most aerial of oceanic birds, and consequently their wing expanse is very great in proportion to the weight of their bodies. They feed on fish and offal that they themselves pick up from the surface of the water, or obtain, after the manner of skuas and jaegers, by robbing other sea birds.

Magnificent Frigatebird *Fregata magnificens*

Local names: Man-o'-War Bird; Hurricane Bird; Scissors-tail; Cobbler; Rabihorcado (Cuba); Tijereta (D.R.); Rabijunco; Tijerilla; Tijereta (P.R.); Frégate; Queue-en-Ciseaux.

Description: 38–41″. A long-winged, short-necked sea bird. The tail often appears pointed, but in reality is deeply forked. Male entirely black, glossed above with green and purple; bill bluish; feet black; distensible throat-patch orange, red in breeding season. The female has a white breast and brownish lesser wing-coverts; feet red. The immature has white underparts and a white head. Fig. 14.

Habitat: Usually seen soaring high above the sea near shore.

Fig. 14 Magnificent Frigatebird (female)

Nidification: Nests in colonies, often on windward side of small cay. The roughly built platforms are either situated in bushes, or trees, such as mangroves, or on rocks. One white egg is laid. Red gular pouches of males are inflated during breeding season.

Range: Throughout the West Indies. Widespread in tropical American seas; also Cape Verde Islands and off adjacent coast of Africa.

HERONS & BITTERNS *Ardeidae*

These waterfowl comprise a large, cosmopolitan family. All of the species native to North America, north of Mexico, occur in the West Indies, and all but one of these, the American Bittern, breed in this region.

Most herons inhabit swamps and marshes. They procure their food by wading out in shallow water until unwary fishes or amphibians approach near enough to be caught by rapid thrusts of their bills. Notable exceptions are the Cattle Egret, which feeds on insects, spiders, and occasionally frogs and lizards, and the Yellow-crowned Night Heron, which feeds largely on crabs.

A heron may readily be recognised in normal flight from ibises and storks, for the head and neck are drawn back on to the shoulders, not outstretched.

Great White Heron   *Ardea occidentalis*

Local names: White Gaulin; Garzón Blanco.

Description: 46–54″. A large pure white heron with a heavy, yellow bill and *yellowish legs*. Similar in size to Great Blue Heron, and now considered merely a colour-phase of that species.

Habitat: Primarily coastal. Most numerous in the West Indies among the cays off southern Cuba known as the "Archipiélago de los Canarreos". Usually seen in shallow water well out from the mangroves, but also in interior saline lagoons.

Nidification: Like that of Great Blue Heron.

Range: Cuba and the Isle of Pines; casual elsewhere in Greater Antilles and Bahamas. Also Florida Keys, coast of Yucatán Peninsula, and islands in southern Caribbean Sea, particularly Los Roques.

Great Blue Heron   *Ardea herodias* 4/4/97 DR

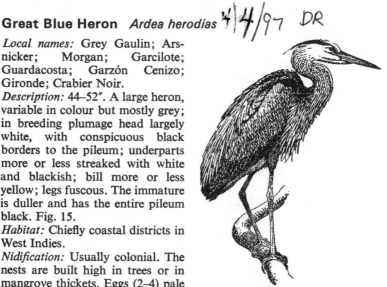

Local names: Grey Gaulin; Arsnicker; Morgan; Garcilote; Guardacosta; Garzón Cenizo; Gironde; Crabier Noir.

Description: 44–52″. A large heron, variable in colour but mostly grey; in breeding plumage head largely white, with conspicuous black borders to the pileum; underparts more or less streaked with white and blackish; bill more or less yellow; legs fuscous. The immature is duller and has the entire pileum black. Fig. 15.

Habitat: Chiefly coastal districts in West Indies.

Nidification: Usually colonial. The nests are built high in trees or in mangrove thickets. Eggs (2–4) pale bluish green.

Fig. 15 Great Blue Heron

Range: West Indies, but known to breed only in Greater Antilles (e.g. Cuba, Jamaica, Puerto Rico, St. Thomas, Anegada). Also North America, including Mexico, extralimital Caribbean islands and the Galápagos Islands. North American individuals winter in West Indies.

~4/4/97 DR

Green Heron *Butorides virescens*

Local names: Little Gaulin; Lees Pond Gaulin; Water Witch; Poor Joe; "Bitlin"; Aguaita Caimán; Martinete; Caga-leche; Cagón; Cuaco; Kio; Cra-cra; Racrac; Valet de Caïman; Caäli; Crabier.

Description: 16–19". A very small, dark heron; one of the commonest of West Indian water birds. Plumage mostly glossy green above, with some violet on back;

Fig. 16 Green Heron

neck, sides of head and breast chestnut, with a broken streak of white from chin to lower breast; posterior underparts ashy; legs and toes greenish yellow. Immature birds have the underparts whitish, streaked with dusky. There is a rufous phase in Cuba. Fig. 16.

Habitat: Virtually anywhere near fresh or salt water.

Nidification: Nest situated in a bush, tree or bamboo (rarely in reeds), usually in a swamp, though sometimes a considerable distance from water. Eggs (usually 3) pale bluish green.

Range: Throughout the West Indies. Also from temperate North America south to extreme northern South America.

Little Blue Heron *Florida caerulea*

4/4/97 DR

Local names: Blue Gaulin; White Gaulin (immat.); Garza Azul; Garza Común; Garza Pinta; Garza Blanca (immat.); Crabier Noir; Crabier Blanc (immat.); Aigrette Bleue; Aigrette Blanche (immat.).

Fig. 17 Little Blue Heron

Description: 22–28″. Head and neck chestnut; rest of plumage very dark slate-grey; bill blue-grey, the tip black; legs greenish. The immature is white, with the tips of the primaries dusky, the plumage in older individuals becoming more like that of the adult. Fig. 17.

Habitat: Swamps, lagoons, rivers.

Nidification: Like that of Great Egret.

Range: Throughout the West Indies. Also tropical and temperate America.

Cattle Egret 4/2/97 DR
Bubulcus ibis

Local names: Cattle Gaulin; Garrapatosa; Garza Africana; Garza Ganadera; Crabier Garde-boeuf.

Description: 21–25″. A comparatively small white heron with a rather short neck and bill. Has tufts of pinkish buff feathers on pileum, lower neck and back when in fully adult breeding plumage, at other times with only the crown buffy; bill yellow, sometimes with a reddish tinge; legs yellow or pinkish. The immature is entirely white with a yellow bill; legs darker than those of adult. Fig. 18.

Habitat: Usually found in flocks *among cattle*, but often associated with other herons when nesting.

Plate 1 **PARROTS**

Nidification: In West Indies, breeds in colonies on coastal islets and in mangrove swamps. Nests like those of preceding species, but eggs (2–3) paler.
Range: Widespread in the West Indies, but not recorded from this region prior to 1948. A recent arrival in the New World, first recorded from the Guianas. Now occurs in North, Central and South America. An Old World heron that has been undergoing a phenomenal extension of range; inhabits Europe, Asia, Africa and Australia. Abundant in Greater Antilles, Antigua and Trinidad.

Fig. 18 Cattle Egret

Plate 2 **PIGEONS & DOVES**

1 Ring-tailed Pigeon	102
2 Red-necked Pigeon	102
3 Plain Pigeon *Hispaniola*	103
4 Zenaida Dove *Lesser Antillean race*	104
5 Violet-eared Dove	103
6 Grenada Dove	106
7 Caribbean Dove *Grand Cayman race*	105

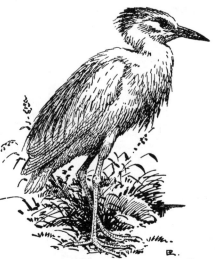

Reddish Egret *Dichromanassa rufescens*

Local names: Gaulin; Garza; Crabier.

Description: 27–32″. A rather chunky heron. Body plumage dark slate-grey, paler on the underparts; head and neck brownish; *bill distinctly bicoloured*, the basal half flesh-colour, the anterior portion black; legs mostly slate-blue, the toes black. There is a white phase that is approximately as numerous in the West Indies as the dark. The bicoloured bill and shaggy appearance of the neck are the most obvious field characters, but young birds have basal part of bill darker. Fig. 19.

Fig. 19 Reddish Egret

Habitat: Primarily a coastal heron.

Nidification: Like that of Great Egret.

Range: The Bahama Islands, Cuba, including the Isle of Pines and coastal cays, Hispaniola; rare or casual in Jamaica, Puerto Rico, St. Croix, and St. Martin. Also extralimital islands in Caribbean Sea, Peninsula of Yucatán, Paraguaná Peninsula (Venezuela), and southern North America.

Great Egret
4/4/97 DR
Egretta alba

Local names: White Gaulin; White Morgan; Garzón; Garzón Blanco; Garza Blanca; Garza Real; Crabier Blanc.

Description: 36–41″. A rather large, long-necked heron. Entirely white; in nuptial plumage with beautiful dorsal plumes; bill yellow; *legs blackish.* Fig. 20.

Habitat: Fresh-water and salt-water swamps, marshes and lagoons.

Nidification: Colonial. The nests are situated in trees, usually mangroves. Eggs (2–3) bluish green.

Range: Virtually throughout the West Indies, but rare in the Lesser Antilles. The species is found on every continent.

Fig. 20 Great Egret

Snowy Egret *Egretta thula* 4/4/97 DR

Fig. 21 Snowy Egret

Local names: White Gaulin; Garza Blanca; Garza de Rizos; Garza Real; Crabier Blanc; Aigrette Blanche.
Description: 21–27″. A pure white heron, strikingly plumed in nuptial plumage; bill black, *yellow at base*; legs (tarsi) black, yellowish green posteriorly when young; *toes bright yellow*. When feeding, more active than Little Blue Heron. Fig. 21.
Habitat: Swamps, lagoons, rivers.
Nidification: Like that of Great Egret.
Range: Virtually throughout the West Indies, although rare in the Lesser Antilles. North American individuals of this and other herons winter on the islands.

Tricoloured Heron *Hydranassa tricolor* 4|5|97 DR

Local names: Gaulin; Switching-neck; Garza de Vientre Blanco; Garza Pechiblanco; Garza Morada; Crabier.
Description: 24–28″. A slender, long-necked heron. Plumage mainly dark slate-grey; throat white, becoming rufous on upper foreneck; *posterior underparts conspicuously white*; bill blackish, the basal part of lower mandible yellow; legs black, greenish posteriorly; toes yellow. The immature has the grey largely replaced by chestnut, but the abdomen is white as in the adult. Fig. 22.
Habitat: Swamps, lagoons, rivers.
Nidification: Like that of Great Egret.

Fig. 22 Tricoloured Heron

Range: Bahamas and Greater Antilles; also Grand Cayman, Old Providence and St. Andrew; rare or casual in Lesser Antilles. Also southern North America, Central America and northern South America.

Black-crowned Night Heron *Nycticorax nycticorax* 4|6|97 DR

Local names: Gaulin; Night Gaulin; Crab-catcher; Guanabá Lominegro; Guanabá de la Florida; Yaboa Real; Rey Congo; Gallinaza (immat.); Coq de Nuit; Coq d'Eau; Crabier.

Description: 23–28″. A stocky, largely nocturnal heron with comparatively short legs.
Pileum, mantle and scapulars glossy black;
occipital plumes white; rest of upperparts,
including wings and tail, grey; underparts
vary from white to very pale grey; tarsi and
toes yellow. The immature has the upperparts
dull brown, spotted and streaked with buffy;
underparts white, streaked with sooty brown.
Fig. 23.

Voice: A loud *woc*, usually heard after dark.
Most herons croak or squawk.

Habitat: Salt-water and fresh-water swamps
and marshes.

Nidification: Nests in colonies in reeds or
mangroves. Eggs (2–4) pale bluish green.

Range: Occurs virtually throughout the West
Indies, but most individuals are probably
visitants from North America. Widespread in
the Americas and the Old World.

Fig. 23 Black-crowned
Night Heron

Yellow-crowned Night Heron   *Nyctanassa violacea*

Fig. 24 Yellow-crowned
Night Heron

Local names: Night Gaulin; Grey Gaulin; Crab-catcher; Crab-eater;
Yaboa; Guanabá; Guanabá Real; Rey Congo; Gallinaza (immat.);
Crabier Gris; Crabier de Bois; Crabier de Montagne; Coq de Nuit; Coq
d'Eau.

Description: 22–28″. Plumage mainly grey with black streaks on back and wings; *head black, the crown and a broad stripe below eye white or buffy;* yellow legs rather long, extending beyond tail when bird is in flight. The immature is darker than the young of *Nycticorax,* the crown black, streaked with white. Fig. 24.

Voice: A short *woc,* less harsh than that of preceding species.

Habitat: Mainly swamps, but often found far from water. Active by day as well as by night.

Nidification: Nests in trees. Less apt to colonise than the Black-crowned Night Heron. Eggs similar.

Range: Throughout the West Indies. Also temperate and tropical America, including the Galápagos Islands.

Least Bittern *Ixobrychus exilis*

Fig. 25 Least Bittern

Local names: "Bittlin"; Gaulin; Garcita; Martinete; Martinetito; Martín García; Crabier.

Description: 11–14″. Adult male has pileum, tail and most of back glossy black; hindneck and sides of head chestnut, paler on cheeks; *wings mostly buffy and chestnut,* thus differing strikingly from larger Green Heron, which has dark wings; underparts white, washed with cinnamon; a blackish patch on each side of breast; bill and feet yellow or yellowish. Female and immature have brown backs. Largely terrestrial, but sometimes seen perched in mangroves or other low vegetation. Might be mistaken for a rail, for often flushes from underfoot in swamp grass. Flight seldom sustained for more than a few yards. A bittern sometimes tries to avoid detection by standing with bill pointed skyward in attempt to simulate its surroundings. Fig. 25.

Voice: A low *cucucucucu;* sometimes cackles when flushed.

Habitat: Marshes and swamps.

Nidification: Nest a small and slight structure, usually situated in a clump of grass. Eggs (2–5) pale bluish white.
Range: Greater Antilles, Guadeloupe, Marie Galante and Dominica; at least winter residents in Bahamas. Also from North to South America.

American Bittern *Botaurus lentiginosus*

Local names: Guanabá Rojo; Ave Toro.
Description: 23–34″. Very variable in size. Upperparts brown, mottled with buffy and black; primaries blackish, showing as *black wing-tips* in flight; underparts mostly buffy with wedge-shaped brown streaks; throat white, except medially; a broad black streak from side of throat to side of neck; tarsi and toes yellowish green. Wing-beats rather rapid. A terrestrial species, that *very seldom alights in trees.*
Habitat: Marshes and swamps.
Range: North America. Winters south to Panama and in small numbers in the Bahamas and Greater Antilles, in particular Cuba; casual in Lesser Antilles (e.g. Barbados) (Sept. 23–late April).

STORKS *Ciconiidae*

Storks are best represented in the Old World. Three species inhabit the Americas, and of these only the Wood Stork occurs in the West Indies where it is rare and local. These birds feed, as do the ibises, on a variety of animal matter.

Wood Stork
Mycteria americana

Local names: Cayama (Cuba); Faisán; Coco (D.R.).
Description: 35–47″. A very large water bird. Head and neck bare (blackish); remiges, primary coverts and tail glossy greenish or purplish black; rest of plumage white; legs and decurved bill variable in colour. The immature has the body plumage more or less greyish; head and neck paler, and to some extent feathered. *Flies with head and neck outstretched* and often soars. Fig. 26.

Fig. 26 Wood Stork

Habitat: Swamps and coastal lagoons.

Nidification: The nests resemble those of herons and are situated in trees, frequently mangroves. Eggs (3–5) white.

Range: Cuba and Dominican Republic, including Saona Island; casual in Jamaica and Bahamas. Also southern North America to Argentina.

IBISES & SPOONBILLS *Threskiornithidae*

There are three West Indian species of this family which is best represented in the Old World. One other, the beautiful Scarlet Ibis (*Eudocimus ruber*) has occurred in this region as a stray (see "List of Vagrants").

In the field, ibises may readily be distinguished from herons by their curved bills, different manner of flight (a few wing-beats followed by a scale) and by having head and neck outstretched. Like herons, they are highly gregarious.

Glossy Ibis *Plegadis falcinellus* 4|6|97 DR

Local names: Coco; Coco Oscuro; Coco Prieto; Cigüeña; Pêcheur.

Description: 22–25″. Head, neck, upper back, lesser wing-coverts and underparts chestnut; rest of plumage glossed green and purple; bill and legs dark olive-brown. *Appears entirely black at a distance.* Young are duller than adults, and the head and neck are streaked with white. Fig. 27.

Habitat: Fresh-water and salt-water swamps and lagoons.

Fig. 27 Glossy Ibis

Nidification: Nests in colonies in trees at moderate elevations. Eggs (3–4) rather dark blue.

Range: Bahama Islands (rare), Cuba, Hispaniola, Jamaica and Puerto Rico; casual on Grand Cayman, St. Andrew's Island, Virgin Islands and Lesser Antilles. Widespread in Old and New World.

White Ibis *Eudocimus albus*

Local names: Coco; Coco Blanco; Gant Blanc.

Description: 22–28″. Plumage white, the four outermost primaries tipped with glossy black and thus shows *black wingtips* in flight; bill, bare skin of head, and legs pinkish to red. The immature has the mantle, wings and tail mostly brown, but the rump and upper tail-coverts are white; head and neck white, mottled with dusky; breast and abdomen white; bill and legs dull coloured. Fig. 28.

Habitat: Fresh-water and salt-water swamps and lagoons.

Nidification: In colonies. Nests in trees. Eggs (3–4) heavily spotted, the ground colour greyish white or greenish white.

Range: Cuba, the Isle of Pines, Jamaica, Hispaniola, and the Bahama Islands; casual elsewhere. Also from southern North America to northern South America.

Fig. 28 White Ibis

Roseate Spoonbill *Ajaia ajaja* 4/5/97 DR

Fig. 29 Roseate Spoonbill

Local names: Spoonbill; Sebiya; Cuchareta; Espátula; Spatule.
Description: 26–32″. Head and throat bare, mostly greenish yellow; neck and mantle white; tail and patch in front of wing buff; rest of plumage pink, the lesser wing-coverts and tail-coverts nearly crimson. Very young individuals are white, and the crown and throat are feathered. The pink colouring is obtained gradually, the bird not fully adult until approximately three years of age. Spoonbills are easily recognised in any plumage by their flat, spatulate bills. In flight they glide less frequently than ibises. Fig. 29.
Habitat: Coastal swamps and lagoons.
Nidification: In colonies. Nests are usually in mangroves. Eggs (normally 3) dull white, heavily spotted.
Range: Cuba, Isle of Pines, Hispaniola and nearby islands, and Great Inagua; vagrant elsewhere in West Indies. Also southern North America, Central and South America.

FLAMINGOS *Phoenicopteridae*

Flamingos are highly gregarious water birds, and are rather wary and seldom allow one a close approach. When feeding, they wade out into shallow water, scrape up the mud and silt with a dancing movement and, immersing head and neck, turn the bill inwards. Their food in the West Indies consists to a great extent of mollusks of the genera *Cerithidea* and *Cerithium*.

Only one species of this small and remarkable family inhabits the West Indies, where it is decidedly local in distribution.

Roseate Flamingo ~~4|4|97 DR~~
Phoenicopterus ruber

Local names: Flamingo; "Filly-mingo"; Flamenco; Flamant.
Description: 42–48″. An unmistakable, slender, long-legged and long-necked, rose-pink water bird with black-tipped wings. The immature is mostly greyish white, more or less marked with dusky on the upperparts. Fig. 30.

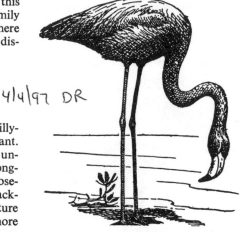

Fig. 30 Roseate Flamingo

Voice: Loud and goose-like.
Habitat: Chiefly coastal lagoons, and brackish lakes and ponds.
Nidification: Colonial. The nests are built on the ground and are composed mostly of mud that is scooped up with bill and feet; lake weed and, at times, sticks are used for reinforcement. They vary in height from four to twenty inches. Eggs (usually 1, rarely 2) white.
Range: Bahama Islands (e.g. Abaco, Andros, Acklin and Great Inagua; largest breeding colony on Great Inagua), Cuba, Hispaniola, including Gonâve and Beata; casual elsewhere in West Indies. Also Yucatán, islands in south Caribbean, Galápagos Islands, and northern South America.

SWANS, GEESE & DUCKS *Anatidae*

Although this cosmopolitan family is well represented in the West Indies, most of the species that occur in this region are winter residents that breed in North America. There are at least six native species of West Indian ducks. These are rare on most of the islands, and are decreasing in numbers due to excessive shooting and to the taking of their eggs.

Fulvous Tree Duck *Dendrocygna bicolor*

Local names: Redhead; Yaguasín; Vingeon Rouge.
Description: 18–20″. Mainly rufescent, with considerable black on upper-parts and wings; upper tail-coverts white, and shows white on sides and flanks; bill blackish; feet blue-grey.
Voice: A shrill whistling, resembling that of *D. arborea.*
Habitat: Rice plantations, swamps, and lagoons.
Nidification: Usually in coarse grass, or (in Cuba) rice plantations. Eggs (11–18) buffy white.
Range: Southern North America to South America, and tropical regions of the Old World. Breeds in Cuba (first recorded in 1943) and Hispaniola; has occurred widely in the West Indies as a vagrant.

Black-bellied Tree Duck *Dendrocygna autumnalis*

Description: 18–21″. Distinguished from West Indian Tree Duck by the black abdomen, large *white patch on wing*, orange bill and pink legs. The South American race (*D. a. discolor*), which is found in the West Indies, has the upper back and breast greyish, not brown as in Central American birds. The latter have been introduced in Cuba, whence there have been recent records.
Range: Southern North America, Central America and northern South

America. Vagrant to Lesser Antilles (e.g. Barbados, Mustique, St. Vincent, St. Lucia, Martinique, Guadeloupe and Grenada), Virgin Islands (e.g. St. Croix) and Puerto Rico; also Cuba; sight record from Andros. West Indian records during all seasons of year.

West Indian Tree Duck *Dendrocygna arborea*

Local names: Whistling Duck; Whistler; Mangrove Duck; Night Duck; Yaguaza; Chiriría; Vingeon; Gingeon; Canard Siffleur.

Description: 19–22″. A large, goose-like duck with relatively long legs that extend beyond the tail in flight. Upperparts mostly brown with pale edgings to the feathers; rump and tail blackish; throat white; lower neck streaked with blackish; chest more or less rufescent; posterior underparts white, spotted with black, particularly on the sides; bill black; legs greenish. Fig. 31.

Tree ducks are largely nocturnal, and may often be seen flying over swamps at dusk. The West Indian species often perch high in trees.

Fig. 31 West Indian Tree Duck

Voice: A shrill whistling.

Habitat: Fresh-water and salt-water swamps.

Nidification: The nest is situated on the ground, in a cavity of a tree, or in a cluster of bromeliads high above the ground. Eggs (up to 14) milky white.

Range: The Bahama Islands, Greater Antilles (including Grand Cayman) and northern Lesser Antilles (e.g. Barbuda). Accidental at Bermuda, and casual elsewhere in West Indies.

Mallard *Anas platyrhynchos*

Local name: Pato Inglés (Cuba).

Description: 20–25″. The glossy green head, white ring around neck and reddish brown chest readily distinguish the drake. Female dusky brown above with pale edgings to most of the feathers; a glossy violet alar speculum is conspicuously bordered with white.

Habitat: Fresh-water and salt-water ponds and lagoons.
Range: Europe, Asia and North America. Winters (in New World) south to Mexico, casually to Panama. Rare winter resident in Cuba and in the Bahamas; casual on Jamaica, Puerto Rico and St. Croix; records from Hispaniola and the Lesser Antilles are unsatisfactory (Oct. 22–March 14).

Gadwall *Anas strepera*

Description: 19–21″. Drake appears greyish in the field, although most of the body feathers are heavily vermiculated with white; a *white alar speculum* and chestnut patch on upper wing, with black between; abdomen white; tail-coverts black; legs yellow. Female resembles female Northern Pintail but has the white mark on wing and yellow legs.
Habitat: Chiefly rather deep fresh-water lakes and ponds (e.g. Lake Ariguanabo, near Havana).
Range: North America, Europe, Asia and northern Africa. Winters (in New World) south to Mexico, New Providence, Cuba, Jamaica and Puerto Rico; rare in West Indies (Oct. 8–March 13).

Northern Pintail *Anas acuta*

Local names: Pato Pescuecilargo; Pato Guineo; Canard Pilet.
Description: 22 (♀)–29 (♂)″. A comparatively large, but slender, long-necked duck. The drake may be recognised by its brown head, white underparts and *pointed tail.* Female largely greyish brown like a female Mallard, but slenderer and lacks the white-bordered violet alar speculum; bill greyish; tail pointed but not elongated as in drake. Fig. 32.
Habitat: Like that of Blue-winged Teal.
Range: North America, Europe and Asia. Winters (in New World) south to northern South America. A fairly common winter resident in the West Indies east to Hispaniola; rather rare in Puerto Rico and casual in Virgin Islands and Lesser Antilles (Sept. 29–April).

Fig. 32 Northern Pintail

White-cheeked Pintail *Anas bahamensis* 4|6|97 DR

Local names: Summer Duck; White-head; White-throat; White-jaw; Brass-wing; Pato Quijada Colorada; Pato de la Orilla; Canard Tête-blanche.

Description: 15–19″. A small, greyish brown duck with *white cheeks and throat*, and light fawn-coloured, pointed tail. The sexes are similar in colour. Fig. 33.

Fig. 33 White-cheeked Pintail

Voice: Drake has low, squeaky call; female quacks.

Habitat: Fresh-water and salt-water ponds and lagoons.

Nidification: Nest concealed in thick growth of grass or weeds or under mangrove roots. Eggs (5–12) buff.

Range: Bahama Islands and Cuba east through Hispaniola and Puerto Rico to the Virgin Islands and northern Lesser Antilles (south to Guadeloupe). Also islands off northern South America (including Trinidad and Tobago), the Galápagos Islands and continental South America; casual in Florida.

Green-winged Teal *Anas crecca* 4|6|97 DR

Local names: Teal; Pato Serrano; Pato de la Carolina; Sarcelle.

Description: 13–15.5″. The drake has a brown head, with a broad, glossy green stripe behind eye; throat black; upperparts vermiculated black and white; mostly white below; wings greyish brown with a green speculum. Female differs from female Blue-winged Teal in having a glossy green alar speculum; no blue on wing. Sometimes found in company with Blue-winged Teal. Flight of both species rapid and tortuous.

Habitat: Like that of Blue-winged Teal.

Range: North America, Europe and Asia. Winters (in New World) south to Colombia and Tobago. Rare winter resident in the West Indies, apparently most numerous in Cuba (October–April).

Blue-winged Teal *Anas discors* 4/5/97 PR

Local names: Teal; Pato de la Florida; Pato Zarcel; Sarcelle.
Description: 15–16″. The drake is recognised by the lunate white mark in front of eye, and by the blue middle and lesser wing-coverts. Small size,

Fig. 34 Blue-winged Teal

and blue wing-patch bordered with white serve to identify the female; blue of wing is apt to appear whitish when bird is in flight. In eclipse plumage, acquired in summer, males resemble females, this plumage lasting through autumn. Drakes of other migrant ducks have attained full breeding plumage by late September. Fig. 34.
Habitat: Mainly shallow-water swamps and lagoons.
Range: North America. Winters south to Argentina and Chile. Found throughout the West Indies, where it is the commonest of winter resident ducks (late August to early May; occasional in June and July).

American Widgeon *Anas americana*

Local names: Pato Lavanco; Pato Cabeciblanco; Moñi-blanco.
Description: 18–22″. The white crown, *large white patch on forepart of wing* and small bill (blue, tipped with black) will readily distinguish the drake. Females browner, with much less white on wing; entire head spotted black and white giving a greyish effect in contrast with rest of plumage.
Habitat: Lakes and lagoons.
Range: North America. Winters south to northern South America. Occurs virtually throughout the West Indies (Aug. 7–May 18).

Northern Shoveler *Spatula clypeata*

Local names: Spoonbill; Shovel-mouth; Pato Cuchareta; Canard Souchet.
Description: 17–21″. Drake has glossy green head, white chest, the posterior underparts reddish brown; wing like that of Blue-winged Teal. Female resembles female Blue-winged Teal, but larger; blue of wing very dull; bill longer (over 2″), and wider (over 1″) distally. Swims in a squat position with head depressed.
Habitat: Lakes and lagoons.
Range: North America, Europe and Asia. Winters (in New World) south to Trinidad and Colombia. Found virtually throughout the West Indies (September–May).

Wood Duck *Aix sponsa*

Local name: Huyuyo.
Description: 17–20″. The male is one of the most beautiful of ducks, highly iridescent and with a complicated colour-pattern. The female has the crested head mostly greyish with considerable white about the

Plate 3   QUAIL DOVES

eyes, giving the bird a spectacled appearance; throat white. Male in eclipse plumage resembles female but lacks white about eyes, and greyish of sides of head broken by white streak to throat; bill more brightly coloured. Fig. 35.

Voice: A variety of shrill, squeaking notes.

Habitat: Chiefly shady streams and lagoons in western Cuba (e.g. Laguna La Deseada in Pinar del Río).

Nidification: Nests in cavities in trees or palm stubs. Eggs (8–14) buffy white.

Fig. 35 Wood Duck

Range: Cuba (where a permanent resident), the United States and southern Canada. Winters, in West Indies, south to the northern Bahamas (recorded from Grand Bahama, New Providence, Eleuthera, San Salvador) and probably western Cuba; casual on Jamaica, Puerto Rico and Saba.

Plate 4 TROGONS, PARAKEETS & KINGFISHER

1	Cuban Trogon	139
2	Hispaniolan Trogon *2a, Male. 2b, Female*	139
3	Ringed Kingfisher *Male. Lesser Antillean race*	140
4	Olive-throated Parakeet *Jamaica race*	112
5	Cuban Parakeet	112
6	Hispaniolan Parakeet	112
7	Caribbean Parakeet	112

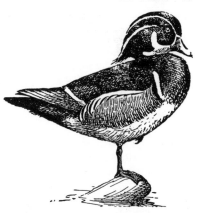

Redhead *Aythya americana*

Description: 19–23″. The drake has a reddish brown head; forepart of body black, changing to black and white vermiculation on the mantle, scapulars and sides (appearing grey in the field); centre of abdomen white. Female largely greyish brown with a grey alar speculum; chin and centre of abdomen white.

Note: Diving ducks of the genus *Aythya* do not spring into the air when flushed as do the "shoal-water" ducks, but patter along the water before rising. In the hand they may be recognised by the large lobe on the hind toe.

Habitat: Deep-water lakes or ponds.

Range: North America. Winters south to Mexico, the Bahamas (e.g. New Providence; Andros), Cuba and Jamaica (Nov. 11–March 5).

Ring-necked Duck *Aythya collaris*

Local names: Black Duck; Pato Negro; Pato del Medio; Cabezón.

Description: 16–18″. The drake resembles the male Lesser Scaup, but back black; chin and band in front of wing white; alar speculum grey; a conspicuous white band across bill; an inconspicuous chestnut ring around neck. Female resembles female Redhead, but smaller; usually has a distinct whitish band across upper mandible; upperparts darker brown, without a trace of white vermiculation that gives the Redhead a greyish brown appearance: distinguished from female Lesser Scaup by the pale band on bill, grey speculum and whitish throat; feathers about base of upper mandible merely whitish.

Habitat: Mainly fresh-water lakes.

Range: North America. Winters south to Central America and the West Indies, whence recorded as far south as Barbados, St. Lucia and St. Andrew; also Trinidad and Margarita Island (October–March).

Canvasback *Aythya valisineria*

Description: 20–24″. Resembles the Redhead, but drake has neck reddish brown; pileum blackish; black vermiculation on back and sides very fine, these areas appearing white in the field. The female resembles the female Redhead, but is somewhat rufescent about the head and neck. The best field characters are the low forehead and almost straight culmen, the bill appearing wedge-shaped in profile.

Habitat: Lakes and lagoons.

Range: North America. Winters south to Mexico, casually to Guatemala. Rare autumnal and winter visitant to Cuba and Puerto Rico; of doubtful occurrence in Jamaica.

Lesser Scaup *Aythya affinis*

Fig. 36 Lesser Scaup

Local names: Black Duck; Black-head; Pato del Medio; Pato Turco; Pato Morisco; Canard Tête-noire.

Description: 15–18″. The drake has a black head (glossed with purple and slightly with green) and forepart of body; back and sides barred black and white; abdomen white; a white alar speculum. Female mostly dusky brown, white on lower breast and abdomen; a white alar speculum and feathers at base of upper mandible conspicuously white. Fig. 36.

Habitat: Lakes and lagoons.

Range: North America. Winters south to northern South America. A common winter duck in the Bahamas and Greater Antilles, but rare in the Lesser Antilles (Sept. 23–May 26).

Ruddy Duck *Oxyura jamaicensis* 4/6/97 DR

Fig. 37 Ruddy Duck

Local names: Rubber Duck; Diving Teal; Red Diver; Pato Chorizo; Pato Espinoso; Pato Rojo; Canard Plongeon; Coucouraime.

Description: 14–17″. A small, chunky duck with thick neck and broad blue or black bill. The drake in full plumage (seen during all seasons in West Indies) has bright *reddish brown upperparts*, neck and throat, black pileum, and *white cheeks*. In eclipse plumage reddish parts replaced by dusky, in this respect resembling female, but cheeks white. Female mostly dark greyish brown above, whitish below; a dusky streak across whitish cheeks. Tail often held erect. Flight bee-like. Fig. 37.

Voice: Utters weak, clucking notes during courtship.

Habitat: Lakes and lagoons. Now very rare on, or absent from, most of the Lesser Antilles.

Nidification: Nest usually in clump of sedges in shallow water; occasionally in mangrove swamps. Eggs (4–12) whitish; very large. Breeds during all seasons of the year.

Range: The West Indies. Also North America and northern Central America.

Masked Duck *Oxyura dominica*

Fig. 38 Masked Duck
(young male)

Local names: Quail Duck; Squat Duck; Pato Chorizo; Pato Chico; Pato Criollo; Pato Espinoso; Pato Codorniz; Pato Agostero; Canard Zombie; Canard Routoutou.

Description: 12–14″. Drake differs from male Ruddy Duck in having the forepart of head black (*no white on head*): upperparts heavily marked with black; a white alar speculum. Female differs from female Ruddy Duck in having the back distinctly barred with buff; underparts mostly ochraceous buff; a black streak through eye, another below eye; *a white alar speculum*; tail longer, but bill smaller, narrower and brighter blue. More secretive than Ruddy Duck. Both species often submerge like grebes when disturbed. Unlike Ruddy Duck, flushes with comparative ease. White on wing conspicuous in flight. Fig. 38.

Voice: A hen-like clucking. Also a clearer, short note, and a soft *du-du-du*.

Habitat: Fresh-water lakes and ponds; rice plantations; mangrove swamps. Seldom found far from cover.

Nidification: Nests in rice plantations, and in clumps of vegetation in fresh-water lakes or ponds. Eggs (8–18) smaller and smoother than those of Ruddy Duck, and buffy white in colour. Downy young distinguished by pale superciliary stripe (facial markings as in adult female) and four (not two) pale spots on back.

Range: Virtually throughout the Antilles, including Grand Cayman and Swan Island, but rare east of Hispaniola. Also Mexico, Central and South America, including Trinidad. Casual in Bahamas.

Hooded Merganser *Mergus cucullatus*

Description: 16–19″. Drake black and white with rufous on sides and flanks; head black, with a fan-shaped white crest, the feathers tipped with black. Female mostly blackish above, the crest buffy brown; a white alar speculum; neck, upper breast, sides and flanks greyish; rest of underparts white. Mergansers have narrow, "toothed" bills.

Habitat: Lakes and lagoons.

Range: North America. Winters south to Mexico, and a rare winter visitant to the West Indies, whence recorded from the Bahama Islands, Cuba, Puerto Rico, St. Croix and Martinique (Nov. 16–February).

Red-breasted Merganser *Mergus serrator*

Description: 20–25″. Drake has black, crested head, glossed with green on sides; neck mostly white; rest of upperparts largely black, becoming grey posteriorly; much white on wing; rest of underparts white with a broad dark band (ochraceous and black) across lower neck; a narrow red bill; feet red. Female somewhat resembles female Hooded Merganser but larger and paler; more white on wing; sides of head and upper neck cinnamon; *bill red.*

Habitat: Primarily a salt-water species.

Range: North America, Europe and Asia. In America, winters chiefly along the coasts of the United States; common during this season in Florida, but casual in the West Indies, whence recorded from the Bahama Islands, Cuba and Puerto Rico (Oct. 14–Feb. 16).

AMERICAN VULTURES OR CONDORS *Cathartidae*

The American vultures comprise a small family of seven species, only one of which, the Turkey Vulture, is known from the West Indies. There are sight records of the smaller Black Vulture (*Coragyps atratus*) from Cuba and from the southern Lesser Antilles (see List of Vagrants).

Since these birds feed on carrion, they are highly beneficial, particularly in the Tropics where sanitary conditions are not at their best.

Turkey Vulture   *Cathartes aura*

Fig. 39 Turkey Vulture

Local names: Crow; John Crow (Jamaica); Carrion Crow (Bahamas); Aura; Aura Tiñosa.

Description: 27–32″. An unmistakable, great black bird with a bare, crimson head. Young have the skin of the head blackish. Usually seen soaring, the wings held above horizontal. Fig. 39.

Habitat: Found chiefly in open country and in large towns (e.g. Havana and Kingston). Introduced in Puerto Rico from Cuba (about 1880), and only recently established in Hispaniola, where now known from both the Dominican Republic and Haiti. Does not breed in Bahamas or Cayman Islands.

Nidification: The (1–2) spotted eggs are deposited among rocks in the side of a cliff, in a hollow log or stump, or on the ground in a thicket.

Range: Cuba (including coastal cays), Isle of Pines, Cayman Islands, Jamaica, Hispaniola, Puerto Rico; also north-western Bahamas (Grand Bahama, Abaco, Andros); casual on Bimini, New Providence, and St. Croix. Also North, Central and South America, including Trinidad.

HAWKS & EAGLES   *Accipitridae*

This cosmopolitan family is well represented in the West Indies, particularly in Cuba. However, a number of the species are rare or local and are not apt to be seen unless definite search be made. The Osprey has recently been included in the Accipitridae.

Swallow-tailed Kite *Elanoides forficatus*

Description: 20–26″. Head, neck and underparts, including under wing-coverts, white; back, tail and most of wing dark and glossy; *tail deeply forked.* A slender, graceful hawk of rare occurrence in the West Indies.
Range: South-eastern North America, Central and South America, including Trinidad. North American individuals migrate to South America via Cuba, Grand Cayman, and Jamaica (Aug.–Oct. 27; Feb. 21).

Hook-billed Kite *Chondrohierax uncinatus*

Local name: Snail Hawk.
Description: 15–17″. Approximately the size of a Broad-winged Hawk, from which it (Grenada race) may be distinguished by its larger, deeply hooked bill; underparts evenly barred tawny and white, and an ochraceous nuchal collar; shows *black barring on under-surface of wing.*
Habitat: Occurs at all elevations; often seen in early summer over xeric woodland in southern Grenada; feeds on small snails.
Nidification: Nests high in a tree. Eggs elsewhere 2–3 spotted.
Range: Grenada. Also Southern Texas, Mexico, Central America and South America, including Trinidad.

Cuban Kite

Chondrohierax wilsonii
Local names: Gavilán Caguarero; Gavilán Sonso.
Description: A little smaller than the Hook-billed Kite. Male has upperparts grey, the tail barred with black; underparts evenly barred greyish and white. Female resembles the Grenada form of the Hook-billed Kite, but brown barrings on underparts less rufescent; bill larger (also deeply hooked) and mostly yellowish. A comparatively tame hawk. Feeds chiefly on tree snails of the genus *Polymita.*
Fig. 40. Perhaps conspecific with *C. uncinatus.*
Habitat: Found most frequently along rivers or streams below 1500 feet.
Nidification: Unknown.
Range: Eastern Cuba.

Fig. 40 Cuban Kite

Snail Kite   *Rostrhamus sociabilis*

Fig. 41 Snail Kite

Local names: Gavilán Caracolero; Babosero; Gavilán Babosero.

Description: 16–18″. Male sooty black with considerable *white at base of tail*, and pale tips to tail feathers. Female sooty brown above; underparts buffy, heavily streaked with blackish; a whitish superciliary stripe and, like male, white at base of tail. Bill slender and deeply hooked; legs red. Flies leisurely over the marshes like a Marsh Hawk, but flight more direct, less wavering; soars at times. Feeds on snails of the genus *Pomacea*. Fig. 41.

Voice: A rasping chatter.

Habitat: Marshes and open swamp land.

Nidification: Nests at low or moderate elevations above the ground. Eggs (2–3) spotted.

Range: Cuba and Isle of Pines. Also southern North America, and Central and South America.

Sharp-shinned Hawk   *Accipiter striatus*   4/3/97 DR

Local names: Halcón; Halconcito; Gavilán Colilargo; Garrapiña (Cuba); Guaraguaíto de Sierra (Dom. Rep.); Halcón de Sierra (P.R.); Emouchet (Haiti).

Description: 11–14″. Variable in markings. Head small; tail long, narrow and square-ended; wings rather short and rounded, thus differing from Sparrow Hawk and Pigeon Hawk which have pointed wings. As in many hawks female decidedly larger than male. Flight rapid and direct. Feeds mainly on small birds. Fig. 42.

Voice: Utters a shrill cackling in vicinity of nest.

Habitat: Forested areas, chiefly at high elevations; found in lowlands as well as on high mountains in Cuba.

Nidification: Nest situated in a tree or palm. Eggs (2–3) spotted and washed with various shades of brown.

Range: Breeds in Cuba, Hispaniola and Puerto Rico. Also North, Central and South America. A few North American individuals winter in the Bahamas (Feb. 22–April 17) and in the Greater Antilles.

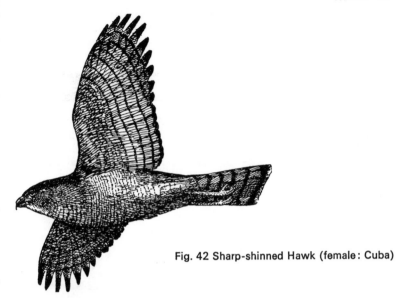

Fig. 42 Sharp-shinned Hawk (female: Cuba)

Gundlach's Hawk *Accipiter gundlachi*

Local names: Halcón; Gavilán Colilargo; Gavilán Rabilargo.
Description: 17–20″. Similar in form to Sharp-shinned Hawk, but larger and tail appears rounded at tip in flight; cheeks and sides of upper breast greyish in adult. Young of both species are heavily streaked on underparts. Closely resembles the North American Cooper's Hawk (*A. cooperii*), a species that has not been recorded from the West Indies.
Voice: Cackling less shrill than that of Sharp-shinned Hawk.
Habitat: Woodland; locally numerous in the Zapata Swamp.
Nidification: Like that of Sharp-shinned Hawk, but nests always high in trees, and eggs (3–4) not spotted.
Range: Cuba.

Red-tailed Hawk *Buteo jamaicensis* 4/4/97 DR

Local names: Chicken Hawk; Macaw; Gavilán del Monte; Guaraguao; Malfini.
Description: 18–24″. A large, thick-set hawk with broad wings and tail, the latter appearing comparatively short and rounded in flight. Upperparts

mostly sooty brown, the *tail rufous* in adults; underparts mostly white, the *abdomen heavily streaked with blackish* in contrast with white of breast. One of the common West Indian hawks, *usually seen soaring*. Preys on rodents and on young poultry.

Voice: A rasping scream.

Habitat: Widespread, but most numerous in mountains.

Nidification: Nest usually in tall tree; occasionally on side of cliff. Eggs (2–3) immaculate or obscurely spotted.

Range: Bahama Islands (Grand Bahama, Abaco and Andros; casual, possibly winter visitant from North America, on New Providence, Eleuthera, Great Inagua), Greater Antilles and some of northern Lesser Antilles (Saba, St. Eustatius, St. Kitts, Nevis; also reported from St. Martin and Montserrat). Also North and Central America.

Broad-winged Hawk   *Buteo platypterus*

Local names: Chicken Hawk; Chicken-eater; Gavilán Bobo; Guaraguao de Bosque; Malfini; Manger-Poulet.

Description: 13–16″. Similar in form and habits to the Red-tailed Hawk but smaller; tail with wide black and whitish bands (adults); no contrasting dusky and white areas on underparts. The immature has the underparts white, broadly streaked with blackish. Fig. 43.

Voice: Weaker and higher pitched than that of Red-tailed Hawk. A shrill rising squeal.

Habitat: Chiefly wooded areas in mountains and lowlands.

Nidification: Nests in trees. Eggs (2–3) either immaculate or spotted.

Range: Cuba (most numerous in Oriente Province), Hispaniola (one

Fig. 43 Broad-winged Hawk (Grenada)

record), Puerto Rico (rare), Antigua, and from Dominica to Tobago; casual on Barbados. Also North America; continental individuals winter for the most part in Central and northern South America, including Trinidad.

Ridgway's Hawk *Buteo ridgwayi*

Fig. 44 Ridgway's Hawk

Local names: Guaraguaíto; Malfini Savane.

Description: 14–16″. Much smaller than the Red-tailed Hawk, the only other hawk of its genus known to inhabit Hispaniola. Upperparts mainly dark brownish grey; chestnut on bend of wing; underparts grey, more or less tinged with rufous; thighs rufous. The immature has the underparts buffy white with dusky and tawny streaks; thighs rufescent. Fig. 44.

Voice: Utters a shrill squealing, reminiscent of the closely related Red-shouldered Hawk (*B. lineatus*) of North America, which it resembles in other respects.

Habitat: Primarily a lowland hawk. Found in woods and in fairly open country.

Nidification: Nests in trees or palms. Eggs (2) variously spotted.

Range: Hispaniola, including some of the surrounding islands (e.g. Gonâve, Cayemite Is., Ile à Vache, Beata).

Common Black Hawk *Buteogallus anthracinus*

Local names: Black Hawk; Crab Hawk; Gavilán Batista; Halcón Cangrejero.

Description: 20–23″. A large *black* hawk, the Cuban form (sometimes considered a separate species) dark sooty brown, but appearing black in the field; tail banded with white; white on under surface of wing, this particularly extensive in Cuban individuals. The immature has the underparts white to ochraceous, heavily streaked and blotched with black or blackish. A rather tame, sluggish hawk; often soars like a *Buteo*. Feeds chiefly on crabs. Fig. 45.

Voice: A shrill *ba-tis-ta* or *ba-tis-ta-ooo*.

Habitat: Mainly coastal Cuba, abundant on cays off south coast, and in southern Isle of Pines. Inhabits mountain forest on St. Vincent.

Fig. 45 Common Black
Hawk (Cuba)

Nidification: Nests in trees, usually at moderate elevations. Eggs (1–2) spotted.

Range: Cuba, including coastal cays and Isle of Pines; St. Vincent. Also southern North America, Central America and northern South America, including Trinidad; vagrant to Grenada, the Grenadines (Union Island) and St. Lucia.

Northern Harrier *Circus cyaneus*

Local names: Gavilán Sabanero; Gavilán de Ciénaga; Malfini Savane.

Description: 18–24″. A rather slender hawk with considerable wing-spread; bill very short. Adult males are predominantly grey, females brown; *white upper tail-coverts* serve as an excellent field character. The female might be mistaken for a female Snail Kite, but underparts mostly plain tawny, not heavily marked with blackish; upperparts likewise paler. Flies leisurely at low elevations, the wings with an upward slant.

Habitat: Open marshes and savannas.

Range: North America, Europe and Asia. Winters (in New World) south to northern South America. Occurs virtually throughout the West Indies in suitable localities (August 15–April 18).

OSPREYS *Pandionidae*

The Osprey or "Fish Hawk" is usually considered to constitute a family distinct from the Falconidae or Accipitridae. There is only one species, which is of world-wide distribution. Unlike other raptorial birds, the Osprey has a reversible outer toe, doubtless an outcome of its specialised feeding habits.

Osprey *Pandion haliaetus*

Local names: Fish Hawk; Eagle; Sea Eagle; Guincho; Guaraguao de Mar; Aguila de Mar; Halcón Pescador; Malfini de la Mer; Aiglon.

Description: 22–25″. A large sea hawk, dark above and *white below*; feathers of upperparts with white tips and much white on head and hindneck; a conspicuous black streak behind eye. Resident birds have more white on head and hindneck, the dark postocular streak more or less obsolete; they often appear white-headed. Feeds on fish, obtained by plunging into the water. Often hovers while searching for food. In flight shows a decided bend to the wing. Fig. 46.

Voice: A series of short, shrill whistles.

Habitat: Coastal areas.

Nidification: The bulky nest is situated in a tree or on the ground. Eggs (3) beautifully spotted.

Range: Cosmopolitan. Breeds in the Bahamas and on cays off Cuba; possibly also in the Virgin Islands (e.g. St. Croix, Anegada). North American individuals winter throughout the West Indies.

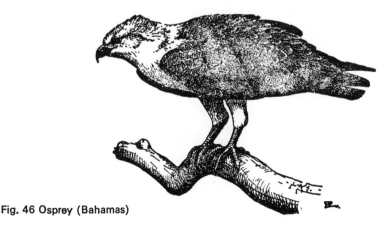

Fig. 46 Osprey (Bahamas)

FALCONS & CARACARAS *Falconidae*

Falcons bear a superficial resemblance to hawks, but are apparently not closely related to the Accipitridae. Some, including the Peregrine Falcon and boreal Gyrfalcon, are noted for their boldness and rapidity of flight when swooping on their prey. Only two species of this family are native to the West Indies: neither is endemic to this region.

Crested Caracara *Caracara plancus*

Fig. 47 Crested Caracara

Local name: Caraira.
Description: 20–24″. A long-legged and long-necked species with a black crest. Upperparts mostly blackish, the hindneck, mantle and tail (except tip) barred with white; primaries largely white basally, showing (in flight) as a *white patch near tip of wing*; throat and foreneck white; breast black and white; *abdomen black*; bare skin of "face" red. The immature is mostly brown, the breast streaked with whitish. Often seen walking in stately fashion on ground. Occasionally soars. Feeds on frogs, lizards, insects, carrion and dead fish. Fig. 47.
Voice: Utters a harsh cackling.
Habitat: Primarily palm-covered savannas.
Nidification: Nests in trees or palms. Eggs (2–3) pale buff to dull rufous, heavily spotted.
Range: Cuba and the Isle of Pines. Also from southern United States, south to southern South America, and a number of islands in southern Caribbean Sea; accidental in Jamaica.

Peregrine Falcon *Falco peregrinus*

Local name: Halcón de Patos.
Description: 16–22″. The largest of the true falcons in the West Indies. Upperparts mostly slaty black; underparts white to ochraceous, spotted, barred or streaked with black; a broad black streak on side of throat; wings long and pointed; tail relatively narrow. Feeds on birds, particularly shore-birds in West Indies.
Habitat: Chiefly lagoons and among small rocky islets.

Range: Cosmopolitan. A winter visitant to the West Indies, found throughout this region (Aug. 8–April 24).

Merlin *Falco columbarius*

Local names: Halcón; Halconito; Emouchet; Gri-gri de Montagne.
Description: 11–13.5". Similar in form to the Peregrine Falcon, but much smaller. Male slate-grey above, the tail barred with black; underparts vary from white to rufous, heavily streaked with black. The female is sooty brown above. Might be confused with an American Kestrel, but stockier in build and flight more rapid and direct; no rufous on upperparts. Feeds on small birds, lizards and large insects.
Habitat: Most frequently seen in vicinity of lagoons.
Range: Northern North America, Europe and Asia. Winters (in New World) south to northern South America. Found throughout the West Indies, where more numerous than the Peregrine Falcon (September–May 2).

American Kestrel *Falco sparverius* 4/6/97 D R

Local names: Killy Hawk; Killy-killy; Bastard Hawk; Cernícalo; Cuyaya; Halcón; Pri-pri; Gri-gri; Gli-gli.
Description: 9–12". The predominantly *rufous back and tail* and different manner of flight distinguish this little falcon from the Merlin. The underparts are either immaculate or spotted with black. A rufescent phase with rufous underparts is found in Cuba and the Isle of Pines. *Hovers* while searching for food; this consists mainly of insects and lizards. *The commonest of Antillean birds of prey,* but rare in the southern Lesser Antilles. Fig. 48.
Voice: A shrill *killi-killi-killi.*

Fig. 48 American Kestrel
(Hispaniola)

Habitat: Mainly open country.

Nidification: Nests in a cavity of a tree or recess in a building; occasionally at the base of a palm frond. Eggs (2–5) heavily speckled or spotted with reddish brown.

Range: Bahama Islands and Antilles, including the Cayman Islands and other small islands in the western Caribbean; of doubtful occurrence on Barbados; North American individuals winter in the Bahamas and Cuba. Widespread in North, Central and South America, including Trinidad, Margarita, Curaçao and Aruba.

CURASSOWS, GUANS & CHACHALACAS *Cracidae*

Only one species of this New World family inhabits the West Indies, where it is confined to the Grenadines. It is possible that it was brought to these islands from Tobago or Venezuela by early European settlers or by the Caribs. However, chachalacas were established on the Grenadines as early as the late seventeenth century. They resemble the species (*O. vetula*) that ranges from southern Texas to Nicaragua.

Rufous-vented Chachalaca *Ortalis ruficauda*

Local name: Cocrico.

Description: 22″. A gallinaceous bird, resembling a broad-tailed pheasant. Upperparts brownish olive, grey on head and hindneck; tail very long and broad, dusky with an iridescent sheen, the outer feathers broadly tipped with chestnut; underparts plain greyish drab, becoming blackish on centre of throat and rufescent on flanks and under tail-coverts; bare skin around eye dark blue; bare sides of throat red. Usually in small flocks.

Voice: A raucous *cocricó*, repeated several times. Also a subdued chuckling when feeding.

Habitat: Largely terrestrial, but seen in shrubbery, trees or coconut palms. Occurs in northern Bequia and western Union.

Nidification: The comparatively small nest is built in a bush or tree at low or moderate elevations above the ground. Eggs (usually 3) white.

Range: Bequia and Union Island (Grenadines), where now rare. Also Tobago, Margarita Island and northern South America.

PHEASANTS, PARTRIDGES & QUAILS *Phasianidae*

Bobwhites may have originally been introduced in Cuba, although the race *cubanensis* is fairly well characterised. Cuban birds have become established in the Dominican Republic, and continental forms elsewhere in the West Indies.

Various other species of this widespread family have been introduced unsuccessfully in various parts of the West Indies; but it is said that feral domestic fowl (*Gallus gallus*) are thriving on the islet of Kick-'em-Jenny in the Grenadines, Mona, and on Little San Salvador.

Northern Bobwhite *Colinus virginianus*

Fig. 49 Northern Bobwhite
(Isle of Pines)

Local names: Quail; Codorniz; Caille.

Description: 8.5–10″. A small game bird with complicated colour-pattern. Native Cuban "quail" are very dark, and closely resemble those from Florida. Males have white, females tawny, throats and superciliary stripes. Usually found in covies or, during breeding season, in pairs. Flight rapid. Fig. 49.

Voice: A clear, whistled *bob-white* or *bob-bob-white*.

Habitat: Mainly fields and open pine woodland.

Nidification: Nests on the ground. Eggs (10–18) white.

Range: Cuba and Isle of Pines; introduced on Andros, New Providence, Eleuthera, Hispaniola, Puerto Rico, St. Croix and, apparently unsuccessfully, on other islands. Also North America and northern Central America.

GUINEA-FOWL *Numididae*

The Common Guinea-Fowl is said to have been brought to the West Indies as early as 1508, and is now domesticated throughout the region, and would doubtless have reverted to a feral state on many of the islands had it not been for the mongoose. It is an important game bird in Cuba and Hispaniola.

The North American Turkey (*Meleagris gallopavo*), of the family Meleagrididae, was introduced on Andros in 1954, but is not established there as a feral species.

E

Common Guinea-Fowl *Numida meleagris*

Local names: Guinea Fowl; Guinea Bird; Guinea; Guineo; Gallina de Guinea; Pintado; Pintade; Pintade Marronne.

Description: The Guinea-Fowl is too well known to require a detailed description. Suffice to state that it is about the size of a domestic fowl, and is greyish black, profusely spotted with white, with a bony crest. Mainly terrestrial, but sometimes alights in tall trees.

Habitat: Most numerous in semi-arid regions, and bush-covered savannas.

Nidification: Nests on the ground. Eggs buffy, the pores darker giving them a speckled appearance.

Range: Africa. Established in a feral state in Cuba, the Isle of Pines, Hispaniola, Puerto Rico and Barbuda.

CRANES *Gruidae*

Cranes comprise a small family that is best represented in the Old World. There are only two species in the New World, the rare Whooping Crane (*Grus americana*) and the Sandhill Crane (*G. canadensis*). A race of the latter inhabits Cuba and the Isle of Pines, and is the largest of native West Indian birds. Its food consists of snakes, frogs, lizards, insects and vegetable matter.

Sandhill Crane
Grus canadensis

Local name: Grulla.

Description: 40″. A heavy, long-legged and long-necked bird. Plumage plain grey, the throat white; lores and crown bare of feathers, the rough, reddish skin covered by short, black "hairs". *Flies with head and neck outstretched*, not drawn back on to the shoulders as in Great Blue Heron. Fig. 50.

Voice: A sonorous, rolling *currooo*, loudest when uttered in alarm.

Habitat: Savannas. Attracted to burnt-over areas.

Nidification: Eggs (1–2) spotted; laid under a bush or tussock of grass.

Fig. 50 Sandhill Crane

Range: Cuba and Isle of Pines. Also North America and north-eastern Siberia.

LIMPKINS *Aramidae*

Limpkins belong to a family closely related to the cranes. There is only one species, which is confined to the Americas. Their food consists mainly of mollusks, but they also eat lizards, frogs and insects.

Limpkin *Aramus guarauna*

Fig. 51 Limpkin (Cuba)

Local names: Clucking Hen; Carrao; Guareao; Colas; Grand Colas; Poule Ajoli.

Description: 27″. Larger and chunkier than a rail, with long dark legs and heavy bill, decurved at tip. Plumage brown, the head, neck and anterior part of body streaked with white. Chiefly terrestrial, and sometimes loth to take to wing. Most active at dawn and at dusk. Fig. 51.

Voice: A wailing *gua-re-ao* or a short *kwaouk*.

Habitat: Marshes, savannas, borders of streams, hillsides, humid forest; often far from water. Most numerous at low elevations, but occurs high in the mountains of Hispaniola.

Nidification: Nests situated at low elevations, but occasionally in trees. Eggs (4–8) spotted.

Range: Cuba, Isle of Pines, Jamaica, Hispaniola, including Gonâve, Tortue and Saona; now very rare or extirpated in Puerto Rico; Eleuthera, but casual elsewhere in the Bahama Islands. Also south-eastern United States and from Mexico to South America.

RAILS, GALLINULES & COOTS *Rallidae*

The present family is distributed throughout the world. Of the various West Indian species only one, the Zapata Rail, is endemic to this region. The Uniform Crake (*Amaurolimnas concolor*), widespread in tropical America, formerly inhabited Jamaica, but has not been recorded from that island since 1881, and is presumably extirpated. This reddish brown crake was known in Jamaica as the "water partridge", although it was more of a "land rail" than other Antillean species of this family. It doubtless fell prey to the mongoose, which was introduced on that island in 1872.

With the exception of gallinules and coots, West Indian Rallidae are more likely to be heard than seen. Rails and crakes are exceedingly wary, and prefer to seek safety by running rather than by flight. Their food consists of snails, crabs, insects and vegetable matter.

King Rail *Rallus elegans*

Fig. 52 King Rail

Local names: Gallinuela de Agua Dulce, Martillera.

Description: Resembles the Clapper Rail but breast darker, like "light phase" of North American King Rails. Would be difficult or impossible to distinguish in the field from brownish breasted Antillean Clapper Rails. Fig. 52.

Voice: In Cuba and Isle of Pines like that of Clapper Rails.

Habitat: Fresh-water swamps, and borders of rivers.

Nidification: The nest and eggs (3–11 in Cuba) resemble those of the Clapper Rail.

Range: Cuba and the Isle of Pines. Also North America.

Clapper Rail *Rallus longirostris*

Local names: Marsh Hen; Mangrove Hen; Gallinuela de Mangle; Gallinuela de Agua Salada; Pollo de Mangle; Pollo de Laguna; Gallineta; Yegua; "Rateau" (prob. corruption of "Râle d'Eau"); Pintade (Guadeloupe).

Description: 13–14″. Upperparts greyish brown and black, the pileum and hindneck dusky; throat white or whitish, becoming greyish, buffy or brownish on breast; posterior underparts barred black and white. Not apt to occur with the King Rail in Cuba.

Voice: A harsh, hollow-sounding chatter.

Habitat: In or near mangrove swamps.

Nidification: Nest usually among mangrove roots. Eggs (5–9) whitish or buffy, spotted.

Range: Bahamas, Greater Antilles and northern Lesser Antilles (viz. Antigua and Guadeloupe). Also from United States to South America, including Trinidad.

Spotted Rail   *Pardirallus maculatus*

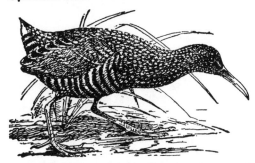

Fig. 53 Spotted Rail

Local names: Gallinuela Escribano; Gallinuela Color-Guineo.

Description: 11″. A strikingly marked rail. Plumage black, heavily spotted with white, the abdomen barred with white; back and wings "washed" with brown; bill green, with a red spot at base of lower mandible; feet red. Fig. 53.

Voice: A deep, chesty grunting; also a clucking *tuk-tuk-tuk*, etc., gradually accelerating.

Habitat: Fresh-water swamps. Common in the Zapata Swamp near Santo Tomás, and in rice plantations.

Nidification: Nest built low in swamp grass. Eggs (3–7) spotted, the markings almost entirely confined to larger ends.

Range: Western Cuba, Hispaniola (Dominican Republic); reported from the Isle of Pines and Jamaica (Black River marshes). Also Mexico, Central America and South America, including Trinidad.

Zapata Rail   *Cyanolimnas cerverai*

Local names: Gallinuela Sin-cola; Gallinuela Escribano; Gallinuela de Santo Tomás.

Description: 11.5″. A dark rail without streaks or spots, except for white tips to flank feathers. Upperparts olive-brown; forehead, sides of head and underparts slate-grey, the flanks greyish brown and centre of throat

Fig. 54 Zapata Rail

whitish; under tail-coverts conspicuously white; bill green, red at base; feet red. Wing very short and flight consequently very weak; tail short and decomposed. Fig. 54.

Voice: A short, limpkin-like *kwaouk*.

Habitat: Dense, bush-covered swamp land in vicinity of Santo Tomás and near the Laguna Tesoro, in company with other rails.

Nidification: Nest on hummock of sawgrass. Eggs (3) white.

Range: Zapata Swamp, Cuba.

Sora or Sora Crake *Porzana carolina*

Description: 9″. Most easily recognised by its short, yellow bill, less than an inch in length. Upperparts olive-brown, the back mottled with black and narrowly streaked with white; a black line along centre of crown; adult male has forepart of head, anterior to eyes, black and a black streak from chin to foreneck, these features less pronounced in females; breast grey, becoming white on abdomen, the flanks barred black and white; feet green. Immature individuals lack the black or blackish markings on face and black throat-stripe; breast and sides of head brownish. Flushes more readily than native rails.

Habitat: Fresh-water and salt-water swamps.

Range: North America. Winters south to northern South America. Occurs throughout the West Indies (Sept.9–May 21).

Yellow-breasted Crake *Porzana flaviventer*

Local names: Twopenny Chick; Gallinuelita; Gallinuela Chiquita; Gallito Amarillo.

Description: 5.5″. A tiny "yellow" crake with remarkably large feet.

Fig. 55 Yellow-breasted Crake

The upperparts are mostly tawny, with some black mottling and white streaks on back and wings; crown blackish, bordered by a white superciliary stripe; underparts white, washed with ochraceous and barred with black on flanks; bill olive-black; feet yellowish. Flight short and weak, much like that of a fledgling sparrow; can seldom be flushed a second time. Fig. 55.

Voice: A high-pitched *peep*, often repeated.

Habitat: Grassy borders of fresh-water lakes or ponds; rice fields; rarely salt-water swamps.

Nidification: Nest loosely built in water plant and presumably also in swamp grass. Eggs (5) sparsely spotted.

Range: Cuba, Jamaica, Hispaniola and Puerto Rico. Also southern Mexico, Central and South America.

Black Crake *Laterallus jamaicensis*

Description: 5.5″. A tiny crake. The head and underparts are blackish, the flanks barred with white; a chestnut band across hindneck; rest of upperparts blackish brown, spotted with white; bill black; feet sooty brown; iris red. A secretive species, difficult to flush, but flight surprisingly strong. Also known as "Black Rail".

Habitat: Marshes. Has evidently suffered from mongoose predation.

Range: United States south to Central America and western South America. Winter resident in Greater Antilles (Cuba, Jamaica, Hispaniola, Puerto Rico) and may breed sparingly; transient in Bahamas (e.g. Eleuthera).

Purple Gallinule   *Porphyrula martinica*   4/97 DR

Fig. 56 Purple Gallinule

Local names: Blue-pated Coot; Plantain Coot; Sultana; Gallareta Platanera; Gallareta Azul; Gallareta Inglesa; Poule Sultana; Poule d'Eau à Cachet Bleu; Cascamiol.

Description: 13″. The only brightly coloured gallinule in West Indies. Adults have the head, neck and underparts violet, the under tail-coverts white; rest of upperparts mostly green; bill red at base, the tip yellowish; frontal shield blue; feet yellow. The immature has the crown and sides of head brown, the rest of upperparts mostly greenish; throat white, the rest of underparts buffy; bill greenish. Fig. 56.

Voice: A variety of cackling or clucking notes.

Habitat: Dense aquatic growth, but sometimes strays from this environment.

Nidification: Nest in cat-tails or sedges, up to six feet above the water. Eggs (3–12) spotted.

Range: Bahama Islands (casual); Greater Antilles east to Puerto Rico; recorded in Lesser Antilles from Barbuda southward. Also southern North America, Central America and South America, including Trinidad and Tobago. Wanders freely among the islands.

Common Gallinule   *Gallinula chloropus*   4/97 DR

Local names: Water Fowl; Red-seal Coot; Gallareta Pico Colorado; Gallareta Pico Rojo; Yagareta; Dagareta; Poule d'Eau; Poule d'Eau à Cachet Rouge.

Fig. 57 Common
Gallinule

Description: 13″. Plumage mainly sooty black, with a brown wash on back; under tail-coverts mostly white and some white on flanks; *frontal shield and basal portion of bill red*; tip of bill greenish yellow; legs green with a red tibial band. Usually seen swimming, when head is jerked backwards and forwards. Fig. 57.

Voice: Emits a variety of sounds, some harsh, others querulous.

Habitat: Fresh-water and salt-water swamps, rivers and streams.

Nidification: Nests on or near the ground or water. Eggs (3–9) spotted.

Range: Cosmopolitan. Found virtually throughout the West Indies.

American Coot *Fulica americana*

Local names: Water Fowl; Coot; Gallareta; Gallareta Pico Blanco; Yagareta; Gallinazo; Dagareta Negra; Judelle.

Description: 15″. Plumage sooty grey, blacker on the head and neck; under tail-coverts mostly white, and a little white on wing noticeable in flight; bill conspicuously white, except at tip, the frontal shield dark red; lobed feet greenish. Usually found on open water, often in flocks. More duck-like and larger headed than Common Gallinule, but swims in similar fashion. An expert diver.

Voice: A variety of cackling or clucking notes.

Habitat: Fresh-water lakes and ponds as well as coastal brackish lagoons. May interbreed occasionally with the Caribbean Coot.

Nidification: Like that of Common Gallinule. Eggs (up to 12), heavily speckled.

Range: Bahamas and Greater Antilles; vagrant to Lesser Antilles. Also

North America, Central America and western South America. Many North American coots winter in the West Indies.

Caribbean Coot *Fulica caribaea* 4/97 DR

Fig. 58 Caribbean Coot

Local names: Coot; White-seal Coot; Water Fowl; Gallareta; Gallareta Pico Blanco; Yagareta; Gallinazo; Dagareta Negra; Judelle (Haiti); Poule d'Eau à Cachet Blanc.

Description: Resembles the American Coot, but frontal shield broader and *entirely white*, though sometimes tinged with yellow. Now considered a phase of *F. americana,* for there is positive evidence of interbreeding on Caribbean islands and in Michigan. Fig. 58.

Range: Widespread in the Antilles, most numerous from Hispaniola eastward; also islands in southern Caribbean, north-western Venezuela, and United States; unrecorded from the Bahamas, Cayman Islands and from small islands in the western Caribbean.

JACANAS *Jacanidae*

Jacanas comprise a small family of six genera, only one of which occurs in the New World. They are characterised by greatly elongated toes that enable them to walk on the surface pond vegetation with ease. The use of the thorn-like spur on the bend of the wing is not known; it would serve as a formidable weapon.

Northern Jacana *Jacana spinosa* 4/97 DR

Local names: Brazilian Coot; Spanish Coot; Banana Coot; Queen Bird; River Chink; Gallito de Agua; Médecin; Poule d'Eau Dorée; Chevalier.
Description: 7.5–9″. A conspicuous plover-like bird. Head, neck and forepart of body black; rest of plumage mostly purplish chestnut; a large

Fig. 59 Northern Jacana

golden yellow patch on wing, and under surface of wing mostly this colour; bill and frontal plate yellow; feet greyish olive. Has a habit of raising its wings after alighting. Immature has white underparts. Fig. 59.

Voice: A noisy cackling.

Habitat: Chiefly fresh-water ponds, swamps and rivers.

Nidification: The shallow, roughly built nest is situated among water plants. Eggs (3–4) buffy brown, heavily scrawled with black.

Range: Cuba, Isle of Pines, Jamaica and Hispaniola; vagrant to Puerto Rico. Also southern North America and Central America.

OYSTERCATCHERS *Haematopodidae*

The oystercatchers comprise a small family of shore-birds, related to the plovers, and are represented on all the continents. They are characterised mainly by their brightly coloured, blade-like bills, adapted for the opening of shellfish. Only one species inhabits the West Indies.

Common Oystercatcher *Haematopus ostralegus*

Local names: Sea Pie (Bahamas); Whelk-cracker; Ostrero; Caracolero.
Description: 17–20″. A large black and white shore-bird with a blade-like
vermilion bill. Head and neck black, the rest of upperparts greyish brown,
with a white patch at base of tail; rest of underparts and *large wing-patch
white*; feet pale pink; eyelids red. Flight swift and powerful. Fig. 60.

Fig. 60 Common Oystercatcher

Voice: A loud, whistled *wheep.*
Habitat: Coastal areas. Most numerous in southern Bahamas and Virgin
Islands.
Nidification: The (1–3) spotted eggs are laid above high-water mark on bare
rock, or on sand or gravel beach; usually on islets.
Range: Breeds in Bahamas, Los Siete Hermanos (Dominican Rep), islets off
Puerto Rico, Virgin Islands and perhaps the Grenadines. Rare elsewhere in
the West Indies. The species is cosmopolitan.

PLOVERS & TURNSTONES *Charadriidae*

Plovers are wading birds of world-wide distribution. Their habits resemble
those of sandpipers, but they are surface feeders. Their bills are not adapted
for probing in soft sand or mud. Turnstones are now classified as sandpipers,
related to the knots.

Semipalmated Plover *Charadrius semipalmatus*

Description: 7.25". Resembles Thick-billed Plover, but smaller, with a *much shorter bill, orange-yellow at base* but black in immature; *legs yellow or yellowish.*
Voice: A plaintive *chew-we.*
Habitat: Coastal beaches, sand and mud flats.
Range: Canada and Alaska. Winters south to southern South America. Most numerous in West Indies as autumnal transient (throughout the year).

Piping Plover *Charadrius melodus*

Description: 7". Resembles Semipalmated Plover, but *upperparts light sandy grey*; chest band seldom complete; bill black in winter.
Voice: A clear, whistled *peep-lo.*
Habitat: Usually found farther back on a beach than the Semipalmated Plover.
Range: United States and southern Canada. Winters mainly along coast of south-eastern United States, sparingly in the Bahamas and Greater Antilles; accidental on Barbados (August–May).

Snowy Plover *Charadrius alexandrinus*

Fig. 61 Snowy Plover

Local names: See Thick-billed Plover.
Description: 6.5″. Resembles Piping Plover, but smaller; breast band reduced to black patches on sides of chest; black bill slenderer and slightly longer; *legs blackish*, not yellow. Most numerous in southern Bahamas; rare in Greater Antilles. Fig. 61.
Voice: A clear, three-syllable whistle.
Habitat: Usually found on sand or mud flats well back from shore.
Nidification: Three spotted eggs are laid on the sand.
Range: Bahama Islands (recorded from Andros, Exuma and Watling's Island southward), Greater Antilles and northern Lesser Antilles; also islands in South Caribbean. A cosmopolitan species.

Collared Plover *Charadrius collaris*

Local names: Little Ploward; Nit; Snipe; Bécassine.
Description: 6.5″. Differs from Semipalmated Plover in smaller size, longer and slenderer black bill, pale pink feet, and a more or less rufous tinge to the upperparts usually most pronounced on crown and sides of neck; always lacks white on hindneck.
Voice: A succession of short, clear whistles.
Habitat: Sandy beaches. Perhaps present in Antilles only in spring and summer, and may not breed on these islands.
Nidification: Two spotted eggs are laid on ground (Trinidad).
Range: Grenada, Grenadines (recorded from Mustique) and Barbados; reported seen at St. Lucia and St. Martin. Also Mexico, Central and South America, including Trinidad and Tobago.

Thick-billed Plover *Charadrius wilsonia*

Fig. 62 Thick-billed Plover

Local names: Sand Bird; Snipe; Little Ploward; Nit; Frailecito; Títire de Playa; Putilla; Cabezón; Corredor; Playante; Playero Marítimo; Bécassine (these names also applied to other small shore-birds).
Description: 7.75". Mostly greyish brown above, with a white "collar" and short superciliary stripe; underparts white, with a broad black or dusky band across chest; a *relatively thick black bill*; *feet greyish pink*. The common small beach plover of the Bahamas and Greater Antilles. Fig. 62.
Voice: A melodious *wheet*.
Habitat: Coastal beaches, sand and mud flats.
Nidification: The (2–4) spotted eggs are laid on the sand.
Range: Virtually throughout the West Indies, but rare or absent in the Lesser Antilles south of Antigua. Also southern North America to northern South America.

Killdeer *Charadrius vociferus* 4|97 DR

Fig. 63 Killdeer

Local names: Soldier Bird; Ploward; Playero Sabanero; Títire Sabanero; Frailecillo Gritón; Collier; Chevalier de Terre.
Description: 10". Differs from other "ringed plovers" by larger size, with much longer tail; *two* black breast-bands; *rump and upper tail-coverts rufescent*, conspicuous in flight. Fig. 63.
Voice: A shrill, oft-repeated *kill-deer*; also a rising *deee*.
Habitat: Primarily an inland plover, found on open fields or savannas and on the borders of lagoons.
Nidification: On the ground. Eggs (3–4) spotted.
Range: Throughout the West Indies as transient or winter visitant; resident in the Bahamas and Greater Antilles. A widespread North American plover that migrates south to northern South America; resident on coast of Peru and northern Chile.

American Golden Plover *Pluvialis dominica*

Description: 10.5". Resembles Black-bellied Plover both in summer and winter plumages, but slenderer; coloration above more uniform, with *no*

white at base of tail; axillars (i.e. long feathers under wing) grey, not black or blackish.
Voice: A whistled *quee* or *queedle*, less melodious than the notes of the Black-bellied Plover.
Habitat: Chiefly inland fields or savannas.
Range: Northern North America and Siberia. Winters (in New World) in southern South America. Transient in West Indies (July 26–Jan. 1: Feb. 16–April).

Black-bellied Plover *Squatarola squatarola* 4/5/97

Description: 12″. In breeding plumage the black underparts, bordered with white anteriorly, distinguish the Black-bellied and Golden Plovers from any other shore-bird. Most Black-bellied Plovers seen in West Indies are in winter plumage, when they might be mistaken for large sandpipers, but they have big heads and short, thick bills: upperparts black, heavily spotted, the tail barred, with white or yellowish; base of tail conspicuously white; underparts white, streaked with dusky.
Voice: A plaintive, whistled *pee-a-wee.*
Habitat: On or near beaches.

Plate 5 HUMMINGBIRDS (1) See also Pl. 8

Range: Arctic America, Europe and Asia. Winters (in New World) south to Brazil and Peru. Most numerous in West Indies in autumn and spring (throughout the year).

Ruddy Turnstone *Arenaria interpres*

Description: 8.5″. A short-legged, robust shore-bird with complicated colour-pattern. In nuptial plumage, characterised by tawny and black back, black and white head, black chest and white wing-patches. In winter plumage, as usually seen in West Indies, more like other small shore-birds, but *posterior upperparts alternately black and white, and white patches on wings*; chest blackish; legs orange.
Habitat: Coastal areas.
Range: Northern North America, Europe and Asia. Winters (in New World) south to Argentina and Chile. Winter resident and transient in the West Indies (throughout the year).

AVOCETS & STILTS *Recurvirostridae*

Avocets and stilts are a small, but cosmopolitan, family of long-legged wading birds. Three species are found in the New World, but only one of these, the Common Stilt, is native to the West Indies, although the American Avocet occurs here occasionally as a vagrant.

Plate 6 **CUCKOOS**

Common Stilt   *Himantopus himantopus*   4|97   OR

Fig. 64 Stilt

Local names: Red-shank; Soldier; Crack-pot Soldier; Telltale; Zancudo; Cachiporra; Arcagüete; Viuda; Echasse; Pète-pète; Pigeon d'Etang.

Description: 14–15″. A graceful, black and white wader, with *very long pink legs*, and long and slender black bill. Crown, hindneck, mantle and wings black; tail pale grey; rump, forehead, markings around eye and underparts white. Females have a sooty brown mantle. Fig. 64.

Voice: A noisy yapping.

Habitat: Lagoons and ponds.

Nidification: Terrestrial. Eggs (3–4) buffy, spotted.

Range: Cosmopolitan. In West Indies breeds in Bahamas, Greater Antilles and northern Lesser Antilles; vagrant among southern Lesser Antilles.

WOODCOCK, SNIPE & SANDPIPERS   *Scolopacidae*

Members of this family are predominantly birds of arctic regions. Only one species, the Willet, is indigenous to the West Indies, although a number of others may be seen on the islands at any time of the year.

Sandpipers are usually found in flocks or small groups on or near beaches and about the borders of lagoons. For the most part they are silent in winter and on migration: the Greater and Lesser Yellowlegs are notable exceptions. Apparently many individuals of the larger species pass over or by the islands on migration without stopping. The popular "bird-guides" covering eastern North America contain coloured illustrations of *all* the species of Scolopacidae that occur regularly as winter residents or transients in the West Indies.

Common Snipe *Gallinago gallinago*

Description: 11″. A well-known game bird with a *long, straight bill*. Upperparts black and brown with pale streaks; in flight shows some rufous on tail; often flushes from underfoot. Flight rapid and tortuous. Fig. 65.

Voice: A rasping note, uttered when flushed.

Habitat: Fresh - water marshes.

Fig. 65 Common Snipe

Range: Northern North America, Europe and Asia. Winters (in New World) south to northern South America. Transient and winter resident in West Indies (Aug. 19–early May).

Long-billed Curlew *Numenius americanus*

Description: 20–26″. Resembles the Whimbrel, but larger with a decidedly longer bill (up to 8″ in length in adult females); most of underparts and pale markings on upperparts cinnamon-buff, the under wing-coverts and axillars cinnamon; no well-marked black streak through eye.

Range: Western North America. Winters from southern United States south to Guatemala. Formerly occurred in West Indies, whence recorded from Cuba and Jamaica; questionable records from Lesser Antilles. Not reported from West Indies during present century but, though uncommon, is evidently increasing as winter resident in Florida. (June–October).

Whimbrel *Numenius phaeopus*

Description: 15–18″. A large, chunky shore-bird with a *long, decurved bill* Plumage black above, with pale mottling and barring; neck and breast streaked with black; two bold black stripes on crown; and black streak through eye. The almost extinct Eskimo Curlew is smaller and slenderer, with a bill under 2.5″ (see "List of Vagrants").

Habitat: Coastal lagoons; borders of mangrove swamps.

Range: Northern North America, Europe and Asia. Winters (in New World) mainly on Pacific coast of South America. Transient and apparently a rare winter resident in the West Indies, recorded during all seasons, the European race twice from Barbados (Sept. 24; Dec. 16).

Upland Sandpiper *Bartramia longicauda*

Description: 12″. A rather large, slim, long necked, long tailed, small headed shore-bird. The upperparts, neck and breast are buffy brown, mottled with black, the rump plain black; bill slender and short (about 1″), mostly yellowish; long legs greenish yellow.
Habitat: Meadows or savannas.
Range: North America. Winters mainly in southern South America. Transient in West Indies (Aug.–Oct. : April–May).

Spotted Sandpiper *Actitis macularia*

Fig. 66 Spotted Sandpiper
(winter)

Description: 7.5″. One of the commonest of small sandpipers in the West Indies. Upperparts brownish olive; underparts white, marked with rounded black spots only in nuptial plumage; lower mandible yellowish. Solitary in habits; never in flocks. More active than Solitary Sandpiper, and constantly teeters. Has characteristic *fluttering flight*, with short wing-beats. Fig. 66.
Voice: Often utters a shrill *peet-wit* when flushed.
Habitat: Anywhere in vicinity of water.
Range: North America. Winters south to southern South America. Transient and winter resident in West Indies (throughout the year).

Solitary Sandpiper *Tringa solitaria* 4/4/47

Description: 8.5″. Resembles the Lesser Yellowlegs but *smaller* and darker; no white at base of tail, but *white bars on outer rectrices* conspicuous in flight; *legs dark olive*. The long, pointed, dark wings, and swift, erratic flight readily distinguish it on the wing from the Spotted Sandpiper. *Usually solitary* and rather tame.

Habitat: Fresh-water ponds and marshes.
Range: Northern North America. Winters almost entirely in South America. Fairly common transient, but rare winter resident, in West Indies (July 21–May 20).

Greater Yellowlegs *Tringa melanoleuca*

Description: 13–15″. Resembles Lesser Yellowlegs, but larger and more robust; bill 2″ or more in length, *slightly* upturned.
Voice: A loud, whistled *kew-kew-kew* or *kew-kew-kew-kew*.
Habitat: Mainly salt-water and fresh-water ponds and lagoons.
Range: Northern North America. Winters south to Patagonia. Transient and winter resident in West Indies, most numerous in autumn and spring (throughout the year).

Lesser Yellowlegs *Tringa flavipes*

Fig. 67 Lesser Yellowlegs

Description: 10–11″. The commonest of the larger shore-birds in the West Indies. As its name implies, its *long legs are yellow*; bill (1.5″) thin and straight; much *white at base of tail*, conspicuous in flight. Fig. 67.
Voice: A short, whistled *cue* or *cue-cue*, less shrill than notes of Greater Yellowlegs.
Habitat: Mainly fresh-water and salt-water ponds or lagoons.
Range: Northern North America. Winters south to Patagonia. Transient and winter resident in West Indies (throughout the year).

Willet *Catoptrophorus semipalmatus*

Fig. 68 Willet

Local names: Tell-bill-willy; Pilly-willick; Long-legs; Pond Bird; Duck Snipe; Laughing Jackass; Chorlo; Zarapico Real; Playero Aliblanco; Bécassine Aile-blanche.

Description: 15″. Resembles a Greater Yellowlegs, but upperparts paler, less contrasted with white of underparts; *legs dark* (plumbeous). In flight readily recognisable by *white wing-patches*. Fig. 68.

Voice: A high-pitched *will-will-willet* in nesting season; also a harsh *kip-kip*, etc., when alarmed.

Habitat: Coastal areas.

Nidification: In the West Indies, nests on beaches, well back from the water's edge. Eggs (4) spotted.

Range: Breeds in Bahamas, Greater Antilles (e.g. Cuba, Grand Cayman, Beata, St. Croix) and northern Lesser Antilles. Also North America. Winters south to Brazil and Bolivia. Occurs as transient or winter resident throughout the West Indies, but rare or lacking on most of the Lesser Antilles.

Red Knot *Calidris canutus*

Description: 11″. Plumages much like those of the Dowitcher, but a more robust bird with a much shorter bill (1.25″).

Habitat: Coastal areas.

Range: Arctic regions. Winters, in the New World, as far south as Tierra del Fuego. Passage migrant in the West Indies, whence recorded from the Bahamas, Greater Antilles and Lesser Antilles (July 17–May 19).

Pectoral Sandpiper *Calidris melanotos*

Description: 9″. Resembles Least Sandpiper, but larger. Foreneck and breast greyish, streaked with blackish, these markings abruptly terminating on upper abdomen, thus sharply contrasted with white of posterior underparts.

Habitat: Borders of lagoons and flooded meadows; occasionally dry, grassy fields, and ploughed land.

Range: Arctic America and north-eastern Siberia. Winters mainly in southern South America. Common fall, but rather rare spring, transient in West Indies; casual in winter (July–May 12).

White-rumped Sandpiper *Calidris fuscicollis*

Description: 7.5″. Distinguishable from other small sandpipers of this group by its white upper tail-coverts, conspicuous in flight, but not easily identified when stationary. Other species have the outer upper tail-coverts white, but the inner feathers are dark. The Curlew Sandpiper (see "List of Vagrants") has white upper tail-coverts, but is readily distinguished by its long, decurved bill.

Habitat: Chiefly borders of lagoons; often associated with Least Sandpipers.

Range: Arctic America. Winters mainly in extreme southern South America. Fairly common fall, but rare spring, transient in West Indies (July– Dec. 4; March 22–June 11).

Least Sandpiper *Calidris minutilla*

4/5/97

DR

Description: 6″. The smallest of West Indian sandpipers. Most closely re-

Fig. 69 Least Sandpiper

sembles Semipalmated Sandpiper, but *legs yellowish* and bill slenderer; usually decidedly darker and browner (less grey) above. Fig. 69.

Habitat: Chiefly about borders of coastal lagoons and fresh-water lakes or ponds; less frequently on beaches than Semipalmated Sandpiper.

Range: Northern North America. Winters from southern United States south to South America. Transient and winter resident in West Indies (July 5–May 30).

Semipalmated Sandpiper   *Calidris pusilla*

Description: 6.25″. A little beach sandpiper that resembles the Least Sandpiper (fig. 69); upperparts average greyer, less brownish; anterior underparts less heavily streaked with dusky, in winter plumage almost immaculate; bill somewhat thicker; *legs blackish*. Usually found in flocks.

Habitat: Borders of lagoons and mangrove swamps; beaches.

Range: Northern North America. Winters south to southern South America. Common fall transient in West Indies, but decidedly less numerous in spring; some winter and a few are found in summer (throughout the year).

Western Sandpiper   *Calidris mauri*

Description: 6.5″. In winter plumage distinguishable from Semipalmated Sandpiper only by longer bill, decidedly decurved at tip. However, the smaller males are indistinguishable at this season from female Semipalmated Sandpipers. In nuptial plumage, more rufous above and underparts more heavily marked with dusky. The bill of the female is so long as to appear cumbersome.

Habitat: Primarily beaches.

Range: Alaska and extreme north-eastern Siberia. Winters south to Peru. Transient and winter resident in West Indies (July–March 26).

Sanderling   *Crocethia alba*

Description: 8″. Whiter than other small sandpipers in winter plumage, when underparts immaculate white and upperparts pale grey; in nuptial plumage (rarely seen in West Indies) brownish above and on anterior underparts; bill (1″) straight and stubby, black as are the legs. In flight shows a white band on wing.

Habitat: Beaches and, to a lesser extent, borders of lagoons.

Range: Arctic regions. Winters (in New World) south to southern South

America. Transient and winter resident in West Indies (throughout the year).

American Dowitcher   *Limnodromus griseus*

Description: 12". Snipe-like in appearance, with a *long, straight bill*; underparts vary from whitish (winter plumage) to pinkish cinnamon (nuptial plumage); *posterior upperparts white* with black spots and bars.
Habitat: Coastal areas; lagoons.
Range: Northern North America and north-eastern Siberia. Winters south to Brazil. Transient and winter resident in West Indies (July 19–June 3).

Stilt Sandpiper   *Micropalama himantopus*

Description: 8.5". In nuptial plumage readily identified by dark, barred underparts and rufous on sides of head. In winter plumage might be mistaken for Dowitcher, but bill shorter, and *legs longer and slenderer*. The *dull greenish legs* distinguish it from the Lesser Yellowlegs. Both Dowitcher and Stilt Sandpiper often wade up to the belly and feed with jerky movements of the head.
Habitat: Borders of lagoons.
Range: Alaska and northern Canada. Winters south to southern South America. Fairly common fall transient in West Indies, but rare in spring; has been reported in winter (July–May).

Buff-breasted Sandpiper   *Tryngites subruficollis*

Description: 8.5". General coloration buff to ochraceous buff, with broad, black centres to the feathers of the upperparts; sides of breast spotted with black, but *underparts otherwise immaculate*; bill short (1.75") and slender; feet yellowish.
Habitat: Fields or savannas.
Range: Arctic America. Winters in southern South America. Rare but widespread on migration through the West Indies, most apt to be seen in early autumn (Sept. 6–Nov. 4; April).

Marbled Godwit   *Limosa fedoa*

Description: 16–20". A very large shore-bird with a long, usually perceptibly upturned, bill; coloration cinnamon-buff, heavily marked with black above; in nuptial plumage barred with black below. Individuals seen in West Indies would probably be in winter plumage with underparts virtually immaculate cinnamon-buff. The large size, distinctive bill and *brownish* coloration are diagnostic.

Habitat: Coastal areas; lagoons.

Range: Interior of North America. Winters south to Chile. Rare in West Indies, whence recorded from Cuba, Jamaica, Hispaniola, Puerto Rico, St. Croix, Anegada, Grenada and Carriacou; questionably from Guadeloupe and Martinique (August–April 12).

Hudsonian Godwit   *Limosa haemastica*

Description: 14–16″. Similar in form to the Marbled Godwit. May always be distinguished by *white* tail-coverts in contrast with *black* of tail; winter plumage greyish rather than brownish. In nuptial plumage the underparts are rufous barred with black.

Habitat: Coastal areas; lagoons.

Range: Northern Canada. Winters in southern South America. Transient in the West Indies, whence recorded from the Bahamas, Cuba, Hispaniola, Puerto Rico, Guadeloupe and Barbados, questionably from Dominica and Martinique (Sept. 9–Nov. 5).

Ruff   *Philomachus pugnax*

Description: 10–13″. Male (much larger than female) has variously coloured ruff in nuptial plumage when unmistakable. Most apt to be seen in winter plumage in West Indies. More chunky in appearance than a yellowlegs, with comparatively short bill and tail; feathers of upperparts, including rump, with white or pale margins; no dusky streaks on underparts; in flight shows white on sides of otherwise dark tail; feet variable in colour.

Habitat: Borders of swamps or lagoons, often in association with yellowlegs. A frequent visitor to Barbados.

Range: Europe and Asia. Winters in Africa and India. Visitant to Antilles; occurs from the Lesser Antilles west to Puerto Rico; casual in Jamaica (July 31–Jan. 28: March 30–May 19).

THICK-KNEES   *Burhinidae*

Thick-knees, or stone-curlews as they are called in England, are a small family of plover-like birds, best represented in the Old World. Only two species occur in the Americas, one of which inhabits Hispaniola. They are most active at night.

Double-striped Thick-knee *Burhinus bistriatus*

Fig. 70 Double-striped Thick-knee

Local names: Búcaro; Coq Savane; Poule Savane.

Description: 15–17″. A crow-sized, plover-like bird of open country. Upperparts a mixture of blackish and buffy brown; underparts mostly white, the breast pale grey with narrow black streaks; a white superciliary stripe and black stripes bordering crown; shows some white on wing in flight. The yellow eyes are large, the bill short and thick, the long legs greenish. *Most active at night.* Runs in spurts like a plover, with head drawn in on shoulders. Does not often take to wing. Most readily found by *riding* through plantations. Fig. 70.

Voice: A series of loud, cackling notes, descending in pitch. Usually heard after sundown.

Habitat: Savannas and open, cultivated country.

Nidification: Lays 2 spotted eggs on the ground.
Range: Hispaniola. Also Central and northern South America, including Margarita Island.

SKUAS & JAEGERS *Stercorariidae*

Jaegers are powerful, falcon-like, pelagic birds of the north, characterised by hooked bills and wedge-shaped tails with elongated central rectrices. By nature they are parasitic, attacking gulls and other sea birds to force them to drop or disgorge their food, although they often feed on floating galley refuse. They are rarely observed in the Caribbean, but are apt to be seen in the Gulf Stream off north-western Cuba and west of the Bahamas. They often follow steamers en route to Havana and remain with these until land is approached, when they veer out to sea.

All three jaegers are known from the West Indies, and there are records of the massive, hawk-like skuas of the genus *Catharacta* from this region (see

"Addenda", p. 241). The Pomarine Jaeger and Parasitic Jaeger have light and dark colour phases.

Parasitic Jaeger *Stercorarius parasiticus*

Fig. 71 Parasitic Jaeger

Description: 16–21". Upperparts sooty brown, darkest on pileum; hindneck and sides of neck straw-yellow; underparts mostly white; considerable white at bases of primaries, conspicuous in flight. Plumage sooty brown in dark phase, but white shows on undersides of wings. Tail wedge-shaped, the central feathers elongated and pointed in adults. Fig. 71.

Range: Chiefly arctic regions. Winters (in New World) south to southern South America. Not uncommon in Gulf Stream north of western Cuba and west of the Bahamas; also recorded from Jamaica, the Morant Cays, Barbados and the Grenadines (Dec. 7–May 12: one July record).

GULLS & TERNS *Laridae*

The Laridae are the most widespread and best known of sea birds, and are well represented in the West Indies, although there is but one indigenous species of gull in this region. All of the West Indian members of this family occur in North America, but the Bridled Tern only as a vagrant.

Unlike gulls, terns feed almost entirely on small fish, which they obtain by plunging into the sea. They may be distinguished from gulls by their straight bills and comparatively narrow wings. The majority are mostly grey above and white below, with black "caps" and forked tails.

Herring Gull *Larus argentatus*

Description: 25". Readily distinguished from the Laughing Gull by its large size, mostly yellow bill and pale pink legs. The immature is greyish brown. The common gull of the North Atlantic, but quite rare in the West Indies.

Habitat: Most frequently seen in the harbours of Havana and Matanzas.
Range: A widespread gull of the Northern Hemisphere. Winters (in New World) south to the Antilles and Panama (Sept. 15–May 21).

Ring-billed Gull *Larus delawarensis*

Description: 19″. Resembles the Herring Gull, but *smaller*; a *black ring around bill*; legs yellowish or greenish (but pinkish first year); in flight shows more black on under side of wing. The immature shows white on basal portion of tail. Young Herring Gull has a blackish ring on bill.
Range: Breeds in interior of North America. Winters south to the Bahamas, Greater Antilles and Panama; vagrant to St. Martin, Martinique and Barbados (Oct. 13–May 13).

Laughing Gull *Larus atricilla* 4/97 DR

Fig. 72 Laughing Gull

Local names: Sea Gull; Laughing Bird; Gullie; Gallego Común; Galleguito; Gaviota Gallega; Gaviota Cabecinegra; Gaviota Boba; Mauve à Tête Noire; Goéland; Pigeon de la Mer; Mangui.
Description: 19″. In breeding plumage, at once distinguished from other West Indian gulls and terns (apart from vagrants) by its *black head.* In winter the head is merely mottled with blackish on the top and sides. In flight shows white border on hind edge of wing. The immature is mainly greyish brown above (white at base of tail) and the breast is dusky. *The only gull apt to be seen in the Antilles.* Fig. 72.
Voice: A raucous "laughter", but more often a querulous *ke-ruh.*
Habitat: Coastal areas.

Nidification: Terrestrial; in colonies. Eggs (3–4) greenish, spotted.
Range: Breeds from North America south to islands in the southern Caribbean Sea. Occurs throughout the West Indies.

Bonaparte's Gull   *Larus philadelphia*

Description: 13–14″. A small, tern-like gull, black headed in breeding plumage; *outer portion of wing mostly white*, appearing as a white band in contrast with grey of inner wing; outer remiges bordered with black. In winter plumage, head mostly white, with a conspicuous blackish spot behind eye. *Bill slender, black*; feet orange-red. The immature resembles winter adults, but has a dusky band along inner part of wing, and a well-defined black tip to white tail; bill paler at base. The slightly larger European Black-headed Gull, a vagrant to the Lesser Antilles, resembles this species, but may be distinguished by paler bill and *broad dusky streak on under side of wing*.

Range: North-western North America. Winters south to Mexico and the West Indies. Recorded from the Bahamas, Cuba, Haiti, Puerto Rico, Martinique and Barbados (Aug. 17–April 29).

Gull-billed Tern   *Gelochelidon nilotica*

Fig. 73 Gull-billed Tern

Local names: Gullie; Egg Bird; Gaviota de Pico Corto; Pigeon de la Mer; Oiseau Fou.
Description: 14″. A chunky tern, pale grey above and white below, with a black "cap" in breeding season; at other times the pileum is whitish, more or less streaked with black, with a black spot before eye and dusky patch on ear-coverts; legs and relatively *thick bill* black; tail forked, but not deeply. Often feeds on insects. Fig. 73.
Voice: A katydid-like *cha-cha-chi* or *cha-chi.*
Habitat: Usually coastal beaches, but sometimes seen "hawking" for insects well back from the shore.
Nidification: Terrestrial; in colonies. Eggs (2–3) spotted.
Range: Cosmopolitan. Summer resident in Bahamas, Virgin Is. (Anegada) and on Sombrero; transient or rare winter resident elsewhere. Winters mainly in western and southern Caribbean.

Forster's Tern   *Sterna forsteri*

Description: 14.5″. In breeding plumage closely resembles the Common Tern, but wings (primaries) silvery white instead of grey; *inner* webs of outermost tail feathers blackish. Those reported from the West Indies have been young or adults in winter plumage when readily identified by broad black stripe through eye in contrast with white of crown and nape. Young do not have a dusky bar on inner portion of wing as in Common Tern. Feeds on insects as well as fish.

Range: North America. Winters south to Guatemala. Rare in the West Indies, whence recorded from the Bahamas, and Greater Antilles (November–April).

Common Tern   *Sterna hirundo*

Local names: Gullie; Egg Bird; Gaviota; Palometa; Petite Mauve.
Description: 15″. Slighter in build than Gull-billed Tern. In breeding plumage, mostly white, with grey mantle and wings and black "cap"; tail deeply forked, the long, outermost feathers with blackish outer webs; bill slender, *red, tipped with black.* In winter plumage, lacks the black cap, but band through eye and across nape sooty black, and crown streaked with black; bill black or mostly black. Young resemble winter adults, but are mottled with dusky above. Often confused with Roseate Tern.
Voice: A harsh, drawling *kee-ar-r-r*; also a short *kik.*
Habitat: Coastal areas.
Nidification: Like that of Roseate Tern, but clutch-size 2–3.
Range: North America, Europe and Asia; may not breed in the West Indies, but indigenous to Dutch and Venezuelan islands in the southern Caribbean. Winters (in the New World) south to northern Argentina; transient and rare winter resident in the West Indies where recorded throughout the year.

Roseate Tern   *Sterna dougallii*

Local names: Gullie; Davie; Gaviota; Palometa; Pigeon de la Mer; Oiseau Fou; Petite Mauve; Mauve Blanche; Carite.
Description: 15.5″. Closely resembles Common Tern, but upperparts paler and black of pileum extends farther on hindneck; bill slenderer and black, except in breeding season and in summer when more or less red basally; *some individuals have most, if not all, of bill orange-red* at this season, and these are often misidentified as Common Terns; tail more deeply forked, the outer feathers entirely white and *extend beyond wings when bird is at rest*; wing shorter (less than 9.25″). Both of these terns are rarely seen in winter.
Voice: A rasping *krek*; less often a plover-like *hew-it.*
Habitat: Coastal areas.

Nidification: Terrestrial; in colonies, usually on small islets. Eggs (1–2, rarely 3) spotted.
Range: Cosmopolitan. Found virtually throughout the West Indies, breeding in Bahamas, Greater Antilles and Lesser Antilles, and on extra-limital islets in the Caribbean.

Bridled Tern *Sterna anaethetus*

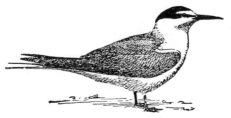

Fig. 74 Bridled Tern

Local names: Egg Bird; Booby; Bubí; Gaviota; Gaviota Oscura; Gaviota Monja; Oiseau Fou (Haiti); Touaou; Dongue.
Description: 15″. Differs from the Sooty Tern in having the back, wings and tail brownish grey in contrast with the deep black

Plate 7 **FLYCATCHERS & COTINGA**

1	Jamaican Becard *Female*	149
2	Stolid Flycatcher *Bahama race*	153
3	Rufous-tailed Flycatcher	154
4	Loggerhead Kingbird *Bahama race*	151
5	Lesser Antillean Pewee *Puerto Rico race*	154
6	Greater Antillean Pewee *Bahama race*	154
7	Jamaican Elaenia	157
8	Yellow-bellied Elaenia	156
9	Caribbean Elaenia	156
10	Greater Antillean Elaenia *Hispaniola race*	157

of the crown; a white streak from base of culmen to above and *behind eye. In flight shows some white on hindneck.* The immature is very different from the young Sooty Tern: head, hindneck and underparts white, the crown streaked with black; rest of upperparts blackish with brown margins to the feathers. The two species often nest on the same cay. Rarely seen in winter. Fig. 74.

Voice: A querulous, high-pitched *erk.*

Habitat: A pelagic tern.

Nidification: Like that of Sooty Tern, but egg usually less exposed.

Range: Tropical seas. Found virtually throughout the West Indies.

Sooty Tern   *Sterna fuscata*

Local names: Egg Bird; Booby; Bubí; Hurricane Bird; Gaviota Oscura; Gaviota Monja; Oiseau Fou; Touaou.

Description: 16″. *Black above* and white below; forehead and streak extending to point above, but not behind, eye white; tail deeply forked, the outer webs of elongated feathers white; bill and feet black. *The immature is sooty brown;* paler and greyer on underparts; back spotted with white. The black upperparts, showing no white on hindneck, dis-

Plate 8   HUMMINGBIRDS (2)

B.W.I.   G

tinguishes the Sooty from the Bridled Tern in flight. Rarely seen in winter.
Voice: A shrill *de-wérra*.
Habitat: A pelagic tern.
Nidification: Terrestrial; in colonies, usually on remote islets. One spotted egg is laid. Breeding season for most part in spring, but at Aves Island and Alta Vela in winter.
Range: Tropical seas. Occurs virtually throughout the West Indies.

Least Tern *Sterna albifrons*

Local names: Kill-'em-Polly; Sea Swallow; Egg Bird; Peterman; Gaviota Chica; Golondrina de Mar; Gaviotica; Pigeon de la Mer; Oiseau Fou; Petite Mauve.
Description: 9″. Somewhat resembles a Roseate Tern, but *much smaller*. In breeding season with a *yellow, black-tipped bill*; a white band from bill to above eye; feet orange-yellow. In autumn the bill is blackish, the feet dusky yellow, and the black "cap" obsolete.
Voice: A short *kip* or *kipic*; also a high-pitched *chereep*.
Habitat: Sea coast and inland lakes or lagoons.
Nidification: Lays 1–3 spotted eggs, usually on beaches above high-water mark, on large islands as well as small.
Range: Cosmopolitan. Common (locally) in West Indies, where a summer resident (April 1–Oct. 17).

Royal Tern *Thalasseus maximus*

Fig. 75 Royal Tern

Local names: Sprat Bird; Gullie; Gabby; Egg Bird; Gaviota Real; Pigeon de la Mer; Oiseau Fou; Mauve; Foquette.

Description: 20″. The *common large tern* of the West Indies, readily recognised by its large, *orange or yellow bill*; feet black; black feathers on nape elongated; tail moderately forked. General colour-pattern like that of Roseate Tern. *The only tern apt to be seen in winter.* Fig. 75.
Voice: A shrill *teerr*.
Habitat: Mainly along the seashore.
Nidification: Nests in colonies on small cays. One (rarely 2) beautifully spotted egg is laid.
Range: Mainly tropical and subtropical American seas; also coast of West Africa. Found throughout the West Indies.

Sandwich Tern   *Thalasseus sandvicensis*

Local names: Gullie; Egg Bird; Gaviota de Pico Agudo.
Description: 15″. Smaller than a Royal Tern, the *bill black with a yellowish tip*; the South American yellowish-billed race interbreeds sparingly in Virgin Island colonies; hybrids have dark, mottled bills.
Voice: A shrill *kir-ik*.
Habitat: Coastal areas. Transient virtually throughout West Indies.
Nidification: Like that of Royal Tern. Eggs (1–2) spotted, and often scrawled.
Range: Widespread in West Indies. Breeds in Europe, the south-eastern United States, Bahamas (Green Cay, Hogsty Reef, Ragged Islands), off Yucatan, Cayo Los Ballenatos south of Cuba, off Culebra and in the Virgin Islands; the South American race, which predominates in the southern Caribbean, breeds south to Argentina.

Caspian Tern   *Hydroprogne caspia*   4/97   DR

Description: 21″. Resembles the Royal Tern, but larger with a *heavier, red bill*; tail less deeply forked—about a quarter, rather than half, its length; under surface of wings darker.
Voice: A hoarse *kaak*, not shrill and high-pitched like that of Royal Tern.
Habitat: Seacoast.
Range: Cosmopolitan. In New World breeds in North America and winters south to Colombia. Visitant to Bahamas and Greater Antilles where it occurs during all seasons.

Black Tern   *Chlidonias niger*

Local names: Gaviota Negra; Gaviota Ceniza.
Description: 9.5″. In nuptial plumage grey, with black head, neck and

underparts, apart from white under tail-coverts. In West Indies, most apt to be seen in winter plumage when dark grey, with white forehead, nuchal collar and underparts, and a black streak behind eye; bill black. A small tern with a slightly forked tail. Flight rather wavering like that of a nighthawk.

Habitat: Fresh-water lakes, ponds, marshes and lagoons.

Range: Breeds in North America, Europe and Asia. Winters (in New World) chiefly off western South America. Rare transient in West Indies (April 11–Nov. 21).

Brown Noddy
Anous stolidus

Fig. 76 Brown Noddy

Local names: Egg Bird; Booby; Black Bird; Lark; Gaviota Boba; Severo; Cervera; Bubí; Moine; Minime; Charles.

Description: 15″. A distinctively coloured tern, mostly sooty brown, with a whitish "*cap*" in adults; *tail rounded*. Not apt to be seen in winter. Fig. 76. See Black Noddy (A. *tenuirostris*), p. 243.

Voice: A dry *kak*, or a hoarse, rook-like growl.

Habitat: A pelagic tern.

Nidification: In colonies on small cays. The single, sparingly spotted egg is laid on the ground, or in a crevice of a rock; in some localities builds a rough nest in a bush, or a low tree.

Range: Mainly tropical seas. Widespread among the West Indies.

SKIMMERS *Rynchopidae*

Skimmers comprise a small family of three species, all belonging to the genus *Rynchops*. One is found in the New World, one in Africa and the third in Asia. They have the peculiar habit of immersing their elongated lower mandibles when flying over the surface of the water. Their food consists of small fish and shrimp obtained for the most part at night or in the evening or early morning.

Black Skimmer *Rynchops nigra*

Fig. 77 Black Skimmer

Local name: Pico de Tijera (Cuba).

Description: 17–20″. Upperparts chiefly brownish black; inner remiges more or less tipped with white; forehead, lores and underparts white; bill narrow and blade-like, red or reddish basally, the distal portion black; *lower mandible decidedly longer than upper;* feet orange-red; wings very long. Fig. 77.

Range: South-eastern North America south to South America, but does not breed in West Indies, whence recorded from the Bahama Islands, Cuba (where numerous at times), off northern coast of Hispaniola, Puerto Rico, Virgin Islands and from Guadeloupe (Nov. 26–April 7). A South American race has been recorded from Grenada (July 31).

PIGEONS & DOVES *Columbidae*

This familiar cosmopolitan family is well represented in the West Indies. One genus (*Starnoenas*) and several species are endemic to this region.

In addition to those described, the extinct Passenger Pigeon occurred as a vagrant to Cuba (see "List of Vagrants"). The domestic Rock Dove (*Columba livia*) and, locally, Old World turtle doves (*Streptopelia*) occur as semi-feral species.

White-crowned Pigeon *Columba leucocephala*

Local names: Bald-pate; White-head; Paloma Cabeciblanca; Paloma Coronita; Paloma Casco Blanco; Torcaza Cabeciblanca; Ramier Tête-blanche.

Description: 14″. A dark grey pigeon with a conspicuous *white crown*. The crown is greyish white in females and smoky grey in immature birds. Highly gregarious. *Moves freely among the islands.* Fig. 78.

Voice: A throaty *crooo-cru-cru-crooo*, reminiscent of European Wood Pigeon.

Habitat: Widespread in woodlands, but most abundant at low elevations.

Nidification: In colonies, usually on cays or in coastal mangroves. Nests are built in trees. Eggs (1–2) white.

Range: Almost throughout the West Indies, but unknown in Lesser Antilles south of St. Lucia, and apparently casual south of St. Martin, St. Bartholomew and Antigua. Also Florida Keys and islands in western Caribbean Sea.

Fig. 78 White-crowned Pigeon

Red-necked Pigeon   *Columba squamosa*   page 33

Local names: Red-necked Pigeon (Jamaica); Blue Pigeon; Paloma Turca; Torcaza Cuellimorada; Ramier Cou-rouge.

Description: 15″. A dark slate-grey pigeon, the head, foreneck and chest dull vinaceous; hindneck chestnut and metallic purple; bare skin about eye reddish in males, yellowish in females; feet and basal part of bill red.

Voice: Closely resembles the cooing of the White-crowned Pigeon, but less guttural.

Habitat: Woodland. Most numerous in humid rain forest, but also occurs in drier lowlands, including Bridgetown, Barbados.

Nidification: Nests usually situated at moderate elevations in trees, rarely in shrubs and in crevices of cliffs. Eggs (1–2) white.

Range: Greater and Lesser Antilles, and some extralimital islands in southern Caribbean Sea.

Ring-tailed Pigeon   *Columba caribaea*   page 33

Local name: Ring-tail.

Description: 16″. Somewhat resembles a Plain Pigeon, but hindneck metallic bronze-green; *no white on wing*; a black band across tail, the distal portion of tail pale drab. No other West Indian pigeon has a bicoloured tail. A heavy, robust species.

Voice: A throaty *cru-cru-crooo*.

Habitat: Forested mountains and hills.

Nidification: Like that of Plain Pigeon.

Range: Jamaica.

Plain Pigeon *Columba inornata* 4/3/97 ♪R   page 33

Local names: Blue Pigeon (Jamaica); Paloma Boba; Torcaza Boba; Torcaza Cenicienta; Paloma Ceniza; Paloma Sabanera; Ramier Millet.
Description: 15″. Head, forepart of body and underparts vinaceous, and wings washed with this colour; mantle greyish brown; rump and tail grey; *wing-coverts margined with white.* Paler and more purplish than any other pigeon, and other large pigeons lack white on wings.
Voice: A hooting *crooo-cruh-cruh,* repeated a number of times, sometimes preceded by a guttural note.
Habitat: Forested woodland as well as fairly open country in mountains and in lowlands. Rare, except in parts of Hispaniola.
Nidification: Nests in trees at moderate elevations above the ground. Eggs (1–2) white.
Range: Cuba, Isle of Pines, Jamaica, Hispaniola (including Tortue Island), and Puerto Rico.

Mourning Dove *Zenaida macroura* 4/97   ♪R

Local names: Turtle Dove; Paloma; Long-tailed Pea Dove; Rabiche; Tórtola; Tórtola Rabilarga; Fifi; Tourterelle Queue-fine.
Description: 11–13″. Resembles the Zenaida Dove, but slenderer and with a long, pointed tail; no white on wing.
Voice: A mournful *cuácoo-coo-coo;* occasionally a soft *ooá-oo.*
Habitat: More or less open country, both in lowlands and in mountains.
Nidification: Nests at low or moderate elevations in bushes or trees, rarely on ground. Eggs (2) white.
Range: Bahama Islands and Greater Antilles east to Culebra and Vieques; rare or casual east of Hispaniola. Also North and Central America.

Violet-eared Dove *Zenaida auriculata*   page 33

Local names: Trinidad Ground Dove; Tourterelle-Ortolan.
Description: 9–10″. A small dove, resembling the Mourning Dove, but tail short and not as pointed; *no white on tail* of West Indian race; underparts more vinaceous. Also resembles Zenaida Dove, but smaller; upperparts greyer; sides of neck golden bronze; no white on wings or tail. Male has grey crown. Like Mourning and Zenaida Doves, largely terrestrial. Often congregates in flocks.
Voice: A soft *ooa-oo* or *u-ooa-oo,* reminiscent of Zenaida Dove, but low in volume. Does not emit the more protracted cooing characteristic of the Zenaida Dove and Mourning Dove.
Habitat: Semi-arid areas. More numerous and widespread on Tobago.

Nidification: Nests at various elevations in trees, palms or shrubbery, rarely on ground. Eggs (2) white.

Range: Martinique (2 records), St. Lucia, St. Vincent, Barbados (2 records), the Grenadines and Grenada. Also islands in southern Caribbean, including Tobago and Trinidad, and continental South America.

Zenaida Dove *Zenaida aurita* page 33

Local names: Wood Dove; Seaside Dove; Mountain Dove; Pea Dove; Tórtola; Cardosantera; Bobona; Rolón; Sanjuanera; Guanaro; Tourterelle; Tourterelle Rouge; Grosse Tourterelle; Gros Tourte.

Description: 11–12″. A stocky dove, brown above and vinaceous below; more or less cinnamon about head and neck; black spots on wings; dark violet-blue (appearing black) streaks above and below ear-coverts; sides of neck more or less purple; tips of outer secondaries white and *broad, white tips to outer tail-feathers.* The underparts vary in intensity of colour.

Voice: A mournful *cuácoo-coo-coo* like a Mourning Dove, but usually slightly more curtailed; also a short *ooá-oo*, more resonant than that of Violet-eared Dove.

Habitat: Fairly open country; particularly in lowlands. Does not occur in dense forest. Found in Bridgetown, Barbados.

Nidification: Nests in shrubbery and trees at low or moderate elevations; sometimes on ground. Eggs (2) white.

Range: Virtually throughout the West Indies. Also coast of Yucatán Peninsula and adjacent islands; formerly Florida Keys; not present on Swan Islands, Old Providence and St. Andrew.

White-winged Dove
Zenaida asiatica

Local names: Whitewing; Lap-wing; Aliblanca; Tourterelle Aileblanche; "Barbarin".

Description: 12″. Approximately the same size as Zenaida Dove; underparts duller; *a conspicuous white band along edge of wing*; no black spots on wings. Arboreal in habits. Fig. 79.

Voice: An explosive *cur-*

Fig. 79 Whitewinged Dove

uca-cao-cola-cao-cola-cao-cola, frequently followed by a softer *cura-curoo.*
Habitat: Lowlands and lower wooded hills.
Nidification: Nests in shrubs or trees at low or moderate elevations. Eggs
(2) white.
Range: Southern Bahamas (rare), Cuba, Isle of Pines, Jamaica, Cayman
Islands, Swan Island, Old Providence, St. Andrew, Hispaniola and adjacent
islands, Mona, Puerto Rico, Vieques; casual on St. Croix. Also southern
North America to western South America.

Common Ground Dove
Columbina passerina

4/3/97 DR

Local names: Ground Dove;
Stone Dove; Tobacco Dove;
Rola; Rolita; Tortolita; To-
josa; Palomita de la Virgen;
Ortolan.
Description: 6–7″. A tiny,
terrestrial dove, not much
larger than a sparrow. Rufous
on wings apparent in flight
that is whirring and of short
duration; feathers of foreneck and breast with dusky
centres, presenting a scale-

Fig. 80 Common Ground Dove

like effect. Female duller than male. The most widespread of West Indian
birds. Fig. 80.
Voice: A soft *wa* or *oo-a,* with rising inflection.
Habitat: Open country, chiefly in lowlands, but found high in mountains
of Hispaniola.
Nidification: In shrubbery near the ground; nest sometimes on ground.
Eggs (2) white.
Range: Virtually throughout West Indies, but absent from Swan Islands,
Old Providence and St. Andrew. Also Bermudas and from southern United
States south to Brazil and Ecuador.

Caribbean Dove *Leptotila jamaicensis*   page 33

Local names: White-belly; Ground Dove (St. Andrew).
Description: 12–13″. A terrestrial dove, distinguished from the Zenaida
Dove by white forehead, largely white underparts and absence of any
black or white on wings. Fig. 81.

Voice: A plaintive *cu-cu-cu-oooo*.
Habitat: Mainly lowlands. Most numerous in semi-arid districts.
Nidification: Nests in shrubbery; occasionally on the ground. Eggs (2) white.
Range: Jamaica, Grand Cayman, St. Andrew; introduced on New Providence. Yucatán Peninsula and islands; Bay Islands.

Fig. 81 Caribbean Dove

Grenada Dove   *Leptotila wellsi*

page 33

Local name: Unknown.
Description: 12″. A rare, terrestrial dove about the size of a Zenaida Dove, but duller with *no black or white markings on wings*; forehead white; bare skin around eyes red; no blackish spots on sides of head, and little white at tips of outer tail feathers.
Voice: A mournful, descending *oooo*, repeated after intervals of about eight seconds. Resembles cooing of White-bellied Dove, but lacks short preliminary notes.
Habitat: Scrubby hillsides of southern Grenada; occurs near Grand Anse.
Nidification: Unknown.
Range: Grenada.

Crested Quail Dove   *Geotrygon versicolor*   page 48

Local names: Blue Dove; Blue Partridge; Mountain Witch.
Description: 12″. A gaudily coloured dove, with a short but distinct crest. Forehead black; rest of pileum and most of underparts greyish; a conspicuous cinnamon malar stripe; hindneck iridescent light bronzy; mantle and wing-coverts iridescent purple; most of primaries and posterior underparts rufous; rest of plumage glossy blackish; bill black; feet pink. Fig. 82.

Fig. 82 Crested Quail Dove

Voice: A doleful *cooo-cu*, the second note softer and lower in pitch.
Habitat: Forest undergrowth. Most numerous in Blue Mountains.
Nidification: Nests in forest undergrowth; occasionally on ground. Eggs (2) buff.
Range: Jamaica.

Grey-headed Quail Dove   *Geotrygon caniceps*   page 48

Local names: Camao; Azulona (Cuba); Paloma del Suelo; Perdiz Coquito Blanco (Dom. Rep.).
Description: 11″. A beautiful quail dove with variegated colours. Head and underparts mostly grey; mantle purple; rump violet-blue; lower abdomen and under tail-coverts tawny; some rufous on wing; bill and feet pink. The Hispaniolan race has a white forehead. Unlike any other dove of Cuba and Hispaniola.
Voice: A low *hup*, repeated rapidly, and suddenly changing to a drawnout, throbbing *cooo* (Hispaniola).
Habitat: Forested regions of Cuba and mountain forest in Dominican Republic.
Nidification: In low undergrowth. Eggs (1–2) buff.
Range: Cuba and Dominican Republic; not definitely known from Haiti.

Ruddy Quail Dove   *Geotrygon montana*   page 48

Local names: Partridge; Red Partridge; Mountain Perdrix; Perdiz (except Cuba); Boyero; Torito; Quejosa; Perdrix Rouge (male); Perdrix Noire (female); Perdrix Grise (female).
Description: 10–12″. Sexes dissimilar. *Male:* Rufous above, vinaceous buff below, with a buffy streak below eye. *Female:* Mainly dark olive-brown above, paler below. Bill and feet red or reddish. Birds from Guadeloupe to St. Lucia are larger than those from elsewhere, St. Vincent individuals intermediate in size.
Voice: A prolonged, booming note, reminiscent of the doleful sound of a fog-buoy.
Habitat: Chiefly humid forest, and coffee and cacao plantations.
Nidification: Nests at low elevations in undergrowth; occasionally on ground. Eggs (2) buff.
Range: Greater Antilles east to Vieques Island; Lesser Antilles (Guadeloupe, Dominica, Martinique, St. Lucia, St. Vincent, Grenada). Also tropical Central and South America.

Key West Quail Dove *Geotrygon chrysia* page 48

Local names: Partridge; Barbiquejo (Cuba); Perdiz; Torito; Perdrix.

Description: 11–12″. Mainly rufous above, but crown, hindneck and upper mantle glossed with green and purple, and some purple gloss on back and wings; underparts largely white, the breast pale vinaceous; a white streak below eye, bordered below by rufous; bill and feet reddish. Might

Fig. 83 Key West Quail Dove

be mistaken for *male* Ruddy Quail Dove; best distinguished by *white* stripe below eye, whitish underparts and iridescent upperparts. Fig. 83.

Voice: A protracted booming note like that of Ruddy Quail Dove, but less resonant.

Habitat: Chiefly semi-arid woodland and lowland scrub. Numerous in and near Hispaniola, but rare on islands elsewhere in the Antilles as well as in the Bahamas.

Nidification: Nests at low elevations in undergrowth; occasionally on ground. Eggs (1–2) buff.

Range: Bahamas (unrecorded from many southern islands), Cuba (including Isle of Pines and cays), Hispaniola and adjacent islands, Mona (?), southern Puerto Rico; vagrant to Florida.

Bridled Quail Dove *Geotrygon mystacea* page 48

Local names: Barbary Dove; Marmy Dove (Virgin Islands); Wood Hen (Saba); Partridge; Perdrix Croissant.

Description: 12″. Resembles Key West Quail Dove, but darker; most of upperparts, apart from iridescent anterior portion, dusky olive-brown; rufous confined to wings (primaries, outer margin of wing and under wing-coverts) and outer tail feathers; underparts buffy brown, the throat and *stripe below eye white*. Might be mistaken for *female* Ruddy Quail Dove, but shows some rufous on wing, and has white or whitish stripe below eye.

Voice: Like that of Key West Quail Dove.

Habitat: Woodland and rain forest, but favours drier localities than Ruddy Quail Dove.

Nidification: Nests usually at low elevations. Eggs (1–2) buff.
Range: Culebra, Vieques, Virgin Islands (excluding Anegada and most of smaller cays), and Lesser Antilles from Saba and Barbuda south to St. Lucia.

Blue-headed Quail Dove *Starnoenas cyanocephala* page 48

Local names: Perdiz; Paloma Perdiz.
Description: 12–13″. A large, brown quail dove with a blue crown, and a blue and black white-bordered "bib"; a black stripe through eye and a white stripe below eye; no rufous on wings. Unlike any other Cuban dove. Fig. 84.
Voice: A rapid *hup-up*, rather deep, like a soft fog horn.
Habitat: Woodland undergrowth.
Nidification: In shrubbery on or near ground. Eggs (1–2) white.
Range: Cuba and the Isle of Pines.

Fig. 84 Blue-headed
Quail Dove

PARROTS, PARAKEETS & MACAWS *Psittacidae*

Parrots and parakeets are widely distributed, particularly in tropical countries. Only two genera are native to the West Indies, one comprising parrots of the genus *Amazona*, the other parakeets of the genus *Aratinga*. Formerly there were macaws in this region, but specimens are extant of only the Cuban Macaw (*Ara tricolor*), which became extinct during the 19th century. South American parakeets have been introduced successfully in Puerto Rico (see p. 239) and Jamaica.

Members of this family feed chiefly on fruit, and some of the commoner species cause considerable damage to plantations of banana, guava, etc. They are usually found in pairs or flocks, particularly early in the morning or late in the afternoon. In flight the shallow, rapid wing-beats are characteristic.
Voice: Parrots squawk (*waak-waak*), parakeets screech (*creek-creek*), parrotlets chatter softly.
Nidification: In cavities of trees or palms, sometimes (parrots) in rock crevices. The Olive-throated and Caribbean Parakeets and the Guiana Parrotlet often excavate holes for this purpose in termite nests. Eggs of parrots (2–4), parakeets (2–6) and parrotlets are white.

Imperial Parrot *Amazona imperialis* page 32

Local name: Sisserou.
Description: 18–20″. The larger of the two parrots of Dominica. Upperparts mostly green, greenish blue on head; a dark violet band across hindneck, appearing as black; tail and *underparts mostly purplish violet*; a red alar speculum, and red on bend of wing.
Habitat: Mountain forest, chiefly at high elevations.
Range: Dominica.

St. Vincent Parrot *Amazona guildingii* page 32

Local name: Parrot.
Description: 16–18″. A large, beautifully coloured parrot. Head white, yellow and violet; neck mostly green; *body plumage mostly golden brown*, washed with green; wings variegated; tail green and violet-blue, broadly tipped with yellow. Some individuals are greener, less brown. *The only parrot on St. Vincent.*
Habitat: Chiefly mountain forest, but has been found nesting not far above sea level near windward coast.
Range: St. Vincent.

St. Lucia Parrot *Amazona versicolor* page 32

Local names: Jacquot; Perroquet.
Description: 16.5–18″. Mostly green, the head bluish; underparts in adults washed with maroon, the foreneck more or less red; a conspicuous red patch on wing. *The only parrot on St. Lucia.*
Habitat: Mountain forest. Apparently now restricted to the central part of the island; formerly widespread.
Range: St. Lucia.

Red-necked Parrot *Amazona arausiaca* page 32

Local names: Jacquot; Perroquet.
Description: 15–16″. Resembles the St. Lucia Parrot, but slightly smaller and darker; no maroon wash on underparts. *Red neck-patch usually well developed in contrast with green of remainder of underparts.* The smaller of the two parrots of Dominica.
Habitat: Mountain forest, for the most part at lower elevations than the Imperial Parrot.
Range: Dominica.

Cuban Parrot *Amazona leucocephala* page 32

Local names: Parrot; Cotorra; Loro; Cotica; Perico.
Description: 11–13″. Mostly green, with *red throat, foreneck and cheeks*; anterior part of head white; primaries largely blue; abdomen more or less maroon.
Habitat: Found in remote woodlands in Cuba, both in mountains and in low country; elsewhere in dense scrubby woods near sea level.
Range: Bahama Islands (now confined to Abaco, Acklin [no recent report] and Great Inagua), Cuba, Isle of Pines and the Cayman Islands.

Hispaniolan Parrot *Amazona ventralis* 4/2/97 D R page 32

Local names: Cotorra; Jacquot.
Description: 11–12″. Resembles the Cuban Parrot, but white on head restricted to forehead; no red on throat, foreneck or cheeks, this area green like the breast.
Habitat: Woodland. Reported introduced on Puerto Rico and Culebra.
Range: Hispaniola, Grande Cayemite, Gonâve and Saona.

Yellow-billed Parrot *Amazona collaria* page 32

Local name: Yellow-billed Parrot.
Description: 11–12″. Mostly green; forepart of head and ear-coverts bluish, the feathers at base of upper mandible white; throat and foreneck maroon, and some maroon at base of tail; outer margin of wing blue; bill yellowish, but sometimes stained darker.
Habitat: Forested hills and mountains, but rare in Blue Mountains. More widespread than Black-billed Parrot.
Range: Jamaica.

Puerto Rican Parrot *Amazona vittata* page 32

Local name: Cotorra.
Description: 12–13″. Green above and below; a narrow, red band on forehead; outer margins of wings and tail blue.
Habitat: Confined to the Luquillo National Forest; almost extinct.
Range: Puerto Rico, formerly Culebra Island and Vieques Island.

Black-billed Parrot *Amazona agilis* page 32

Local name: Black-billed Parrot.
Description: 10.5–11.5″. Resembles the Yellow-billed Parrot, but entire

upperparts (apart from wings) and underparts green; ear-coverts blackish; *a red alar speculum*; bill blackish.

Habitat: Wooded hills and cattle country of Jamaica, but apparently absent from eastern part of island (Blue Mountains and John Crow Mountains). In some localities (e.g. Cockpit Country) found with Yellow-billed Parrot.

Range: Jamaica.

Hispaniolan Parakeet *Aratinga chloroptera* page 49

Local names: Periquito; Perico; Perruche; Maîtresse.

Description: 12–13″. Plumage green, sometimes with one or more scattered red feathers; under wing-coverts red, this colour showing as a streak along bend of wing; a golden tinge to under surface of remiges and tail; *tail long and pointed.*

Habitat: Most numerous in mountains, but sometimes seen in lowlands.

Range: Hispaniola; one collected in 1892 on Mona Island; apparently formerly inhabited Puerto Rico.

Cuban Parakeet *Aratinga euops* Page 49

Local names: Periquito; Perico; Catey.

Description: 9.5–10.5″. Resembles the Hispaniolan Parakeet, but smaller; red on bend of wing barely apparent; usually more scattered red feathers, particularly on the head. A rather small, green parakeet with a pointed tail.

Habitat: Wooded regions, but occasionally found in open country in the lowlands.

Range: Cuba; formerly the Isle of Pines.

Olive-throated Parakeet *Aratinga nana* page 49

Local name: Parakeet.

Description: 9–10″. Mostly green, but with some blue on the wing, and brownish olive from throat to abdomen. Readily distinguished from the Jamaican parrots by smaller size, pointed tail, and more rapid flight.

Habitat: Chiefly wooded hills and lower mountain slopes.

Range: Jamaica. Also Mexico and Central America.

Caribbean Parakeet *Aratinga pertinax* page 49

Local name: Parakeet.

Description: 9–10″. Upperparts green; forehead, sides of head, throat and centre of abdomen orange-yellow; rest of underparts mostly yellowish; some blue on wing. Similar in form to Olive-throated Parakeet.

Habitat: Scrubby woods or thickets in the hills, descending at times to feed on seasonable fruits. Most numerous in eastern St. Thomas.

Range: St. Thomas (apparently introduced from Curaçao). Also islands in the southern Caribbean Sea, Panama, and northern South America.

Guiana Parrotlet   *Forpus passerinus*

Local names: Parakeet; Love-bird.

Description: 5.5″. A tiny, short-tailed, green parakeet, about the size of a sparrow. Male has more or less blue on the wings and, when adult, the rump is blue. Fig. 85.

Habitat: Steadily increasing its range since its introduction in Jamaica; now widespread in rather open country in

Fig. 85 Guiana Parrotlet

lowlands on the southern side of island. Rare and evidently decreasing on Barbados, whence recently reported from Christchurch and St. Philip.

Range: Jamaica (introduced near Old Harbour, about 1918), and Barbados (introduced during early part of present century); its introduction in Martinique has apparently been unsuccessful. Native to South America, including Trinidad.

CUCKOOS & ANIS   *Cuculidae*

Cuckoos, though best represented in the Old World, range widely through the Americas. Four genera inhabit the West Indies, and of these two (*Hyetornis* and *Saurothera*) are endemic to this region.

The West Indian species of this family are rather sluggish and sometimes difficult to locate, though they are quite tame. They are more often heard than seen. Their food consists mainly of insects, but lizard-cuckoos are known to eat small lizards occasionally and even mice! They are among the most beneficial birds of the islands.

Anis belong to a distinct subfamily (Crotophaginae) and are very different in appearance from other cuckoos.

B.W.I.   H

Mangrove Cuckoo   *Coccyzus minor*   4/97   OR

Fig. 86 Mangrove Cuckoo

Local names: Rain Bird; Rain Crow; May Bird; Four o'Clock Bird; "Mani-coco"; Coffin Bird; Go-go; Pájaro Bobo; Boba; Arrierito; Arriero Chico; Guacaira; Carga-Agua; Primavera; Petit Tacot; Coucou-Manioc; Gangan.

Description: 11–12". Upperparts grey or brownish grey; outer rectrices black, broadly tipped with white; ear-coverts black; throat and breast vary from whitish to rich ochraceous; *posterior underparts always ochraceous*; lower mandible yellow or orange, tipped with black. Fig. 86.

Voice: A guttural *ga-ga-ga-ga-ga-ga-gau-gau-gau-go*. Starts like that of Yellow-billed Cuckoo, but does not slow up suddenly. Less resonant than the voice of a lizard cuckoo.

Habitat: Mangrove swamps and woodlands. Most abundant in semi-arid country in lowlands. Rare in Cuba, except on some cays.

Nidification: At low or moderate elevations above the ground in a tree or shrub. Eggs (2–3) light bluish green.

Range: Virtually throughout the West Indies; in Lesser Antilles from Barbuda, Antigua and Montserrat south, excluding Barbados; vagrant to St. Martin; unknown from Isle of Pines. Also extralimital islands, Central America, northern South America and southern Florida.

Yellow-billed Cuckoo   *Coccyzus americanus*

Local names: See Mangrove Cuckoo.

Description: 11–12". Resembles the Mangrove Cuckoo, but underparts white with *no ochraceous wash*; primaries more or less rufous, but this colour sometimes confined to inner webs and thus not apparent; ear-coverts dusky, not black. Bahaman and Cuban Mangrove Cuckoos have rather white breasts, but the posterior underparts are ochraceous.

Voice: Higher pitched and less guttural than that of Mangrove Cuckoo, and terminating as a rather deliberate *cow-cow-cow-cow*.

Habitat: Mainly lowland scrub and woodland in coastal areas. Rarely seen at high elevations.

Nidification: Like that of Mangrove Cuckoo.

Range: Breeds in the Greater Antilles and probably on some of the

Bahamas and northernmost Lesser Antilles; mainly transient in this region. Also breeds in North America and in northern Central America; winters in South America (Feb. 17–Dec. 4).

Black-billed Cuckoo *Coccyzus erythropthalmus*

Description: 11–12″. Resembles the Yellow-billed Cuckoo, but browner above; no rufous on primaries; under surface of tail feathers grey with indistinct and narrow white tips; *lower mandible black* or mostly black; *naked skin about eye red*, rather than greyish.

Range: Eastern North America. Migrates chiefly through Mexico and Central America and winters in northern and north-western South America. Transient in West Indies (May [May 11]: September 5–November 15).

Chestnut-bellied Cuckoo *Hyetornis pluvialis* page 81

Local names: Old Man Bird; Hunter; Rain Bird.

Description: 20–22″. A large cuckoo with a long tail and rounded bill; upperparts dark olivaceous, more greyish on head; *underparts with contrasted colour-pattern*, the throat white, chest pale grey, the lower breast, abdomen and under tail-coverts chestnut; broad white tips to tail feathers; apart from under wing-coverts, no rufous on wing.

Voice: A guttural, accelerating *ú-ak-ú-ak-ak-ak-ak-ak-ak-ak*.

Habitat: Thickets in rather open districts in the hills and mountains.

Nidification: At low or moderate elevations in bushes or trees. Eggs (2–4) white.

Range: Jamaica.

Bay-breasted Cuckoo *Hyetornis rufigularis* page 81

Local names: Pájaro Bobo; Cua; Tacó; Tacot; Tacot Cabrite.

Description: 17–20″. Upperparts grey; *chin to breast dark chestnut*, the posterior underparts ochraceous; primaries mostly chestnut, appearing as a rufous patch on wing; like other West Indian cuckoos (apart from the ani) has broad white tips to tail feathers. Fig. 87.

Voice: Like that of Chestnut-bellied Cuckoo; also emits a bleating suggestive of a rather large lamb.

Habitat: Found locally from arid lowlands to mountain rain forest.

Nidification: Nests at moderate elevations in trees. Eggs (2) white.

Range: Hispaniola and Gonâve Island.

Fig. 87 Bay-breasted Cuckoo

Great Lizard Cuckoo *Saurothera merlini*

Local names: Rain Crow; Big Rain Crow; "Kataw"; Arriero; Guacaico; Tacó.
Description: 18–22". A large, long-tailed cuckoo. Above olive-brown (Cuba), greyish brown (Isle of Pines) or greyish (Bahamas); primaries more or less rufous; anterior underparts whitish; posterior underparts buff (Bahamas) or ochraceous; tail feathers, apart from central pair, with whitish tips and black subterminally; bare skin around eye red; bill long and rather straight. Other cuckoos of

Fig. 88 Great Lizard Cuckoo

Cuba and the Bahamas are *much smaller*. Races of *S. merlini* from the Bahamas are smaller than Cuban form. Fig. 88.
Voice: A throaty *ka-ka-ka-ka-ka-ka-ka-ka-kau-kau-ko-ko*, louder and less guttural than voice of Mangrove Cuckoo; suggestive of notes of a flicker, but of cuckoo-like quality. Also a guttural *tuc-wuh-h*.

Habitat: Widespread in woodland and thickets.
Nidification: The four species of *Saurothera* nest at low or moderate elevations above the ground. Eggs (2–3) white.
Range: Bahama Islands (Andros, New Providence, Eleuthera), Cuba and the Isle of Pines.

Hispaniolan Lizard Cuckoo *Saurothera longirostris*　　page 81

Local names: Pájaro Bobo; Tacó; Tacot.
Description: 16–18″. Upperparts grey, the primaries mostly chestnut, forming *a rufous patch on wing*; throat variable, whitish (Gonâve Island) to ochraceous; *breast pale grey*, the posterior underparts ochraceous; white tips to outer tail feathers, these black subterminally; bare skin about eye red. The common cuckoo of Hispaniola.
Voice: Like that of Great Lizard Cuckoo.　　4/3/97 ＤＲ
Habitat: Like that of Great Lizard Cuckoo.
Range: Hispaniola, including Gonâve, Tortue and Saona.

Jamaican Lizard Cuckoo *Saurothera vetula*　　page 81

Local names: May Bird; Old Woman Bird; Rain Bird.
Description: 15–16″. Differs from Hispaniolan Lizard Cuckoo in having the anterior upperparts brown; throat and foreneck white, the remainder of underparts ochraceous. The white tips to the tail feathers are very wide and even the central feathers are tipped with white. Readily distinguished from the smaller Mangrove Cuckoo and larger Chestnut-bellied Cuckoo by its long, almost straight bill, and by the rufous wing-patch.
Voice: Like that of other lizard cuckoos.
Habitat: Dense woodland in the hills, and in semi-arid country; apparently does not occur in mountain rain forest.
Range: Jamaica.

Puerto Rican Lizard Cuckoo *Saurothera vieilloti*　　page 81

Fig. 89 Puerto Rican
　　　　Lizard Cuckoo

Local names: Pájaro Bobo; Pájaro de Agua.
Description: 16–18″. Resembles Hispaniolan Lizard Cuckoo, but upperparts rufescent; underparts darker, but throat whitish; posterior underparts tawny; *no rufous evident on wing*. The long, straightish bill and bicoloured under-

parts distinguish this species from other Puerto Rican cuckoos. Fig. 89.
Voice: Like that of other lizard cuckoos.
Habitat: Woodland, coffee plantations, and brush-covered limestone hills.
Range: Puerto Rico, and possibly Vieques Island.

Smooth-billed Ani *Crotophaga ani*

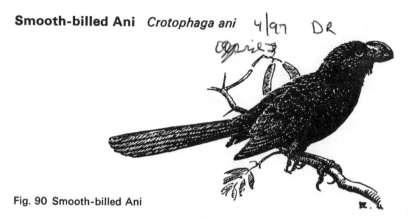

Fig. 90 Smooth-billed Ani

Local names: Black Daw; Black Witch; Long-tailed Crow; Tick Bird;
Savanna Blackbird; Old Arnold; Chapman Bird; Judío; Garrapatero;
Bourse-Tabac (Haiti); Corbeau; Merle Corbeau; Juif; "Bilbitin"(=corruption of "Bout de Petun").
Description: 14–15". A long-tailed, glossy black cuckoo. Distinguished
from other black birds by its extraordinary bill, deep at base, the ridge of
the culmen high and thin. Flight slow, with alternate flaps and glides.
Fig. 90.
Voice: A shrill, drawling *weu-ik*, *weu-ik*, often emitted on wing.
Habitat: Mainly bush-covered fields, pastures, plantations, gardens.
Nidification: At moderate elevations in bushes or trees. Several females
usually lay in a nest, the eggs deposited in layers, more or less separated by
leaves; those at the bottom fail to hatch even if fertile. As many as 29 eggs
have been found in a nest; these are blue, covered with a white, chalky
deposit.
Range: West Indies; absent from Barbados and from most of the Lesser
Antilles north and north-west of Montserrat (recorded from St. Eustatius),
although widespread on the Virgin Islands that are considered part of the
Greater Antilles (see p. 11). Also southern Florida (rare), islands in
western Caribbean Sea, Panama, and South America, including Trinidad
and Tobago.

OWLS *Strigidae*

Owls are distinguished by their large-headed, neckless appearance. The majority are nocturnal, and thus are rarely seen in daytime. Their flight is noiseless. The larger species feed mostly on small mammals, but also to some extent on birds and insects, the smaller ones mainly on insects.

I have followed the British "Check-list" (1952) in combining the "Tytonidae" (barn owls) with the Strigidae. Among West Indian genera, two (*Gymnoglaux* and *Pseudoscops*) are endemic to this region.

Barn Owl *Tyto alba*

Fig. 91 Barn Owl
(Hispaniola)

Local names: Owl; Screech Owl; Night Owl; Death Owl; Death Bird; Jumbie Bird; Lechuza; Frezaie (Haiti); Chat-huant (Lesser Antilles).

Description: 12–17". A long-legged owl with a heart-shaped face. In light forms (found on islands north and west of Hispaniola and on extralimital islands) largely white. The upperparts are washed with ochraceous and mottled with dusky and white; underparts white, lightly speckled with blackish. Native Barn Owls of Hispaniola and the Lesser Antilles are much darker and smaller, the white replaced by ochraceous. Fig. 91.

Voice: A hissing scream, similar in all forms; also a loud clicking.

Habitat: Caves, old buildings, ruins, and dense thickets in daytime. Often seen coursing fields or marshes at dusk.

Nidification: Nests in caves, abandoned cars, recesses in buildings, and in cavities of trees. Eggs (2–8) white.

Range: Bahama Islands and Greater Antilles, including the Cayman Islands, east to Hispaniola; also Dominica, St. Vincent, the Grenadines and Grenada. A cosmopolitan species. The North American race is a vagrant to the Greater Antilles. There is no satisfactory evidence that two species are indigenous to Hispaniola.

Puerto Rican Screech Owl *Otus nudipes*

Local names: Cuckoo Bird (Virgin Is.); Múcaro.
Description: 9–10″. Resembles a North American Screech Owl (*Otus*

asio), but lacks ear-tufts. Mostly brownish grey or rufescent (two phases), the posterior underparts white, streaked with black or dark brown. The only other owl in Puerto Rico is the much larger Short-eared Owl. Fig. 92.

Voice: A protracted quavering trill; also a loud *coo-coo* like Burrowing Owl, and on occasions a hoarse croaking; and other sounds.

Habitat: Found in densely foliaged trees, thickets or caves during the day. Rare east of Puerto Rico.

Nidification: In caves, crevices in limestone cliffs, under the eaves of houses or in cavities of trees. Eggs (2–3) white.

Range: Puerto Rico, Culebra, Vieques, St. Thomas, St. John, Tortola, Virgin Gorda and St. Croix.

Fig. 92 Puerto Rican
Screech Owl

Bare-legged Owl *Gymnoglaux lawrencii*

Local names: Cotunto; Sijú Cotunto; Cuco.
Description: 8–9″. Somewhat resembles a Burrowing Owl, but upperparts less heavily spotted with white and *underparts streaked*, not barred; tarsi bare. Occasional individuals are rufescent. Fig. 93.

Voice: An accelerating and rapid trill reminiscent of the Puerto Rican Screech Owl, sometimes answered by an alto *hui-hui-hui-hui*; also a short *cu-cu*.

Habitat: Mainly limestone country. During day time found in densely foliaged trees, thickets or caves.

Nidification: In a cave or cavity of a tree or palm. Eggs (2–3) white.

Range: Cuba and the Isle of Pines.

Fig. 93 Bare-legged Owl

Burrowing Owl *Speotyto cunicularia*

Fig. 94 Burrowing Owl

Local names: Cuckoo Bird (Bahamas); Cucú; Coucou; Coucouterre.
Description: 9″. A terrestrial, long-legged owl, heavily spotted with white above, and *barred* with greyish brown and white below. Flight rapid and bounding, but seldom sustained for more than a few yards. Has a habit of bobbing up and down when agitated. Largely diurnal when breeding. Fig. 94.
Voice: A mellow, rather high-pitched *coo-co-oo*. By day utters a cackling chatter when disturbed.
Habitat: Thickets and semi-open, scrub-covered land. On New Providence, sometimes found on golf course.

Nidification: In burrows excavated in banks. Eggs (2–5) white.
Range: Bahama Islands, Cuba (breeds in west), Hispaniola including Gonâve and Beata; formerly St. Kitts, Nevis, Antigua, Marie Galante: recorded in 1956 from Redonda. Also North, Central and South America.

Cuban Pygmy Owl
Glaucidium siju

Local names: Sijú; Sijucito; Sijú Platanero.
Description: 6–7″. The smallest West Indian owl, and the commonest of Cuban owls. Upperparts greyish brown, with a rufous collar across hindneck; pileum spotted, the back, wings and tail barred, with white or whitish; underparts white, marked chiefly on the lower

Fig. 95 Cuban Pygmy Owl

throat and breast, with dusky or brownish; *tarsi feathered*. Largely diurnal. Fig. 95.

Voice: A startlingly shrill *ku-ku-ku-se-se-si-si-si*, rising in tone; also a soft, slowly repeated *too, too, too*.

Habitat: Woodland.

Nidification: In cavities of trees, usually old woodpecker holes. Eggs (3–4) white.

Range: Cuba and the Isle of Pines.

Short-eared Owl   *Asio flammeus*

Local names: Carabo; Lechuza de Sabana; Múcaro Real; Múcaro de Sabana; Chat-huant.

Description: 14–17″. A large, terrestrial owl, largely diurnal. Ear-tufts short and inconspicuous. General coloration buff to ochraceous buff, heavily marked with blackish above, and with blackish streaks on underparts; toes mostly bare in resident races, feathered in North American birds.

Voice: A short, emphatic *kee-aw*, also more owl-like sounds.

Habitat: Savannas, upland pastures and marshy grassland.

Nidification: Terrestrial. Eggs (2–4) white.

Range: Cosmopolitan. Breeds in Cuba, Hispaniola and Puerto Rico. North American vagrants reported from Grand Turk and St. Bartholomew.

Stygian Owl   *Asio stygius*

Local names: Siguapa (Cuba); Lechuza Orejita (D.R.); Maître-bois (Haiti).

Description: 16–18″. A large, dark owl with *prominent ear-tufts*. Upperparts sooty black, more or less mottled with white or buffy; underparts buff to ochraceous buff, heavily spotted and streaked with sooty black. Fig. 96.

Voice: A loud *hu* or *hu-hu*.

Habitat: Woodland, both in semi-arid and humid regions.

Nidification: In Cuba on the ground or in the deserted nest of another species in a tree. Eggs (2) white.

Fig. 96 Stygian Owl

Range: Cuba, Isle of Pines, Hispaniola and Gonâve Island. Also Mexico, Central and South America.

Jamaican Owl *Pseudoscops grammicus*

Fig. 97 Jamaican Owl

Local names: Brown Owl; Potoo; Patoo.
Description: 12–14″. Plumage tawny, vermiculated with black; underparts streaked with dusky brown; remiges and rectrices irregularly barred with blackish; short but conspicuous ear-tufts. Fig. 97.
Voice: A guttural *gurrr*; occasionally a high-pitched quavering *whoooo*.
Habitat: Woodland, and more open, park-like country.
Nidification: Nests in a cavity of a tree, or in a crotch of a tree well hidden by foliage. Eggs (2) white.
Range: Jamaica.

POTOOS *Nyctibiidae*

The potoos comprise a small tropical American family of nocturnal birds, related to nightjars. The five species are all members of the genus *Nyctibius*. Only one of these occurs in the West Indies.

In habits potoos differ from nightjars by perching in a more or less upright position. They feed on insects, which they obtain in a flycatcher-like manner, rather than by "hawking" as is customary with nightjars.

Common Potoo *Nyctibius griseus*

Local names: Potoo; Patoo (Jamaica); Don Juan (Dom. Rep.); Chathuant (Haiti).
Description: 17–18″. A large grey or tawny grey bird, the plumage spotted and streaked with black and with irregular black barring on remiges and rectrices; *tail very long* (about 8.5″) *and legs very short.*

Fig. 98 Common Potoo

Difficult to locate during the day, for it blends with the bark of trees. Most apt to be seen at dusk on flight to its feeding grounds. Fig. 98.

Voice: Utters a guttural *ho-wow*; also a hoarse *waark-cucu*. The loud and eerie descending half-hoots, half-whistles of South American races have not been recorded in the Antilles.

Habitat: Occurs for the most part at elevations below 3000 feet in both arid and humid areas.

Nidification: Lays a single spotted egg on top of a stub, and incubates in its usual upright posture with eyes shut. A "nest" found near Mandeville was on a mahoe tree stub about twenty feet above ground.

Range: Jamaica, Hispaniola and Gonâve Island. Also Mexico, Central America and South America, including Trinidad and Tobago.

NIGHTJARS *Caprimulgidae*

There are only three West Indian genera of this widespread family of nocturnal birds. Of these *Siphonorhis* is endemic to the Greater Antilles. This genus includes the Least Pauraque (*S. brewsteri*) and the Jamaican Pauraque (*S. americanus*). The latter, a larger (9–10″) and darker bird endemic to Jamaica, is presumably extinct, having been last recorded in 1859, thirteen years before the introduction of the mongoose on that island. Considering habitat requirements of the Least Pauraque, it is possible that the Jamaican species still exists in the semi-arid and little known Hellshire Hills.

Nightjars are seldom seen during the day when they rest on the ground or lengthwise on the limbs of trees, their mottled plumages blending with their surroundings. They may readily be located after sundown when their vocal efforts are persistent. Some ornithologists consider the Whip-poor-will of Puerto Rico and Nighthawks of the West Indies as representing distinct species (viz. "*Caprimulgus noctitherus*" and "*Chordeiles gundlachii*") mainly because of differences in voice, although morphologically they are difficult to distinguish from Whip-poor-wills and Nighthawks of eastern North America.

Chuck-will's-widow *Caprimulgus carolinensis*

Description: 12–13". Plumage grey to ochraceous buff, barred, streaked and spotted with black. Males have immaculate patches on outer tail feathers. In the hand may at once be distinguished from other West Indian nightjars by the presence of lateral filaments on rictal bristles.
Voice: Rarely vocal in West Indies in spring.
Habitat: Woodland.
Range: South-eastern North America. Winters south to Colombia, Venezuela, the Greater Antilles and Bahama Islands; vagrant to St. Martin, Saba and Barbuda (Aug. 28–May 15).

Rufous Nightjar *Caprimulgus rufus*

Local names: Cent-coups-de-couteau; Jacques-pas-papa-vous.
Description: 11". Closely resembles the Chuck-will's-widow, a species not known from St. Lucia, but darker and more rufescent; folded wing less than 7.75", rather than 8" or over.
Voice: Like that of Chuck-will's-widow and recalled by its vernacular names. The accent is on the fourth syllable *Jacques-pas-papá-ou*, repeated many times.
Habitat: Woodland in wilder parts of St. Lucia (e.g. near Grand Anse, Petit Anse, Cacoli, Anse-la-Raye, Piton Flore).
Nidification: Terrestrial. Eggs (2) indistinctly spotted.
Range: St. Lucia. Widespread in South America.

Whip-poor-will *Caprimulgus vociferus*

Local names: Guabairo (Puerto Rico); Guabairo Chico (Cuba).
Description: 9". Much smaller than any other Greater Antillean species of *Caprimulgus*. The Puerto Rican form resembles, but is slightly smaller than, continental Whip-poor-wills.
Voice: A repeated *rip* (not "*purple rip*" as in continental races), very different from utterances of other nightjars of Caribbean islands.
Habitat: Mainly scrubby woodland of south-western Puerto Rico, particularly in the Guánica State Forest.
Nidification: On ground. Eggs (2) in Puerto Rico profusely but indistinctly spotted.
Range: Puerto Rico. Also North and Central America; rare or casual as winter resident in Cuba.

Fig. 99 Greater Antillean Nightjar (Cuba)

Greater Antillean Nightjar *Caprimulgus cubanensis*

Local names: Guabairo; Pitanguá; Pétonoi.
Description: 11″. Resembles the Chuck-will's-widow, but darker and greyer above; underparts decidedly darker, more blackish, but with irregular whitish spots on breast. Males have the outer tail feathers *broadly tipped* with white. Fig. 99.
Voice: An oft-repeated *guabairo* (Cuba) or *pitanguá* (Hispaniola).
Habitat: Woodland. Apparently most numerous on borders of swamps (e.g. Ciénaga de Zapata, Ciénaga de Lanier); rare in Hispaniola.
Nidification: Terrestrial. Eggs (2) indistinctly spotted.
Range: Cuba, Isle of Pines, and Hispaniola.

White-tailed Nightjar *Caprimulgus cayennensis*

Local names: Coré; Cohé.
Description: 8–9″. Adult male strikingly marked, with rounded tail, the outer feathers mostly white; *a white band on wing*. Females are rather nondescript, browner (less grey) and with no white on wings and tail, the primaries with ochraceous spots. Nighthawks have longer wings that extend to end of tail when perched, and have forked tails.
Voice: A plantive, high-pitched whistle.
Habitat: Occurs at low elevations in Martinique; apparently most numerous in southern half of island, favouring grassy hillsides covered with low shrubbery. Apt to be seen on roads after sundown.
Nidification: Terrestrial. Eggs (1 or 2) uniformly spotted, and with a few black scrawls.
Range: Martinique. Also Tobago, Trinidad, Margarita, Bonaire, Curaçao Aruba, and South America and southern Central America.

Least Pauraque *Siphonorhis brewsteri*

Fig. 100
Least Pauraque

Local names: Torico; Grouiller-corps.
Description: 7–8″. A tiny nightjar, smaller and paler than Greater Antillean Nightjar; a white band across foreneck and narrow, white tip to tail; bill short and rounded; feet relatively long. Sexes virtually similar. Fig. 100.
Voice: A croaking, half-whispered *guëk*, followed by a drawn-out, guttural *pau-rá-kay*; also a clear, rising whistle.
Habitat: Semi-arid districts in lowlands, ranging up into the hills to elevations of approximately a thousand feet. Numerous in scrubby woods on Gonâve Island (e.g. near Pointe-à-Raquette) and between Copey and Manzanillo Bay. May be found between L'Arcahaie and Mont Rouis, north of Port-au-Prince.
Nidification: Terrestrial. Eggs (2) indistinctly spotted.
Range: Hispaniola and Gonâve Island.

Common Nighthawk
Chordeiles minor

Local names: Piramidig; Killy-dadick; Gie-me-me-bit; Mosquito Hawk; Querequeté; Querequequé; Gaspayo; Capacho.
Description: 8–10″. The only nightjar apt to be seen in the West Indies. Usually observed when in flight in late evening; occasionally active on cloudy days. The long, narrow, *white-banded wings* distinguish this species. Male has

Fig. 101 Common Nighthawk

white tail-band. Flight erratic, with occasional swoops during breeding season. Fig. 101.

Voice: A characteristic *pity-pit pit*, resembling the sound of a katydid. North American individuals emit a nasal *peernt*. Both cries may be heard in spring in the West Indies.

Habitat: Open country.

Nidification: Terrestrial. Eggs (1–2) distinctly spotted.

Range: Breeds in Bahama Islands and Greater Antilles, including Cayman Islands, east to the Virgin Islands (e.g. St. Thomas). Also North America and Mexico. Winters in South America. North American individuals occur as transients throughout the West Indies.

SWIFTS *Apodidae*

Swifts are members of a cosmopolitan family represented in the West Indies by four genera and six indigenous species. The Antillean Palm Swift is usually considered to constitute a genus endemic to these islands. These are the most aerial of land birds. They are highly gregarious, usually associating in flocks and nesting in colonies. Their food consists entirely of insects, captured on the wing.

Plate 9 WOODPECKERS (Males)

Chimney Swift *Chaetura pelagica*

Description: 5.25″. Upperparts dark sooty, slightly paler on the rump and upper tail-coverts; remiges black; chin and throat greyish white, becoming darker, ashy brown, on posterior underparts. May be distinguished from the Black Swift by smaller size, tailless appearance and more rapid wing-strokes. The Chimney Swift has a short, rounded tail, the Black Swift a slightly forked tail.

Range: North America, east of the Rocky Mountains. Winters in South America. Recorded from Bahamas, Cuba, Hispaniola, Tortue, Jamaica, Cayman Islands and Swan Island (Aug. 22–Oct. 23; April 13–May 18).

Short-tailed Swift *Chaetura brachyura*

Local name: Rain Bird.

Description: 4″. Similar in shape to Chimney Swift. Shorter from bill to end of tail than Lesser Antillean Swift, but with longer wings. Posterior upperparts from rump to tail, and under tail-coverts pale grey, in striking contrast with the rest of the plumage which is blackish. Other small Lesser Antillean swifts do not show such contrast and do not have such stubby tails. Fig. 102.

Habitat: Found in Kingstown as well as in interior hills.

Plate 10 SWALLOWS & GRASSQUITS

Nidification: Nest a half-saucer, composed of sticks glued together with salivary secretions, and attached to the vertical surface of a chimney or the inside of a cave. Eggs (3–6) white.

Range: St. Vincent; of doubtful occurrence on Grenada; accidental on St. Croix. Also South America, including Trinidad and Tobago.

Fig. 102 Short-tailed Swift

Grey-rumped Swift
Chaetura cinereiventris

Local names: Rain Bird; Oiseau de la Pluie.

Description: 4.5". A small, mostly black, swift with ashy grey rump and underparts. The tail is longer than that of the Short-tailed Swift and is black, not pale grey. Has been considered conspecific with *C. martinica*.
Habitat: Forested hills.
Nidification: Probably in hollow trees or caves, and possibly in chimneys occasionally as in South America, where nest like that of Short-tailed Swift. Eggs (2–4) white.
Range: Grenada. Also South America, including Trinidad and Tobago, and southern Central America.

Lesser Antillean Swift *Chaetura martinica*

Local names: Rain Bird; Oiseau de la Pluie; Hirondelle; "Chique-sol"; Petit Martinet Noir.
Description: Resembles the Grey-rumped Swift, but plumage duller with a brownish tinge, the underparts decidedly darker. The two "species" would be indistinguishable in the field, but do not occur together.
Voice: All West Indian *Chaeturae* utter a soft "chippering" on the wing.
Habitat: Found chiefly in the forested mountains, but occasionally at sea level.
Nidification: A nest of this swift, similar in construction to that of a Short-tailed Swift, was attached to the inside of an old oven; normal site probably in a hollow tree or cave. Eggs (3) white. Breeds in early summer.

Range: Guadeloupe, Dominica, Martinique, St. Lucia, and St. Vincent; a questionable sight record from Nevis.

Collared Swift
Streptoprocne zonaris

Local names: Rain Bird; Gowrie; Ringed Gowrie; Vencejo de Collar; Golondrina; Oiseau de la Pluie.
Description: 8–8.75″. A large black swift with a *white ring around the neck*. The immature has the white "collar" more or less obscured. *Flight exceedingly rapid.* Fig. 103.
Voice: A shrill *screee-screee*, reminiscent of European swifts.
Habitat: Usually found in the mountains, but occurs at times at low elevations.
Nidification: Sometimes colonial; nest a shallow, saucer-shaped structure composed chiefly of moss, situated on a rocky ledge or niche adjacent to a waterfall or cascade. Two white eggs comprise a clutch.
Range: Cuba, Isle of Pines (casual). Hispaniola, Tortue Island, and Jamaica; rare visitant (May–October) to Grenada; Grenadines; casual Vieques, Saba. Also Mexico to South America.

Fig. 103 Collared Swift

Black Swift *Cypseloides niger*

Local names: Swallow; Black Swallow; Rain Bird; Vencejo Negro; Hirondelle de Montagne; "Chique-sol"; Oiseau de la Pluie; Gros Martinet Noir.
Description: 6.5″. Plumage sooty black, darker above than below; forehead more or less white. Larger than a Chimney Swift, with much longer wings and tail. Flight less erratic than that of any of the smaller Lesser Antillean swifts with which it associates at times. Fig. 104.

Fig. 104 Black Swift

Voice: A soft *chip-chip.*

Habitat: Forested hills and mountains; occasional in lowlands, particularly in rainy weather.

Nidification: In small colonies. The shallow cup-shaped nest is situated on the face of a cliff or precipitous ravine and is composed of mud and moss. One relatively large white egg is laid.

Range: Cuba, Jamaica, Hispaniola, Puerto Rico, St. Croix (vagrant), St. Kitts, Guadeloupe, Dominica, Martinique, St. Lucia, St. Vincent; Grenada (transient); Barbados (transient); doubtful on Isle of Pines. Only summer resident in Lesser Antilles (March–September): individuals from these islands apparently winter in Guyana. Also breeds in Central America and in western North America.

Antillean Palm Swift *Tachornis phoenicobia* 4/3/97 ᵱ ᴿ

Local names: Swallow; Palm Swallow; Vencejito; Vencejo Chico; Vencejo de Palmar; Golondrina de Palmar; "Jolle-jolle"; "Petit Rollé"; Hirondelle.

Description: 4–4.5″. A very small swift with distinctive markings. Upperparts black, *the rump conspicuously white*; underparts mostly white, with *a broad black band across breast.* Flight tortuous and batlike. The Bank Swallow is much paler above, and lacks the white rump; its flight is more graceful and slower. Both birds have a dusky band across a white breast. Fig. 105.

Voice: A weak twittering.

Habitat: Found chiefly in lowland, settled districts, including towns.

Nidification: In colonies in palms. Nest composed of soft materials cemented together with saliva, situated in a hollow palm spathe or attached to the underside of a drooping frond; globular in shape with the entrance near the bottom. Eggs (3–5) white.

Range: Cuba, Isle of Pines, Jamaica, Hispaniola, Saona, Beata, Ile-à-Vache; accidental Puerto Rico and Key West.

Fig. 105 Antillean Palm Swift

HUMMINGBIRDS *Trochilidae*

Hummingbirds comprise a large family confined to the New World where they occur from Alaska to Chile and Argentina. Most of the species are very small and exquisitely coloured, with highly iridescent plumage. They range in size from 2.5 inches to 9 inches; the smallest is the Bee Hummingbird of Cuba, the largest the Giant Hummingbird (*Patagona gigas*) of the Andes. Their food consists of nectar and minute insects obtained by probing blossoms with their delicate bills. Their flight is rapid and bee-like. Six of the West Indian genera, and all but three of the species, are endemic to this region.

Nidification: Nests are dainty little cups of plant fibres and plant down, often decorated externally with lichen. They are situated in vines, or in bushes or trees usually at low or moderate elevations above the ground; sometimes (habitually in the case of Rufous-breasted Hermit) the nest is attached to the underside of a leaf, palm frond or fern. Eggs (1–2) white.

Rufous-breasted Hermit *Glaucis hirsuta* page 97

Local names: Brown Hummingbird; Brown Doctor Bird.

Description: 5". A rather large hummingbird with a *long, decurved bill,* the lower mandible yellow. Upperparts green; underparts mostly brown, more rufescent in female; tail tipped with white, all but central feathers chestnut basally, black subterminally. No other Grenada hummingbird has brown on underparts and tail.

Voice: A shrill, high-pitched *sweep.*

Habitat: Primarily forested hills on Grenada. Occurs near the Grand Etang.

Range: Grenada. Also South America, including Trinidad and Tobago, and southern Central America (Panama).

Puerto Rican Emerald *Chlorostilbon maugaeus* page 80

Local names: Zumbador; Zumbadorcito.

Description: 3.5–4". Male: Glossy green, with a blackish, forked tail; basal part of lower mandible pinkish. Female: Upperparts green, the rectrices violet distally, the outer tail feathers tipped with greyish white; lores and ear-coverts more or less dusky; underparts whitish with some green on sides. The common *small* hummingbird of Puerto Rico.

Habitat: Widespread, occurring from coastal mangroves to forested mountain summits; most abundant in forested hills and in coffee plantations.

Range: Puerto Rico.

Hispaniolan Emerald *Chlorostilbon swainsonii* page 80

Local names: Zumbador; Zumbaflor; Ouanga-Négresse.

Description: 4–4.5". Male: Green, with dark greenish bronze, forked tail; a velvety black patch on breast: lower mandible mostly pinkish. Female: Green above, becoming dusky toward tip of tail, the outer rectrices with whitish tips; underparts dull greyish with some green on sides: resembles female Antillean Mango, but smaller and *no rufous at base of tail,* and lower mandible paler.

Habitat: Forested hills and mountains, and shrub-covered mountain slopes. Most numerous at high elevations.

Range: Hispaniola.

Cuban Emerald *Chlorostilbon ricordii* page 97

Local names: Hummingbird; God Bird; Zunzún; Zumbador; Picaflor; Colibrí.

Description: 4–4.5". Male: Green, with blackish tail and white under tail-coverts; lower mandible mostly pinkish; tail forked. Female; Green to bronze-green above, becoming dusky violet on tail; underparts greyish, green on the sides; ear-coverts more or less dusky; both sexes have a white spot behind eye. The common hummingbird of Cuba.
Habitat: Woodland and copses.
Range: Northern Bahama Islands (Grand Bahama, Abaco, Andros; vagrant to New Providence), Cuba and Isle of Pines; vagrant to southern Florida.

Blue-headed Hummingbird *Cyanophaia bicolor*   page 97

Local names: Frou-frou Bleu; Colibri Tête-bleue (♂); Colibri Falle-blanc (♀).
Description: 4.5". Male: Green, the tail and *most of head violet-blue*; basal part of lower mandible pinkish. Female: Upperparts green with a bronze sheen on mantle and at bases of central tail feathers which are tipped with dark violet; outer rectrices mostly bluish, grey at bases and with *broad whitish tips*: lores and ear-coverts black or dusky; underparts greyish white with some green on sides.
Habitat: Chiefly confined to mountains where found in forest as well as fairly open country.
Range: Dominica and Martinique.

Green-breasted Mango *Anthracothorax prevostii*

Local names: Doctor Bird; Hummingbird.
Description: 5". Green above, the underparts variable, with an admixture of black, green and violet-blue, the males darker than females; much purple on tail, except on central pair of rectrices. Immature birds are white, or brown and white, below, with a black median stripe.
Habitat: Most numerous about the settlements.
Range: Old Providence (including Santa Catalina Island) and St. Andrew; vagrant (?) to Albuquerque Cay. Also Mexico, Central America and northern South America.

Jamaican Mango *Anthracothorax mango*   page 80

Local names: Hummingbird; Doctor Bird.
Description: 5". A sturdy hummingbird, dark greenish bronze above, *black below*; *outer tail feathers purple*, edged with black and sides of head and neck glossy purple. Immature birds have bluish green gorgets.

Habitat: Usually found in rather open, sunny places in the hills and lowlands. Common in semi-arid woodland.
Range: Jamaica.

Antillean Mango *Anthracothorax dominicus*   page 80

4/2/97 DR

Local names: Hummingbird; Doctor Bird; Zumbador Dorado; Zunzún Dorado; Zumbaflor; Ouanga-Négresse.
Description: 4.5–5″. Male: Resembles the Jamaican Mango, but upperparts green; an iridescent green gorget; no purple on sides of head and neck; in smaller Puerto Rican and Virgin Island race, black of underparts becomes grey on abdomen. Female: Chiefly green above and greyish white below; outer tail feathers largely violaceous chestnut basally (Hispaniola) or brownish grey (Puerto Rico and Virgin Islands), and tipped with white. The immature male is more or less intermediate.
Habitat: Widespread in Hispaniola, where found in semi-arid as well as humid regions; mostly lowlands of central and western Puerto Rico.
Range: Hispaniola, including adjacent islands, Puerto Rico; extirpated on Vieques, Culebra, Culebrita, St. Thomas (?), St. John and Anegada.

Green Mango *Anthracothorax viridis*   page 80

Local names: Zumbador Verde; Zunzún Verde; Colibrí Verde.
Description: 5″. A comparatively large, green hummingbird with a blue-black tail. The sexes are similar.
Habitat: Mainly confined to upland country; often seen in coffee plantations. Of rare occurrence in coastal areas.
Range: Puerto Rico.

Purple-throated Carib *Eulampis jugularis*   page 97

Local names: Doctor Bird; Ruby-throat; Colibri; Colibri Madère; Colibri Falle-rouge.
Description: 5″. A sturdy, very dark hummingbird. Plumage largely black; gorget purplish red; tail and upper tail-coverts bluish green; wings metallic green. Sexes similar. At times appears entirely black in the field, but the *green wings are usually conspicuous* (other hummingbirds have blackish wings).
Habitat: Mountain forest and clearings; often seen in banana plantations. Less numerous at low elevations.
Range: Lesser Antilles-Saba, St. Eustatius, St. Kitts, Nevis, Montserrat, Antigua, Guadeloupe, Marie Galante, Dominica, Martinique, St. Lucia,

St. Vincent, Grenada; apparently casual on Barbuda, Désirade, Iles des Saintes, Bequia and Barbados.

Green-throated Carib *Sericotes holosericeus* page 97

Local names: Doctor Bird; Green Doctor Bird; Zumbador de Pecho Azul; Colibri Falle-vert; Colibri Vert.
Description: 4.75″. Less robust than Purple-throated Carib. Plumage predominantly green; *a violet-blue patch on breast* (rather extensive in Grenada race), bordering green gorget; abdomen blackish, glossed with green, tail violet-black. Sexes alike.
Habitat: Most abundant at low elevations. In some localities (e.g. Martinique) occurs commonly with Purple-throated Carib in mountain clearings.
Range: Puerto Rico, excluding western part, eastward through Vieques, Culebra and the Virgin Islands, and virtually throughout the Lesser Antilles (absent from southernmost Grenadines).

Antillean Crested Hummingbird page 97
Orthorhyncus cristatus

Local names: Little Doctor Bird; Zumbadorcito; Frou-frou; Colibri Huppé.
Description: 3.5″. Male: Green above, the tail and underparts blackish; *conspicuous crest* green, or green and blue, but on the Grenadines, Grenada and Barbados distinctly violet-blue distally. Female: Green above, greyish or whitish below, with whitish tips to the tail feathers; often appears crested.
Habitat: Widespread from sea level to mountain forest, but most abundant in lowlands.
Range: Extreme eastern Puerto Rico (e.g. near Fajardo) eastward through Vieques, Culebra and the Virgin Islands, and throughout the Lesser Antilles.

Streamertail *Trochilus polytmus* page 80

Local names: Doctor Bird; Long-tail Doctor Bird; Hummingbird.
Description: 4.25–10″. The adult male is the most spectacular West Indian hummingbird, often with *two long black tail feathers* (when emits a whirring sound in flight). When lacking "streamers", easily identified by bright green plumage with *black crown*, the lateral feathers of the nape elongated to form tufts; bill mostly red, except in extreme eastern Jamaica where entirely black (intermediates occur at Port Antonio). Females lack

"streamers" and have green upperparts, *mostly white underparts*; outer tail feathers tipped with white. Female of red-billed race has much darker bill than male—dull reddish brown with black tip, often appearing entirely black in field.

Voice: A loud, deliberate *tee-tee-tee*, continued indefinitely.

Habitat: The most abundant and widespread bird in Jamaica, ranging from semi-arid lowlands to the highest mountains.

Range: Jamaica.

Bahama Woodstar   *Calliphlox evelynae*   page 97

Local names: God Bird; Hummingbird.

Description: 3.5–3.75″. Male: Mostly green above, *the deeply forked tail black and rufous*; gorget (and, in birds from southernmost islands, forehead) reddish violet; chest white, the posterior underparts rufescent. Female: Differs in having a rounded tail, and both throat and chest are white. The *brown markings* are the most distinctive features in both sexes.

Habitat: Scrubby woodland, coppets, gardens. The common hummingbird of the Bahamas, often seen in Nassau.

Range: The Bahama Islands.

Ruby-throated Hummingbird   *Archilochus colubris*

Description: 3.5″. Resembles the Bee Hummingbird, but *decidedly larger*. The male has *green upperparts*, and the lateral feathers of the iridescent gorget are not elongated.

Range: North America, east of the Rocky Mountains. Winters mainly in Mexico and Central America. Rare winter resident in the Bahamas and Cuba; casual in Hispaniola, Grand Cayman, Jamaica (Nov. 22–May 15).

Bee Hummingbird   *Mellisuga helenae*   page 80

Local names: Zunzuncito; Zumbete; Pájaro Mosca; Trovador.

Description: 2.5″. Male has the pileum and throat fiery red, the iridescent gorget with elongated lateral plumes; rest of upperparts bluish; rest of underparts mostly greyish white. The female is green above, whitish below, with white tips to outer tail feathers. The *male is the smallest of birds;* the female but slightly larger. More apt to be mistaken for a bee than a bird.

Voice: A prolonged squeaking.

Habitat: Woodland, shrubbery, gardens; occasionally fairly open country.

Range: Cuba and the Isle of Pines.

Vervain Hummingbird   *Mellisuga minima*   4/2/94   DR page 80

Local names: Little Doctor Bird; God Bird; Bee Hummingbird; Zumbadorcito; Zumbaflor; Ouanga-Négresse; Suce-fleurs.
Description: 2.5–2.75″. Another *minute* hummingbird, green above and mainly whitish below. The slightly larger female has the outer tail feathers broadly tipped with white and resembles the female Bee Hummingbird.
Voice: A prolonged squeaking, often emitted on the wing.
Habitat: Widespread, but absent from dense forest.
Range: Hispaniola (including adjacent islands) and Jamaica.

TROGONS   *Trogonidae*

Trogons are tropical birds of resplendent plumage, with long tails and comparatively short wings and bills. The two West Indian species belong to monotypic, endemic genera. In habits they are rather inactive and are easily approached. Their food consists of fruit and insects.

Hispaniolan Trogon   *Temnotrogon roseigaster*   page 49

Local names: Papagayo; Cotorrita de Sierra; Caleçon Rouge; Dame Anglaise; Demoiselle Anglaise.
Description: 11–12″. Differs strikingly from any other bird of Hispaniola. The upperparts are mostly green; anterior underparts grey; *posterior underparts geranium-red;* much white on long tail; short bill honey-yellow. Males have narrow, white barring on wings.
Voice: A loud *cock-craow*, the second note often repeated in nesting season; also cooing and whining sounds.
Habitat: Chiefly mountain forest; local in coastal mangroves.
Nidification: In cavities of trees or stubs. Eggs (2) very pale green.
Range: Hispaniola.

Cuban Trogon   *Priotelus temnurus*   page 49

Local names: Tocoloro; Tocororo; Guatini.
Description: 10–11″. Somewhat resembles the Hispaniolan Trogon, but crown dark violet-blue; wings with conspicuous white bars and spots; breast paler grey and throat white; tail differently shaped, with *a ragged tip;* upper mandible dusky, the lower reddish. Sexes similar. The flight of both trogons is rather short, tilting and noisy.
Voice: A monotonous *toc-coro* or *to co-loro*, softer than notes of Hispaniolan Trogon and repeated more frequently.

Habitat: Widespread in forested country.
Nidification: Like that of Hispaniolan Trogon, but eggs (3–4) white.
Range: Cuba and the Isle of Pines.

KINGFISHERS *Alcedinidae*

Only two of the six New World kingfishers are found in the West Indies, although as many as five occur in Trinidad. Antillean species feed on fish, which they obtain by plunging into the water, and are frequently seen hovering while attempting to locate their prey.

Ringed Kingfisher *Ceryle torquata*   page 49

Fig. 106 Ringed Kingfisher (Female)

Local names: Kingfisher; Martin-pêcheur; Pie; Cra-cra.
Description: 15–16″. Resembles the Belted Kingfisher, but with a very large bill. Male has chestnut breast and abdomen; female is chestnut from lower breast to under tail-coverts, but the upper breast is blue-grey, spotted with white. The extensive chestnut of the underparts and heavy bill are the best field marks that distinguish this species from the Belted Kingfisher. Fig. 106.
Voice: A loud, harsh rattle.
Habitat: Mainly freshwater streams in the Lesser Antilles.
Nidification: Nests in a burrow, excavated in a bank. Eggs (3) white.

Range: Guadeloupe, Dominica and Martinique. Also Mexico, Central America and South America, including Trinidad.

Belted Kingfisher *Ceryle alcyon*

Local names: Kingfisher, Kingfisherman; Martín Pescador; Martín Zambullidor; Pitirre de Agua; Pitirre de Río; Pitirre de Mangle; Pájaro del Rey; Martin-Pêcheur; Pie.
Description: 12–13″. Mainly ashy blue above and white below, with a

broad bluish grey band across chest; female has, in addition, a rather narrow chestnut band across lower breast, and the sides and flanks are chestnut. Both West Indian kingfishers are crested.
Voice: A harsh rattle.
Habitat: Coastal areas, rivers, lakes and lagoons.
Range: Breeds in North America. Winters south to northern South America. Found throughout the year in the West Indies.

TODIES *Todidae*

Todies belong to a family confined to the Greater Antilles, and are the most remarkable and among the most beautiful birds of these islands. Their closest relatives are the motmots, and they are distantly related to kingfishers. They are almost exclusively insectivorous, but are known on occasions to eat minute lizards. They procure their food after the manner of flycatchers, choosing exposed perches from which they dart out after their prey. During flight, a curious whirring rattle may be heard. All five todies are closely related and comprise what is termed a "superspecies".
Nidification: In burrows in the ground about a foot in length; often in a roadside bank. Eggs (2–5; usually 3–4) white.

Cuban Tody *Todus multicolor*   page 176

Local names: Pedorrera, Cartacuba; Barranco-Río.
Description: 4.25″. A tiny bird with vivid *green upperparts and red throat*; underparts mostly white, pink on flanks; blue on sides of neck; lores and under tail-coverts yellow; lower mandible orange-red. The feet of todies range in colour from pink (*T. multicolor*) to blackish (*T. subulatus*). Immature todies lack red on underparts, and have dusky green streaks on the breast.
Voice: A simple chatter.
Habitat: Chiefly forest or woodland, and borders of rivers and streams.
Range: Cuba and the Isle of Pines.

Narrow-billed Tody *Todus angustirostris*   page 176

Local names: Barrancolí, Pichuí; Colibrí; Tête-sèche; Chicorette.
Description: 4.25″. Resembles Cuban Tody, but no yellow on lores and no blue on neck; bill narrower and darker, the lower mandible blackish at tip.
Voice: A harsh *tick-cherek*, and a chattering like that of Cuban Tody.
Habitat: Found only in the mountains of Haiti, and primarily a mountain bird in the Dominican Republic but here occurs locally at low elevations

side by side with Broad-billed Tody. A species of dense, damp jungle and mountain shrubbery.
Range: Hispaniola.

Puerto Rican Tody   *Todus mexicanus*   page 176

Local names: San Pedrito; Medio Peso; Papagayo; Barrancolino.
Description: Resembles Narrow-billed Tody, but yellow on flanks instead of pink; bill wider, the lower mandible not tipped with dusky.
Voice: A rather harsh *cherek*.
Habitat: Widespread, ranging from semi-arid coastal regions to humid mountain slopes.
Range: Puerto Rico.

Jamaican Tody   *Todus todus*   page 176

Local names: Robin; Robin Redbreast.
Description: 4.25″. Resembles Puerto Rican Tody, but breast washed with green, becoming yellow on abdomen and under tail-coverts; flanks pink.
Voice: A short *cherek*.
Habitat: Widespread, but most abundant in wooded hills and mountains.
Range: Jamaica.

Broad-billed Tody   *Todus subulatus* 4/2/97 D Ɋpage 176

Local names: Barrancolí; Barranquero; Colibri.
Description: 4.5″. Slightly larger than Narrow-billed Tody (folded wing over 1.8″); underparts darker (greyish white) with a yellowish or pink wash; bill broader, the lower mandible entirely reddish. *Most easily identified by voice.*
Voice: A rather plaintive *terp-terp-terp*, continued indefinitely.
Habitat: Primarily lowlands, but ranges up to 5,000 feet in the mountains. Most numerous in semi-arid localities. Not found in dense rain forest.
Range: Hispaniola and Gonâve Island.

WOODPECKERS, PICULETS & WRYNECKS   *Picidae*

In the West Indies, woodpeckers are best represented in Cuba, where as many as six species occur. The Cuban Green Woodpecker and the Antillean Piculet belong to genera endemic to the Greater Antilles. Other West Indian woodpeckers are congeneric with North American species.

Woodpeckers, other than piculets, are usually seen climbing up the trunks of trees, their sharp, stiff tails used as props. Their flight is undulating.

Nidification: In holes excavated in trees, palms or cacti, rarely (*M. striatus*) in burrows on steep slopes. Eggs (3–6, usually 4) white.

Antillean Piculet   *Nesoctites micromegas*   page 128

Local names: Carpintero de Sierra; Charpentier Cannelle.
Description: 5.5–6.25″. Resembles a nuthatch more than a woodpecker. Upperparts greenish, the crown yellow, centred with red in male; hindneck spotted with white; underparts whitish or yellowish white, streaked with black. Creeps along limbs of trees, often perching in a sparrow-like manner. The tail is soft and not used as a brace in climbing.
Voice: A loud, rapid *kuk-ki-ki-ki-ke-ku-kuk*, woodpecker-like in quality. The sexes often answer each other.
Habitat: Humid forest, both in lowlands and in mountains, and in semi-arid regions; most numerous in latter environment.
Range: Hispaniola and Gonâve Island.

Northern Flicker   *Colaptes auratus*

Local names: Black-heart Woodpecker; Carpintero Escapulario; Carpintero Ribero.
Description: 12–13″. Upperparts mostly greyish brown, barred with black, the crown plain grey and tail mostly black; *rump white, spotted with black* (not immaculate as in North American flickers); a scarlet nuchal collar; underparts mostly buffy, spotted with black, with a large *black patch on chest*; under surface of wings and tail golden; male has a black malar stripe. Unlike northern flickers, rarely seen on ground. Fig. 107.
Voice: A loud *ka-ka-ka-ka-ka-ka-ka-ka-ka-ka*, like North American flickers. Resembles voice of Great Lizard Cuckoo and Mangrove Cuckoo, but higher pitched and without the guttural quality.
Habitat: Woodland, as well as rather open country.
Range: Cuba, Grand Cayman and North America.

Fig. 107
Northern Flicker

Fernandina's Flicker
Colaptes fernandinae   page 128

Local names: Carpintero Churroso; Carpintero Guasuso.
Description: 13–14″. Upperparts, apart from head, black, barred with buffy yellow; underparts yellowish, barred with black, the throat streaked with black; crown and sides of head cinnamon, the pileum streaked with black; under surface of wings and tail golden like Yellow-shafted Flicker, and like that species male has a black malar stripe. A rather tame, usually quiet woodpecker, *without any red on head.* Like northern flickers, often feeds on ground. Fig. 108.
Voice: Chatters like a Northern Flicker.
Habitat: Chiefly palm groves in open, low country.
Range: Cuba.

Fig. 108
Fernandina's
Flicker (female)

Plate 11 VIREOS & WOOD WARBLERS

Puerto Rican Woodpecker
Melanerpes portoricensis

page 128

Local name: Carpintero.
Description: 9–10.5″. Upperparts glossy black with *a white rump* and forehead; underparts mostly red in males, partially red in females, the rest greyish brown. The black mantle, white rump and absence of streaking distinguishes this woodpecker from the Yellow-bellied Sapsucker, a very rare winter resident in Puerto Rico.
Voice: West Indian woodpeckers of the genus *Melanerpes* utter a variety of harsh sounds, such as a rolling *gurrr-gurrr.*
Habitat: Widespread in woodland; coffee and coconut plantations.
Range: Puerto Rico and Vieques Island.

Guadeloupe Woodpecker   *Melanerpes herminieri*   page 128

Local name: Tapeur.
Description: 10–11.5″. Upperparts glossy black; underparts black, suffused with red. *Appears entirely black* in the field.

Plate 12 THRUSHES & PALMCHAT

K

Habitat: Most numerous in wooded hills in north-eastern Guadeloupe proper ("Basse Terre"), as opposed to Grande Terre.
Range: Guadeloupe.

Cuban Red-bellied Woodpecker
Melanerpes superciliaris

page 128

Local names: Woodpecker; "Pecker-wood"; Red-head Woodpecker; Carpintero; Carpintero Jabado.
Description: 9.5–12″. The West Indian representative of the Red-bellied Woodpecker of North America. Upperparts mostly barred black and white; crown to hindneck scarlet in male, but only nape and hindneck red in female; underparts brownish grey, the abdomen red. The commonest Cuban woodpecker.
Habitat: Wooded areas, palms and coppets.
Range: Bahama Islands (Grand Bahama, Abaco, Watling's Island), Cuba (including some cays), Isle of Pines and Grand Cayman.

Jamaican Woodpecker   *Melanerpes radiolatus*   page 128

Local names: Woodpecker; Green Woodpecker.
Description: 10–11.5″. Somewhat resembles the preceding species, but back and wings black, *narrowly* barred with white; centre of abdomen orange, not red; breast and abdomen otherwise darker and somewhat olivaceous. The red pattern of pileum and hindneck is similar. The only Jamaican woodpecker, apart from the sapsucker.
Habitat: Widespread, occurring from lowland copses and coconut plantations to mountain rain forest.
Range: Jamaica.

Hispaniolan Woodpecker   *Melanerpes striatus*   4/3/97 page 128

DR

Local names: Carpintero; Charpentier.
Description: 9–10″. Resembles West Indian Red-bellied Woodpecker, but pale bars on back and wings greenish yellow, not white; upper tail-coverts scarlet; underparts darker (brownish), the abdomen olivaceous; tail black.
Habitat: Widespread in Hispaniola, occurring from lowland mangrove swamps and semi-arid country to the forested mountains. Apparently not present on any of the adjacent islands.
Range: Hispaniola.

Yellow-bellied Sapsucker   *Sphyrapicus varius*

Local names: Woodpecker; "Sook"; Carpintero de Paso; Charpentier.
Description: 8–8.5″. Upperparts black, mottled with white on wings

and back, the upper tail-coverts mostly white; *a broad white band across wing-coverts*; crown red, but black in *some* females; sides of head striped black and white; throat red in male, white in female; a large black patch on foreneck and chest; rest of underparts pale yellow with blackish streaks on sides and flanks. The immature shows more or less the adult characters and has the distinctive white wing-band. Adult males appear to be rather scarce in the West Indies. Fig. 109.

Voice: Occasionally utters a querulous *mew*, but is usually silent during the winter months.

Habitat: Apt to be seen anywhere among trees, both in lowlands and in mountains.

Fig. 109 Yellow-bellied Sapsucker (female)

Range: North America. Winters south to Panama. Not uncommon on most of the West Indies, but rare east of Hispaniola and unknown in Lesser Antilles south of Dominica (Oct. 14–April 18; one July 22 record).

Cuban Green Woodpecker *Xiphidiopicus percussus* page 128

Local names: Carpintero Verde; Carpintero Tajá; Carpintero Roán.
Description: 8.5–10″. A woodpecker with complicated colour-pattern. Crown to hindneck red (crown of female black, streaked with white); *back and wings green*; tail grey; sides of head white with a black stripe behind eye; throat black; a red patch on foreneck; rest of underparts yellow to greenish yellow, streaked on the breast and barred posteriorly with black. *No other Cuban woodpecker has green upperparts.*
Voice: A mewing or squealing, reminiscent of Yellow-bellied Sapsucker.
Habitat: Woodland.
Range: Cuba (including some offshore cays) and the Isle of Pines.

Hairy Woodpecker *Dendrocopos villosus*

Local names: Spanish Woodpecker; "Sook".
Description: 8–9″. A small black and white woodpecker, the upperparts mostly black, the underparts mostly white. The male has a red nuchal band. Fig. 110.

Voice: A rapid whinny, descending in pitch. Call-note a sharp *chink*.
Habitat: Mainly pine woods.
Range: Bahama Islands (Grand Bahama, Mores Island, Abaco, Andros, New Providence). Also North and Central America.

Fig. 111
Ivory-billed
Woodpecker

Fig. 110 Hairy Woodpecker

Ivory-billed Woodpecker *Campephilus principalis*

Local name: Carpintero Real.
Description: 18–20″. A very large crested woodpecker, about the size of a crow. Plumage mostly black; a white stripe from near gape to back and *large white patch on wing*; bill ivory-white; prominent crest black in female, scarlet and black in male. Fig. 111.
Voice: A loud, nasal *pent-pent* or *pent, pent-pent, pent*; occasionally more protracted.
Habitat: Formerly rare but widespread in lowland woods. A few pairs still exist in or near pine lands of north-eastern Oriente Province.
Range: Cuba and south-eastern United States.

COTINGAS *Cotingidae*

Cotingas comprise a varied assortment of birds related to the tyrant flycatchers, and like them are of South American origin. Some are remarkable for their brilliance of plumage, and some are notable in other respects. One of the more plainly coloured species, the Jamaican Becard, inhabits the West Indies where it is confined to Jamaica. Its food consists chiefly of insects and berries. Becards are now placed in the Tyrannidae.

Jamaican Becard *Platypsaris niger*

page 96

Local names: Judy (♂); Mountain Dick (♀); "Kissidy"; "Rickachay"; London City.

Description: 8″. A rather chunky, short-tailed, flycatcher-like bird. The male is glossy black above and sooty black below, with a small patch of white on the wing apparent only in flight. The female is mostly rufescent above, the back greyish; sides of head and throat cinnamon, changing to greyish white on the breast. The thick bill readily distinguishes the male from the Jamaican Blackbird (*Nesopsar*). Fig. 112.

Voice: A rapid *kelelelelee-oh*, the first notes run together and rising, the last falling, prolonged and rather plaintive.

Fig. 112 Jamaican Becard

Habitat: Wooded hills.

Nidification: Nest an enormous mass of vegetable matter with the entrance from below, suspended from the branch of a tree. Eggs (3) heavily spotted.

Range: Jamaica.

TYRANT FLYCATCHERS *Tyrannidae*

The tyrant flycatchers are members of a large family confined to the New World, where they are best represented in South America. They are not related to Old World flycatchers (Muscicapidae), which are allied to thrushes, although in general they resemble these birds in habits. The elaenias are more warbler-like in their actions, and certain species (e.g. *E. martinica*) feed chiefly on berries. Most of the West Indian flycatchers belong to genera that occur in the United States and Canada, and as such will be recognised by visitors from the north

Eastern Kingbird   *Tyrannus tyrannus*

Description: 8.75". A familiar North American flycatcher that resembles races of the Loggerhead Flycatcher with whitish tipped tails, but back dark slate-grey, not greyish-brown; crown-patch orange-red, not yellow; bill much shorter (about .75"). Rounded tail distinctly tipped with white.

Range: North America. Migrates chiefly through Central America and winters in Peru and Bolivia. Rare transient in western part of West Indies, whence recorded from the Bahama Islands, Cuba, the Isle of Pines, Grand Cayman, Jamaica, Swan Island and Old Providence (Aug. 30–Oct. 15: March 31–May 6).

Tropical Kingbird   *Tyrannus melancholicus*

Local names: Yellow Pipiri; Pipiri Jaune.

Description: 9". Differs from Grey Kingbird in having the *posterior underparts yellow*, becoming greenish yellow on chest; back olive-green; bill smaller.

Voice: A rolling *pip-pree*, softer than the notes of the Grey Kingbird.

Habitat: Chiefly semi-arid parts of southern Grenada.

Nidification: Nests are rather loosely constructed, cup-shaped structures situated in trees or shrubs at various elevations above the ground. Eggs (2–3) beautifully spotted.

Range: Grenada; vagrant to Union Island and to Cuba. Also southern North America to South America, including Trinidad and Tobago.

Grey Kingbird   *Tyrannus dominicensis*

Fig. 113 Grey Kingbird

Local names: Petchary; Chinchary; Fighter; "Christomarie"; Pick-Peter; Pipiri; Rain Bird; Pitirre; Pitirre Abejero; Titirre; Pestigre; Pipirite.

Description: 9.25". The commonest West Indian flycatcher and one of the best-known birds of the West Indies. Plumage grey above, white below, the *ear-coverts blackish*; a usually concealed patch of orange-red and yellow on crown; bill large, particularly so in Lesser Antillean individuals; *tail notched.* Fig. 113.

Voice: A loud *pitirre*.
Habitat: Fairly open, settled districts.
Nidification: Like that of Tropical Kingbird. Eggs (2–4).
Range: South-eastern United States and the West Indies south to northern South America. Winters (in part) in northern South America, but chiefly a permanent resident from Hispaniola eastward.

Giant Kingbird   *Tyrannus cubensis*

Fig. 114 Giant Kingbird

Local names: Pitirre Real; Pitirre de la Ciénaga.
Description: 10.25″. Resembles the Grey Kingbird, but decidedly larger, with a very heavy bill; back greyish brown, the crown (apart from orange patch) dark sooty brown. Fig. 114.
Voice: A rolling chatter, not unlike that of the Eastern Kingbird and Loggerhead Kingbird.
Habitat: Woodlands, in particular pine forest. Also wooded borders of swamps.
Nidification: Like that of other kingbirds, but nests never situated at low elevations. Eggs (2–3).
Range: Cuba and the Isle of Pines. Old records from Great Inagua, Caicos Islands, and from Isla Mujeres (Mexico).

Loggerhead Kingbird   page 96   4/3/97
Tyrannus caudifasciatus

Local names: Loggerhead; Fighter; Tom Fighter; Hard-head Bird; Guatíbere; Pitirre Guatíbere; Pitirre Cantor; Manjuila; Clérigo; Pipirite Tête-Police.
Description: 9.25″. Resembles the Grey Kingbird, but back greyish olive or greyish brown, not grey; *crown and sides of head uniformly darker;* crown-patch yellow or mostly yellow; tail (*not notched*)

Fig. 115 Loggerhead Kingbird (Cuba)

with white or greyish tip, excepting races from Hispaniola and Puerto Rico. Fig. 115.

Voice: A harsh, rolling chatter, suggestive of the Eastern Kingbird.

Habitat: More of a woodland species than the Grey Kingbird, but often seen in rather open country.

Nidification: Like that of Grey Kingbird.

Range: Bahama Islands (Grand Bahama, Abaco, Andros, New Providence), Cuba, Isle of Pines, Cayman Islands, Jamaica, Hispaniola, Puerto Rico and Vieques Island. Vagrant to Florida.

Fork-tailed Flycatcher *Muscivora tyrannus*

Description: 9–16″. In full adult plumage, the two elongated tail feathers distinguish this flycatcher. Lacking these "streamers", *the black crown* (with yellow patch) *and sides of head* in contrast with pale grey back and white underparts, and the bedraggled appearance of the tail are diagnostic.

Range: Central and South America. The race from southern South America migrates to northern South America, including Trinidad and Tobago, and to Grenada, Carriacou and Barbados; casual in Cuba and St. Martin (February-November).

Great Crested Flycatcher *Myiarchus crinitus*

Description: 8″. Distinguished from Cuban, Bahaman or Puerto Rican individuals of the Stolid Flycatcher by the conspicuously yellow posterior underparts and rufous margins to remiges; upperparts paler, more olivaceous, than any form of *stolidus*.

Range: North America, east of the Rocky Mountains. Winters mainly in Central America. Rare visitant to the Bahamas, Cuba and Puerto Rico (Oct. 14–April 20).

Rusty-tailed Flycatcher *Myiarchus tyrannulus*

Local names: Loggerhead; Sunset Bird.

Description: 8″. Resembles the Jamaican race of the Stolid Flycatcher but larger. Voice very different from that of any form of *M. stolidus*.

Voice: Much like that of the Great Crested Flycatcher, a harsh *queuk*, *queuk* or a loud *quip*.

Habitat: Open, settled districts and scrubby woods in the lowlands.

Nidification: In cavities of trees and, occasionally, in man-made structures. Eggs (2–4) heavily spotted.

Range: Grenada, the Grenadines and St. Vincent. Also from southern

North America to South America, including extralimital Caribbean islands.

Stolid Flycatcher *Myiarchus stolidus* page 96

Local names: Tom Fool; Billy Green; Bobito Grande; Maroa; Manuelito; Jüi; Louis; Pipirite Gros-tête (Greater Antilles); Loggerhead; Mountain Loggerhead; Gros-tête; Pipiri Gros-tête; Gobe-mouches Huppé; Janeau (Lesser Antilles).

Description: 7.5–8.5". Dark olive-grey above, more dusky on the crown; underparts greyish white anteriorly, white to pale yellow posteriorly; tail with or without rufous. Yellow bellied forms inhabit the Lesser Antilles, Hispaniola and adjacent islands, and Jamaica.

Voice: A whistled *oo-ee, e-oo-ee* or *ee-oo*; also harsher notes.

Habitat: Woodland; also occurs in mangrove swamps in Greater Antilles.

Nidification: In cavities of trees or cacti. Eggs (3–4) heavily spotted.

Range: Bahama Islands, and Greater Antilles (including Grand Cayman) east to St. John, Tortola and Virgin Gorda; St. Kitts, Nevis, Barbuda, Guadeloupe, Dominica, Martinique and St. Lucia.

Dusky-capped Flycatcher
Myiarchus barbirostris

Local names: Tom Fool; Little Tom Fool.

Description: 6.5". Resembles Jamaican Stolid Flycatchers, but smaller; crown blackish, in striking contrast with remainder of upperparts; entire breast yellow, only the chin and throat white; *no rufous on tail*. Fig. 116.

Voice: An emphatic *preëë*.

Habitat: Widespread in woodland and mountain forest.

Nidification: In cavities of trees. Eggs (3–4) heavily spotted.

Range: Jamaica. Also ("*M. tuberculifer*") from southern North America to South America, including Trinidad.

Fig. 116 Dusky-capped Flycatcher

Rufous-tailed Flycatcher *Myiarchus validus* page 96

Local names: Big-head Tom Fool; Big Tom Fool; Red Tom Fool.
Description: 9.5″. Differs from Jamaican Stolid Flycatcher in being larger; throat grey, rather than white; much more rufous on tail and *wing feathers conspicuously margined with this colour.* Not apt to be found with Stolid Flycatchers.
Voice: An emphatic *preëë*, much louder than voice of Dusky-capped Flycatcher.
Habitat: Wooded hills and mountains; rarely found at low elevations.
Nidification: In shallow cavities of trees. Eggs (3–5) heavily spotted.
Range: Jamaica.

Wood Pewee *Contopus virens*

Description: 6.25″. Resembles the Greater Antillean Pewee, but underparts paler and whiter, without the buffy wash; two *conspicuous* whitish wingbars; wing longer (over 3″).
Range: North and Central America. Northern races winter mainly in South America, migrating chiefly through Central America, but also through the western islands of the Caribbean (e.g. Cuba, Isle of Pines, Jamaica, Grand Cayman, Swan, St. Andrew's Island and Albuquerque Cay) and the Bahamas (Aug. 24–Nov. 4: March 26–April 22).

Lesser Antillean Pewee *Contopus latirostris* page 96

Local names: Bobito; Jüi Pequeño; Gobe-Mouches.
Description: Resembles the Greater Antillean Pewee, but underparts more or less ochraceous rather than buff. St. Lucia individuals have the underparts rufescent.
Voice: An emphatic *pree-e-e*, or a high-pitched *peet-peet-peet-peet-peet*.
Habitat: Mountain forest and wooded hills, including coffee plantations. Local in semi-arid, coastal areas.
Nidification: Like that of Greater Antillean Pewee. Eggs (2).
Range: Puerto Rico (rare or lacking in eastern third of island), Guadeloupe, Dominica, Martinique and St. Lucia.

Greater Antillean Pewee *Contopus caribaeus* page 96

Local names: Little Tom Fool; Willie Pee; Flycatcher; Bobito Chico; Maroita; Manjuila; Pipirite Tête-Fou.
Description: 6.25″. A drab little flycatcher with a broad, flat bill, the

lower mandible pale. Upperparts olive-grey, darker on crown; underparts greyish buff. Has a characteristic habit of quivering its tail after perching. See Wood Pewee. Fig. 117.

Voice: Utters a variety of notes, sometimes a plaintive *ee-oo*, at times a rather deliberate *pit-pit-pit-pit*, or *we-we-we-we-we*.

Habitat: Forested areas, borders of clearings on mountain sides, orchards, bushy country, and mangrove swamps.

Nidification: Nest a well constructed little cup, usually "saddled" on a limb of a tree or in fork of tree or shrub; occasionally on beam of building. Eggs (2–4) spotted, the markings often forming a wreath around middle of egg.

Range: Northern Bahamas (Grand Bahama, Abaco, Andros, New Providence, Eleuthera, Cat Island), Cuba, Isle of Pines, Jamaica, Hispaniola and Gonâve Island.

Fig. 117 Greater Antillean Pewee

Acadian Flycatcher *Empidonax virescens*

Description: 6". A plainly coloured little flycatcher that somewhat resembles a Wood Pewee, but *upperparts dull green*, more prominent pale wing-bars, and *whitish eye-ring*; underparts white, slightly washed with olivaceous and yellow.

Range: South-eastern North America. Winters from southern Central America to north-western South America. Rare transient in Bahamas, western Cuba and the Isle of Pines (Sept. 12–Oct. 21 : April).

Euler's Flycatcher *Lathrotriccus euleri*

Description: 5.5". A pewee-like flycatcher with *conspicuous ochraceous wing-bars*. The Grenada race has the upperparts dark olive, the crown dusky; underparts largely yellowish, with a greyish olive band across chest. Excessively rare in Grenada, whence there are but three records.

Voice: A purling *pee-dedeedeedeedee*, the first note higher pitched than the others (Trinidad).

Habitat: Vicinity of the Grand Etang. In Trinidad partial to cacao plantations, and should be sought in such habitat on Grenada.

Nidification: In Trinidad builds a cup-shaped nest in a tree, at times in a knothole. Eggs (2–3) spotted.
Range: Grenada. Also South America, including Trinidad.

Yellow-bellied Elaenia *Elaenia flavogaster* page 96

Local name: Topknot Pipiri.
Description: Closely resembles the Caribbean Elaenia, but posterior underparts distinctly pale yellow in fresh plumage; *usually appears conspicuously crested.* Replaced in mountains of Grenada by Caribbean Elaenia, but both species found in lowlands of St. Vincent.
Voice: Quite different from that of Caribbean Elaenia; a harsh *creup-creup-wi-creup*, or merely a drawn-out *creup*.
Habitat: Thickets and trees in rather open country in the lowlands.
Nidification: Nest better constructed than that of Caribbean Elaenia and lined with feathers; eggs (2–3) usually more heavily spotted.
Range: St. Vincent, the Grenadines and Grenada. Also Central and South America, including Trinidad and Tobago.

Caribbean Elaenia *Elaenia martinica* page 96

Fig. 118 Caribbean Elaenia

Local names: Whistler; Pee-whistler; Cheery-cheer; Judas Bird; Piole; Siffleur; Siffleur Blanc; Jüi Blanco.
Description: 7″. A plainly coloured flycatcher. Upperparts dark olive-grey; underparts greyish white with a yellowish wash, particularly on abdomen; two greyish white wing-bars and a more or less concealed patch of white on crown: sometimes appears slightly crested. Fig. 118.
Voice: A harsh *che-eup*, often followed by *wi-wi-eup*.
Habitat: Widespread in forest, woodland and scrub-covered country.
Nidification: Nest a roughly built cup with no soft interior lining, situated in a shrub or tree. Eggs (2–3) spotted.

Range: Lesser Antilles (rare or lacking on Grenadines), Virgin Islands to Puerto Rico, Cayman Islands, Old Providence, St. Andrew, and extra-limital islands in Caribbean; perhaps coastal Belize.

Greater Antillean Elaenia   *Elaenia fallax*   page 96

Local names: Penny-catcher; Sarah Bird; Maroita Canosa; Chitte Sara.
Description: 6″. Resembles the Caribbean Elaenia but smaller; underparts pale primrose-yellow to greyish white. Much paler below and with smaller bill than Greater Antillean Pewee.
Voice: A harsh *che-eup*, or a sprightly *swee-ip* reminiscent of the Acadian Flycatcher.
Habitat: Borders of rain forest, pine woods, and thickets in more open country of higher hills and mountains.
Nidification: Nest a cup of moss, lined with feathers, situated in a tree or shrub. Eggs (2) sparingly, but distinctly, spotted.
Range: Hispaniola and Jamaica.

Jamaican Elaenia   *Myiopagis cotta*   page 96

Local name: Unknown.
Description: 6″. Resembles the Greater Antillean Elaenia, but chin to foreneck white in contrast with pale yellow of posterior underparts; an ill-defined white superciliary stripe, most prominent above lores; crown-patch of adult yellow instead of white; *no wing-bars*, but shows some greenish yellow on wings. Closely related to the Greenish Elaenia (*M. viridicata*) of tropical Mexico, Central and South America. Fig. 119.

Fig. 119 Jamaican Elaenia

Voice: A high-pitched, rapidly uttered *tse-tse-tse-u*, the last note decidedly lower than the rest.

Habitat: Widespread in Jamaica, both in mountains and low country. Found in rain forest, open park-like country, the Cockpit Country, and in lowland shrubbery.

Nidification: Said to build a cup-shaped nest without an inner lining of feathers, and to lay (3) spotted eggs.
Range: Jamaica.

SWALLOWS *Hirundinidae*

Swallows are the best characterised of passerine birds. In the field they may be confused with swifts, but their flight is not as erratic. Like swifts, they feed entirely on insects, which they capture on the wing. Two of the West Indian genera (*Kalochelidon* and *Callichelidon*) would be endemic to this region, but are now placed in *Tachycineta* as is *Iridoprocene*.

Golden Swallow *Kalochelidon euchrysea* page 129

Fig. 120 Golden Swallow
(Hispaniola)

Local names: Swallow; Rain Bird; Golondrina Verde; Oiseau de la Pluie; "Jolle-jolle".
Description: 5". A beautiful swallow that somewhat resembles the Tree Swallow, but is smaller and more delicate and graceful in appearance, and with relatively longer wings and more deeply forked tail. The upperparts are green, glossed with bluish and, strongly, with gold; *underparts snowy white*. The immature is duller above and has a grey band across the breast. Fig. 120.
Voice: A soft *chi-weet*.
Habitat: Chiefly open areas in mountains of Hispaniola, now rare in Jamaica where found in the Cockpit Country.
Nidification: In cavities of trees or under the eaves of houses. Eggs (3) white.
Range: Hispaniola and Jamaica.

Bahama Swallow *Callichelidon cyaneoviridis*   page 129

Local names: Swallow; Summer Swallow; Golondrina.

Description: 6″. Somewhat resembles a Tree Swallow, but with the *shape of a Barn Swallow.* The anterior upperparts are dull greenish, turning to a violet-blue posteriorly; *underparts white;* tail *deeply* forked. Flight very rapid, like that of a Barn Swallow. Sometimes seen among flocks of Tree Swallows in winter. Fig. 121.

Voice: A soft twittering like that of the Golden Swallow.

Habitat: On breeding grounds, mainly pine barrens. Now rare on New Providence.

Nidification: Like that of Golden Swallow. Sometimes colonial.

Fig. 121 Bahama Swallow

Range: Breeds in the Bahamas, but probably only on the northern, pine-forested islands, some individuals migrating south to eastern Cuba for the winter; vagrant to Florida.

Tree Swallow *Iridoprocne bicolor*

Description: 5.5″. Upperparts glossy greenish blue, appearing dark in the field; underparts white; tail *slightly* forked.

Range: North America. Winters regularly south to the northern Bahamas, Cuba and northern Central America; also reported from Swan Island, Grand Cayman, Jamaica, Hispaniola and Puerto Rico (Sept. 4–June 3).

Purple Martin *Progne subis*   page 129

Local names: Swallow; Martin; Golondrina Grande; Golondrina de Iglesias; Golondrina Azul; Hirondelle.

Description: 8″. Larger than other West Indian swallows. Male dark violet-blue, appearing blackish in the field; a white streak from lower breast to under tail-coverts, except in birds from Cuba, the Isle of Pines and North America. Female duller above; anterior underparts, sides and flanks greyish brown; remainder of underparts white. North American females are not distinctly bicoloured below, the feathers of the breast with hoary margins, presenting a squamated effect, the abdomen with narrow black shaft-streaks; an ill-defined greyish collar, most prominent on sides of neck. Fig. 122.

Voice: A short *chu* or *chu-chu.*
Habitat: Chiefly towns; also sea cliffs and fairly open country. Not often seen in the mountains.
Nidification: Usually in colonies, under the eaves of a building or in crevices of cliffs; occasionally in a deserted woodpecker's hole in a tree or palm. Eggs (3–6) white.

Fig. 122 Purple Martin

Range: Breeds in North America, including Mexico, and in the Antilles (excluding the Cayman Islands and westernmost West Indian islets) and on Tobago. North American martins occur as transients in the West Indies (e.g. Bahama Islands and Cuba) and migrate, as presumably do other forms, to South America. No satisfactory Antillean record for any martin during November and December.

Bank Swallow *Riparia riparia*

Description: 5.25″. A small, dull-coloured swallow. Upperparts greyish brown; underparts white, with a *blackish band across chest.*
Range: North America and Eurasia. Winters (in New World) in tropical South America. Transient in West Indies, and may winter sparingly in Lesser Antilles (Aug. 14–Dec. 10; Feb. 7–June 1).

Rough-winged Swallow *Stelgidopteryx ruficollis*

Description: Resembles the Bank Swallow, but lacks the conspicuous dark band across the breast; throat and breast greyish.
Range: North, Central and South America. The North American race winters chiefly in Mexico and Central America, but a few occur in the West Indies (e.g. north-western Bahamas, Cuba, Jamaica, Grand Cayman and Swan Island) (Aug. 13–April 26).

Barn Swallow *Hirundo rustica* 4/5/97 DR

Description: 6–7.5″. The cinnamon underparts combined with deeply forked tail readily distinguish the adult. However, most Barn Swallows that winter in the West Indies are immature with the posterior underparts (below chest) white or whitish and the tail not deeply forked. Such birds may be distinguished by their bicoloured underparts, with some *blackish on sides of chest and white spotting on tail*.

Range: North America, Europe, Asia and north-western Africa. Winters (in New World) mainly in South America. Transient throughout the West Indies, and winter resident from Puerto Rico eastward through the Lesser Antilles; occurs elsewhere until early January (Aug. 1–June 9).

Cliff Swallow *Petrochelidon pyrrhonota*

Description: Resembles the Cave Swallow, but distinguished by dark chestnut sides of head and throat, black patch on foreneck, and whitish, rather than brown, forehead.

Range: North America. Migrates chiefly through Central America and winters in South America. Rare transient in West Indies (Aug. 30–Nov. 11: March 21–May 6); casual on Barbados in winter.

Cave Swallow *Petrochelidon fulva*   page 129

Local names: Cave Swallow; Rain Bird; Golondrina de Cuevas; Hirondelle.

Description: 5″. A common Greater Antillean swallow, distinguished by

"*square*" appearance of tail (this is only slightly notched) and by *chestnut rump*. Upperparts mostly blue-black with whitish streaks on back and, in adults, a rufous collar and forehead; underparts whitish, more or less washed with rufous. Fig. 123.

Voice: A soft *chu-chu* and chattering notes.

Habitat: Rocky ravines, sea cliffs and settled districts.

Fig. 123 Cave Swallow

Nidification: Nest composed chiefly of mud, attached to the side of a cliff, cave, building or bridge; usually a crescent-shaped half-cup, rarely covered with entrance at side. Eggs (2–5) spotted. Nests in colonies.

Range: Cuba, Isle of Pines, Hispaniola (including Gonâve, Tortue and Ile-à-Vache), Jamaica, Puerto Rico and Vieques Island; apparently to some extent migratory in Cuba and Isle of Pines: October records from Grand Cayman may pertain to Cuban individuals. Also breeds in Texas, Mexico, Ecuador and Peru. Casual in southern Florida.

CROWS, MAGPIES & JAYS *Corvidae*

Crows are a cosmopolitan group of birds, apparently of Old World origin. They do not occur in Central or South America, but are represented in the West Indies by as many as four species. On the other hand, it is remarkable that jays are absent from this region, for they abound in North and Central America.

The food of Antillean crows consists mainly of fruit. They also feed on grain as well as insects and other animal matter. They are excessively abundant in some localities.

Nidification: Nests of all West Indian crows are roughly built structures, situated high in trees or palms. Eggs (3–4) pale green, heavily spotted.

Cuban Crow *Corvus nasicus*

Local names: Crow; Cao; Cao Montero.

Description: 18–19″. Plumage entirely black with a slight violet-blue gloss. Virtually indistinguishable in the field from the Palm Crow, except by voice. The latter species is rare in Cuba.

Voice: Parrot-like squawks and guttural jabbering.

Habitat: Mainly wooded areas, but often seen in villages or settlements where trees are numerous.

Range: Cuba, Isle of Pines, Providenciales to East Caicos.

White-necked Crow *Corvus leucognaphalus*

Local names: Cuervo, Corneille.

Description: 19–20″. Resembles the Cuban Crow, but slightly larger; plumage strongly glossed with violet, particularly on upperparts; basal portions of feathers of neck and body white instead of grey, but appears entirely black in the field. May be distinguished from the Palm Crow by larger size, more graceful, leisurely flight and *very different voice*, which is raucous and raven-like. Fig. 124.

Voice: Resembles that of the Cuban Crow. A common utterance is a throaty *culik-calow-calow.*

Habitat: Occurs from coastal mangroves to mountain pine forest. Much less sedentary than the smaller Palm Crow, and apt to be seen in flocks.

Range: Hispaniola, and formerly Puerto Rico; also recorded from Gonâve and Saona islands.

Fig. 124 White-necked Crow

Jamaican Crow
Corvus jamaicensis

Local name: Jabbering Crow.
Description: 17″. Smaller than the Cuban Crow, and plumage much duller, without gloss; resembles other species of *Corvus* in the field. *The only true crow in Jamaica.*

Voice: A harsh *craa-craa*, as well as a variety of gurgling or jabbering sounds.

Habitat: Wooded areas and park-like country, common near Moneague and in the Cockpit Country.

Range: Jamaica.

Palm Crow   *Corvus palmarum*   4/3/1997   DR

Local names: Cao Pinalero (Cuba); Cao (Haiti and Dominican Rep.).
Description: 17″. Resembles the Cuban Crow, but slightly smaller (folded wing under 10.5″). In the field, *may readily be identified by its voice.*

Voice: A harsh *craa-craa*, reminiscent of North American Fish Crows or European Carrion Crows.

Habitat: Wooded areas both in lowlands and mountains, most numerous in pine forest (Hispaniola). Very local in Cuba; occurs near Matahambre in Pinar del Río Province.

Range: Cuba and Hispaniola.

NUTHATCHES   *Sittidae*

Nuthatches are members of a small family evidently of Old World origin and best represented in southern Asia. Four species, all of the genus *Sitta*, inhabit North America. An insular race of one of these is resident on the island of Grand Bahama.

Brown-headed Nuthatch   *Sitta pusilla*

Fig. 125 Brown-headed Nuthatch

Local name: Unknown.
Description: 4.5″. A small nuthatch with a brownish cap, bordered by a darker brown streak through eye; a white patch on hindneck; back plain slate-grey; underparts whitish. Fig. 125.
Voice: A high-pitched *chi-chi-chi* or excited chattering.
Habitat: Pine barrens, where it may be seen creeping, mouse-like, around the trunks or along the branches of the trees.
Nidification: Nests (on the mainland) in a cavity excavated in a tree or stub, usually at a low elevation. Eggs spotted.
Range: Grand Bahama. Also the south-eastern United States.

WRENS   *Troglodytidae*

This family is believed to have originated in tropical North America' where it is represented by many species. Two species occur in the West Indies, both with notable songs. One of these, the Zapata Wren, constitutes an endemic genus (*Ferminia*), believed to be related to the Bewick's Wren group (*Thryomanes*) of North America.

House Wren   *Troglodytes aedon*

Local names: Rock Bird; Wall Bird; God Bird; Oiseau Bon Dieu; Rossignol.
Description: 4.5–5″. A little brown bird, with wings and tail barred with black; races from St. Lucia and St. Vincent have white underparts. Easily recognised by its small size, perky appearance and constant activity; tail seldom cocked and longer than depicted. Fig. 126.
Voice: One of the best songsters of the Lesser Antilles (and also of Trinidad and Tobago). Song superior to, but at times reminiscent of, those of North American House Wrens; usually a bubbling warble.

Habitat: Widespread in Dominica and Grenada; on latter island, much more of a "house" wren than elsewhere in Lesser Antilles; on St. Lucia apparently now confined to semi-arid woodland at low elevations in the north-east; on St. Vincent inhabits both windward and leeward slopes; on Guadeloupe occurs in the mountains of Basse Terre; apparently extirpated on Martinique (last reported in 1886). Frequents undergrowth, where readily located by its melodious singing.

Nidification. The nest is situated in a crevice in a bank or building, or in a stump or epiphyte; occasionally rather high above the ground in

Fig. 126 House Wren (Grenada)

Grenada. Eggs (2–6; usually 4–5) thickly speckled.

Range: Guadeloupe, Dominica, Martinique, St. Lucia, St. Vincent and Grenada. Also North, Central and South America; casual in Bahamas and western Cuba.

Zapata Wren *Ferminia cerverai*

Fig. 127 Zapata Wren

Local name: Fermina.

Description: 6.25″. The only wren native to the Greater Antilles is characterised by relatively short wings and long tail. Upperparts greyish brown, spotted on the head and barred elsewhere with black; underparts whitish. Rarely takes to wing and flight very weak. Fig. 127.

Voice: A loud, melodious and variable warbling.

Habitat: Dense shrubbery in the Zapata Swamp, in the vicinity of the territory known as "Santo Tomás", ranging west to the Ensenada la Broa.

Nidification: Said to build a globular nest with the entrance at the side, situated in a bush, and to lay as many as six white eggs.
Range: Cuba.

MOCKINGBIRDS & THRASHERS *Mimidae*

The Mimidae comprise a small family of New World birds, apparently of tropical North American origin and related to the thrushes and wrens. The family is well represented in this region. Three genera are West Indian, and of these *Cinclocerthia* and *Ramphocinclus* are confined to the Lesser Antilles. A fourth genus native to these islands is *Mimus*, which includes the mockingbirds, a group widespread in North, Central and South America.

Northern Mockingbird *Mimus polyglottos* 4/3/97 DR

Local names: Nightingale (Jamaica); Mockingbird; English Thrasher (Bahama Islands); Sinsonte (Cuba); Ruiseñor; Rossignol.
Description: 10″. Upperparts chiefly grey, darker on wings and tail; a considerable amount of white on wing, conspicuous in flight, and outer tail feathers white or largely white; underparts white or greyish white.
Voice: Song a series of melodious phrases. Occasionally mimics other species. Utters harsh notes of alarm.
Habitat: Towns, settlements, open country. Unrecorded from a number of remote "out-islands" in the Bahamas, although occurs from Grand Bahama and Abaco to Grand Turk.
Nidification: Nest a roughly built cup, built in a bush or tree. Eggs (usually 3–4) pale greenish, heavily spotted.
Range: Bahama Islands and Greater Antilles (including the Cayman Islands), east to the Virgin Islands. Also North America, including Mexico, south to the Isthmus of Tehuantepec.

Tropical Mockingbird *Mimus gilvus*   page 177

Local names: Mockingbird; Nightingale; Grive Blanche; Grive des Savanes.
Description: Resembles the Northern Mockingbird, but white on wing obsolete and much less white on tail; pileum with faint dusky shaft-streaks. Fig. 128.
Voice: Song like that of Northern Mockingbird, but a little harsher, less melodious.

Fig. 128 Tropical Mockingbird

Habitat: Rather open, settled country in St. Vincent and Grenada; drier areas in Dominica, Martinique and St. Lucia.
Nidification: Like that of Northern Mockingbird.
Range: Guadeloupe (south-east Grande Terre, including offshore islands), Dominica, Martinique, St. Lucia, St. Vincent, the Grenadines and Grenada. Also Central and South America, and extralimital Caribbean islands.

St. Andrew Mockingbird *Mimus magnirostris*

Local name: Nightingale.
Description: 11″. Resembles the Tropical Mockingbird but larger, the *bill much larger*. Now regarded as a race of *M. gilvus*.
Voice: Song like that of Northern Mockingbird but not known to mimic other birds. Alarm notes less harsh.
Habitat: Copses and orchards, chiefly in the hills.
Nidification: Unknown, but doubtless like that of preceding species.
Range: Island of St. Andrew.

Bahama Mockingbird *Mimus gundlachii* page 177

Local names: Spanish Nightingale; Salt Island Nightingale (Jamaica); Spanish Thrasher; Thrasher; Mockingbird (Bahamas); Sinsonte Prieto; Sinsonte Carbonero (Cuba).
Description: 11″. Larger than Northern Mockingbird. Upperparts brownish grey, indistinctly streaked with dusky on head and back; *very little white on wing*; underparts whitish, streaked with dusky posteriorly. Fig. 129.

Fig. 129 Bahama
Mockingbird (Bahamas)

Voice: Song less melodious and less variable than that of Northern Mockingbird, the notes more abrupt. Does not mimic other birds.

Habitat: Semi-arid scrub and about settlements. In Cuban territory known only from cays off the north coast, opposite Caibarién and San Juan de los Perros. Found virtually throughout the Bahamas; rare on Grand Bahama and Great Abaco, but not on Little Abaco and cays north of that island. In Jamaica confined to semi-arid, limestone country in southern St Catherine and Clarendon parishes, from Port Henderson to Portland Ridge.

Nidification: Like other species of the genus. Eggs creamy white or pinkish white, spotted.

Range: Bahama Islands (from Grand Bahama to Grand Turk) and cays off northern Cuba; also southern Jamaica.

Scaly-breasted Thrasher *Margarops fuscus* page 177

Local names: Thrush; Black-billed Thrush; Spotted Grive; Grive; Grivotte; Grive Fine; Grive Cendrée.

Fig. 130 Scaly-breasted
Thrasher

Description: 9″. Upperparts dark greyish brown; inner remiges (in fresh plumage) and all but central pair of rectrices conspicuously tipped with white; underparts white, heavily marked with greyish brown chiefly in the form of squamations; *bill black.* A shy *arboreal* thrasher, thrush-like in appearance. Fig. 130.

Voice: Like that of a mockingbird, but softer and more hesitant.
Habitat: Forested areas; also about settlements and in semi-arid wood-land. Rare on Grenada and Barbados.
Nidification: The cup-shaped nest is situated in a tree. Eggs (2–3) greenish blue.
Range: Lesser Antilles, but not known from Anguilla and St. Bartholomew, and accidental in the Grenadines.

Pearly-eyed Thrasher *Margarops fuscatus* page 177

Local names: Jack Bird; Paw-paw Bird; Soursop Bird; Black Thrasher (Bahamas); Thrush; Wall-eyed Thrush; Zorzal; Zorzal Pardo; Zorzal Oliblanco; Zorzal de Palmares; Pío Juan; Chucho; Truche; Grosse Grive; Grive Corossol

Fig. 131 Pearly-eyed Thrasher

Description: 11″. An arboreal thrasher that resembles the Scaly-breasted Thrasher, but decidedly larger and with a heavy brownish yellow bill; markings on underparts less squamated, the throat and foreneck streaked with brownish. Fig. 131.
Voice: A hesitant *pio-tereu-tsee* with variations. Gives the impression of "tuning up". Also utters a shrill yapping, a low vibrating *craw-craw*, and a harsh *chook*.
Habitat: Mountain forest and scrubby woodland.
Nidification: The bulky cup-shaped nest is situated in a bush or tree, cavity of a tree, or on the side of cave or cliff. Eggs (2–3) greenish blue.
Range: Bahamas (from San Salvador south), Isla Beata, and from Mona eastward through Puerto Rico and the Virgin Islands to the Lesser Antilles, south to St. Vincent; casual on Eleuthera, Hispaniola (Parque del Este); accidental on Jamaica and Barbados. Also Bonaire and (formerly) Horquilla in the southern Caribbean.

Trembler *Cinclocerthia ruficauda* page 177

Local names: Trembler; Trembling Thrush; Brown Bird; Trembleur; Grive Trembleuse; Cocobino.
Description: 9–10″. Upperparts dark brown to olive-grey, becoming dusky anteriorly; underparts buffy greyish brown to greyish white (birds on St. Lucia are palest and greyest); bill long and slender. *Readily identified in the field by its habit of trembling.* Fig. 132.

Fig. 132 Trembler (Dominica)

Voice: A series of phrases, some harsh, others melodious.

Habitat: Chiefly rain forest, but also found sparingly in secondary growth and drier woodland.

Nidification: Nest built in a cavity of a tree or tree fern, or at the base of a palm frond. Eggs (2–3) greenish blue.

Range: Saba, St. Eustatius, St. Kitts, Nevis, Montserrat, Guadeloupe, Dominica, Martinique, St. Lucia and St. Vincent.

White-breasted Thrasher   *Ramphocinclus brachyurus*   page 177

Local name: Gorge-blanche (usually pron. "Gorge-blanc").

Description: 9–9.5″. Upperparts, sides, flanks and under tail-coverts dark sooty brown; sides of head blackish; rest of underparts immaculate white; iris reddish, not whitish as that of the Trembler and other West Indian thrashers. Largely terrestrial. *Twitches* its wings; tail rarely cocked. Fig. 133.

Fig. 133 White-breasted Thrasher

Voice: Song like that of a Catbird but softer; also a sharp *tiok*.

Habitat: Semi-arid woodland. In Martinique apparently confined to the Presqu'île de la Caravelle, in St. Lucia to the northern part of that island. Occurs in scattered colonies.

Nidification: The bulky cup-shaped nests are situated in shrubs or saplings at low or moderate elevations above the ground. Eggs (2) greenish blue.

Range: Martinique and St. Lucia.

Grey Catbird   *Dumetella carolinensis*

Local name: Zorzal Gato.
Description: 9". Plumage slate-grey, paler on underparts; pileum and tail black; under tail-coverts chestnut. Usually found in thickets.
Voice: Utters a characteristic cat-like mewing, but does not sing in West Indies.
Range: North America: a permanent resident on the Bermuda Islands. Winters south to Colombia and winter resident in the West Indies, but very rare east of Cuba and Jamaica whence recorded from Hispaniola, Tortue, Puerto Rico and Anguilla (Sept. 19–May 25).

THRUSHES   *Turdidae*

Thrushes are a cosmopolitan family, and are well represented in the New World. Many of the species have beautiful songs. The food of West Indian thrushes consists chiefly of berries and insects.

Of the genera native to this region, *Mimocichla* and *Cichlherminia* are herein regarded as endemic, but the former has recently been merged with *Turdus*. The genus *Myadestes* is represented in North, Central and South America.

American Robin   *Turdus migratorius*

Description: 9.5". An abundant North American thrush, chiefly greyish above and *rufous on the underparts*; throat white streaked with black.
Range: North America. Winters south to southern Mexico, northern Bahamas and western Cuba; reported from Jamaica, Mona (Oct. 17–April).

Bare-eyed Thrush   *Turdus nudigenis*   page 145

Local names: Yellow-eyed Grive; Yam Bird; Grive à Paupières Jaunes; Grive à Lunettes.
Description: 9–9.5". A plainly coloured thrush, dark greyish olive above, the underparts mostly brownish grey with dusky streaks on the throat. The best field mark is the *bare, yellow patch around the eye*, presenting a "goggle-eyed" effect.
Voice: Song a clear *turé-too-too*, repeated indefinitely and much like that of the American Robin. Also utters a whining *pe-ou-wa*, and a variety of shorter call-notes.
Habitat: Lowland woods, copses and gardens. Also near settlements at higher elevations. Rare on Martinique.

Nidification: The bulky cup-shaped nests are situated in trees at moderate elevations. Eggs (3) light greenish blue, spotted.
Range: Lesser Antilles from Martinique southward, excluding Barbados; apparently a recent arrival on islands north of St. Vincent. Also Tobago, Trinidad, Margarita Island and continental South America.

Cocoa Thrush   *Turdus fumigatus*   page 145

Local names: Black-eyed Grive; Mountain Grive; Grive des Cacaos.
Description: Differs from the Bare-eyed Thrush in having the upperparts dark brown; *no yellow around eye.*
Voice: Song plaintive, usually four-syllabled, the introductory notes higher pitched than the concluding ones. Also utters a loud *wheeo-wheeo-wheeo.*
Habitat: Mountain forest and cacao plantations on St. Vincent and Grenada, but found in lowlands together with Bare-eyed Thrush in Trinidad.
Nidification: Like that of preceding species, but more or less moss used in construction of nest, and ground colour of eggs greener, less blue. Not known to nest on sides of banks as in Trinidad.
Range: St. Vincent and Grenada. Also Trinidad and continental South America.

White-eyed Thrush   *Turdus jamaicensis*   page 145

Local names: Glass-eye; Shine-eye; Fish-eye; Long Day Bird; Long Day Hopping Dick.
Description: 9–9.5″. Head and neck brown with an admixture of white on throat, and foreneck white; remainder of upperparts dark grey, of underparts pale greyish; bill black; iris bluish white. White-chinned Thrush has a white spot on wing and orange bill and feet.
Voice: A superlative songster. Song much like that of the Northern Mockingbird, but louder and sharper. Utters a shrill note of alarm.
Habitat: Mountain forest and wooded hills; rare in lowland valleys.
Nidification: Nest a bulky cup situated in a tree. Eggs (2–3) pale bluish green, heavily speckled.
Range: Jamaica.

La Selle Thrush   *Turdus swalesi*   page 145

Local names: Chocho; Ouète-ouète Noir.
Description: 10.5″. Upperparts black, the back locally brownish; traces of white on throat; chest dusky, turning to *chestnut on lower breast and abdo-*

men, with a median streak of white; bill mostly orange. Readily distinguished from the Red- legged Thrush by its dark plumage and lack of white on tail.

Voice: Song a soft *turé-too*, uttered rather deliberately and continued indefinitely. Also emits a loud *wheury-wheury-wheury* and gurgling notes.

Habitat: High ridge of Morne La Selle, chiefly above 4,500 feet, east to Dominican Republic. Found in dense shrubbery.

Nidification: Nest a bulky cup, composed largely of moss and situated in a bush or low tree. Eggs greenish blue, spotted.

Range: High mountains of Hispaniola, except Massif de la Hotte.

White-chinned Thrush   *Turdus aurantius*   page 145

Local names: Hopping Dick; Jumping Dick; Twopenny Chick; Chick-me-Chick.

Description: 10.5″. A familiar Jamaican thrush. Upperparts dark grey, underparts paler grey, the chin and centre of lower breast and abdomen white; *a conspicuous white spot on wing*, involving innermost greater wing-coverts; bill, feet and iris orange. Frequently seen on roadsides with tail uptilted, suggestive of a Red-legged Thrush.

Voice: Song a robin-like *turé-too-too*, repeated indefinitely, but much richer in tone and more plaintive; also suggestive of song of European Blackbird (*T. merula*). Utters shrill alarm notes.

Habitat: Wooded areas and gardens, chiefly in hills and mountains.

Nidification: Nest a bulky and rather untidy cup, situated in a tree. Eggs (2–3) dull whitish or pale greenish, spotted.

Range: Jamaica.

Grand Cayman Thrush   *Mimocichla ravida*   page 145

Local name: Thrush.

Description: 11″. Plumage slate-grey, becoming white on abdomen and under tail-coverts; tips of outer tail feathers largely white; bill, feet and bare eye-ring coral-red.

Voice: A subdued warbling, like that of Red-legged Thrush. Also emits chattering notes in flight when alarmed.

Habitat: Formerly inhabited dense woodland. Now exceedingly rare, if not extinct.

Nidification: Unknown.

Range: Grand Cayman.

Red-legged Thrush *Mimocichla plumbea* page 145

Local names: Blue Thrasher; Red-legged Blue Thrasher; Thrush; Blue Jane; Robin; Zorzal Azul; Zorzal de Patas Coloradas; Chua-chuá; Ouète-ouète; Couète-couète; Pierrot Vantard.
Description: 10–11″. The most widespread of West Indian thrushes. There is much geographical variation in colour of underparts, but always recognisable by the predominantly slate-grey colour, black tail with broad white tips to outer feathers, and red feet. The chin and throat are variously black and white, the bill more or less reddish; in central and western Cuba, the

Fig. 134 Red-legged Thrush (Bahamas)

Isle of Pines and Cayman Brac, these thrushes have the abdomen ochraceous. Fig. 134.
Voice: Song prolonged but comparatively weak and hesitant. Utters a loud *wet-wet* when alarmed.
Habitat: Forested districts both in mountains and lowlands; wooded plantations; gardens.
Nidification: Nest a bulky cup usually in a bush or tree. Eggs (3–5) whitish to pale greenish, spotted.
Range: Bahamas (Grand Bahama, Abaco, Andros, New Providence, Eleuthera, Cat Island, Exuma Cays?, Great Inagua?), Cuba, Isle of Pines, Swan Islands (formerly), Cayman Brac, Hispaniola, Gonâve, Tortue, Saona, Mona (casual), Puerto Rico and Dominica.

Forest Thrush *Cichlherminia lherminieri* page 145

Local names: Yellow-legged Thrush; Mauvis; Grive à Pieds Jaunes.
Description: 10.5″. Plumage mainly brown, with large, drop-shaped white spots on underparts; feet and bare orbital space yellow; bill yellow or yellowish. Somewhat resembles the Pearly-eyed Thrasher, but browner, darker on underparts, and *lacks white on tail*. An exceedingly shy thrush, very rare on St. Lucia.
Voice: Song a melodious warbling; also a sharp *chuk* or *chuk-chuk*.
Habitat: Forest, ranging from the undergrowth to the tops of tall trees.
Nidification: The bulky cup-shaped nest is composed externally of moss and is situated in a bush, tree fern, or tree, at low or moderate elevations above the ground. Eggs (2–3) greenish blue.
Range: Montserrat, Guadeloupe, Dominica and St. Lucia.

Wood Thrush   *Hylocichla mustelina*

Description: 8″. Upperparts olive-brown becoming *rufous on the hindneck and pileum*; underparts white with prominent, round, blackish spots on breast, sides and flanks; feet and basal portion of lower mandible flesh-colour. In winter plumage the anterior underparts are tinged with buff.
Range: Eastern half of the United States and south-eastern Canada. Winters chiefly in Central America. Very rare transient in the Bahamas (e.g. Grand Bahama, New Providence and Cay Lobos) and Cuba (Sept. 14–Dec. 12; March 1–April 18).

Olive-backed Thrush   *Catharus ustulatus*

Description: 7″. Differs from the Wood Thrush in having the entire upperparts olive-brown; underparts less distinctly spotted, and sides and flanks washed with greyish olive; anterior underparts, including cheeks, tinged with buff; *eye-ring decidedly buff*, giving the bird a "goggle-eyed" appearance when viewed with a binocular.
Range: North America, chiefly the Canadian zone. Winters south to Argentina. Migrates for most part through Central America. Rare transient in the West Indies; recorded from the Bahama Islands, Cuba, Isle of Pines, Swan Island, St. Andrew, Jamaica and Hispaniola (Sept. 14–Nov. 28; March 19–May 10).

Grey-cheeked Thrush   *Catharus minimus*

Description: Closely resembles the Olive-backed Thrush, but throat white and cheeks not buffy, and lacks buffy ring around eye.
Range: North-eastern Siberia, Alaska, Canada and the north-eastern United States. Winters chiefly in northern South America. Mainly rare transient in the West Indies, but individuals of the south-eastern race ("Bicknell's Thrush") winter in Hispaniola, Mona. Recorded in the West Indies from the Bahamas, Cuba, Swan Island, Jamaica, Hispaniola, Puerto Rico and Martinique (Sept. 14–May 16).

Veery   *Catharus fuscescens*

Description: Differs from preceding species of this genus in having the *entire upperparts tawny brown* (*C. f. fuscescens*); markings on underparts smaller and indistinct and do not extend to lower breast.
Range: North America. Winters in South America. Migrates chiefly through Central America. Rare transient in the West Indies, whence

recorded from the western Bahama Islands and from Cuba, Grand Cayman and Jamaica (Sept. 12–Oct. 22; early April–May 20).

Common Bluebird *Sialia sialis*

Description: 7″. The male is bright blue above, some of the feathers with rusty tips in winter; anterior underparts, sides and flanks rufous; rest of underparts white. The female is duller, the anterior upperparts decidedly brownish.

Range: North America (including Bermuda) south to Nicaragua. Rare winter resident in western Cuba (Nov. 30–early April).

Cuban Solitaire *Myadestes elisabeth*   page 145

Local name: Ruiseñor.

Description: 7.5″. A slender, rather long-tailed, plainly coloured bird with somewhat the appearance of a flycatcher, but gentle and unobtrusive in habits. Upperparts chiefly dark greyish olive, becoming brownish on wings; a prominent black spot on wing; underparts white, more or less washed with grey; *a conspicuous white eye-ring and outer tail feathers tipped with white.*

Voice: Song unhurried and flute-like. One of the most remarkable songsters of the West Indies.

Plate 13 HONEYCREEPERS & TODIES

Habitat: Forested hills and mountains of western and eastern Cuba. In Isle of Pines found sparingly in dense woods bordering the Ciénaga Lanier.
Nidification: The cup-shaped nest is situated on the side of a bank or steep mountain slope. Eggs (3) spotted.
Range: Cuba and the Isle of Pines.

Rufous-throated Solitaire   *Myadestes genibarbis*   page 145

Local names: Mountain Whistler; Fiddler (Jamaica); Soufrière Bird (St. Vincent); Jilguero (Dom. Rep.); Oiseau Musicien (Haiti); Siffleur de Montagne (Lesser Antilles).
Description: 7.5″. Mostly grey, with rufous throat, foreneck and posterior underparts; breast much paler than back; lower eyelids and chin white; *much white on outer tail feathers*; feet yellow. St. Vincent solitaires are black above, the rump greyish olive.
Voice: Whistling less prolonged than, but not inferior to, that of Cuban Solitaire. In winter, solitaires usually emit only a single note, a drawn-out *teut*.
Habitat: Mountain forest, some individuals descending to lower elevations in Jamaica and Hispaniola in winter.

14 ORIOLES, WEAVER & SALTATOR

M

Nidification: The cup-shaped nest is situated in the side of a bank, among vines covering a boulder, in a cavity of a stub or in the heart of a tree fern or bromeliad. Eggs (2) white or bluish white, spotted.

Range: Jamaica, Hispaniola, Dominica, Martinique, St. Lucia and St. Vincent.

OLD WORLD WARBLERS, GNATCATCHERS & KINGLETS *Sylviidae*

The Sylviidae, a large Old World family related to the thrushes, is poorly represented in the Americas. Of the New World members, gnatcatchers are the most widely distributed and are the only ones native to West Indies.

Blue-grey Gnatcatcher *Polioptila caerulea*

Local names: Cat Bird; Chew Bird; Spain-Spain; Cotton Bird; Rabuita.
Description: 4.5″. A tiny bird with a long black and white tail that is often uptilted like that of a wren. Upperparts blue-grey; underparts whitish; a black streak from forehead to border of crown (male); a prominent white eye-ring. The central tail feathers are black, the outer ones largely white. Females are duller than males.
Voice: Song rather rasping, but not unpleasant. Often scolds an intruder with a wheezy *spee-spee*, etc.
Habitat: Mainly undergrowth and scrubby thickets.
Nidification: Nest a neat, compact cup, situated in a bush or low tree (in a crotch or "saddled" on a branch) or small palm. Eggs (3) very pale bluish green, spotted.

Range: Breeds in the Bahamas and from southern North America south to Honduras. North American individuals winter (Aug. 10–May 4) in the Bahamas, Cuba, the Isle of Pines and Cayman Islands.

Fig. 135 Cuban Gnatcatcher

Cuban Gnatcatcher
Polioptila lembeyei

Local name: Sinsontillo.
Description: 4.25″. Resembles

the Blue-grey Gnatcatcher but smaller; upperparts grey (male) or greyish (female); no black on forehead and borders of crown, but *a black streak on side of head*. Fig. 135.

Voice: Song surprisingly loud and more melodious than that of Blue-grey Gnatcatcher.

Habitat: Semi-arid scrub in southern Cuba, east of Cienfuegos Bay; most numerous in southern Oriente Province. Also occurs on north coast of Camagüey Province (e.g. Playa Santa Lucía).

Nidification: Like that of preceding species.

Range: Cuba.

WAXWINGS *Bombycillidae*

These are only three species of waxwings, one of which occurs in the West Indies. These birds are so named because some of the inner remiges are often tipped with wax-like appendages. Waxwings feed mainly on berries, and are apt to be seen in small flocks.

Cedar Waxwing *Bombycilla cedrorum*

Description: 7″. Plumage mostly greyish brown, with *a prominent crest* of this colour; a black streak from forehead through eye; tail grey broadly tipped with bright yellow; posterior underparts pale yellow; the wax-like appendages on wings (when present) are red. Arboreal in habits. Fig. 136.

Range: Breeds in temperate North America. Winters south to northern South America, uncommon in the West Indies east to the Virgin Islands; casual in Lesser Antilles whence recorded from Guadeloupe and Dominica (October 14–May 22).

Fig. 136 Cedar Waxwing

PALMCHATS *Dulidae*

The Palmchat belongs to a family endemic to the West Indies. The single species is rather distantly related to the waxwings, the behaviour of flocks away from their nests often reminiscent of these birds.

The plumage of the Palmchat is coarser than that of a waxwing, and the feet are much larger. Its nesting habits are very different. On the other hand, like waxwings, the Palmchat is gregarious and feeds on berries and on blossoms of various flowering plants.

Palmchat *Dulus dominicus*   3/30 DR   page 145

Local names: Sigua Palmera; Sigua de Palma; Oiseau Palmiste; Esclave.
Description: 8″. Upperparts greyish olive to olive-brown, with some green on wing; underparts buffy white, *boldly streaked with dusky*. An active, noisy, arboreal bird, often found in flocks.
Voice: Possesses no true song, but utters a variety of notes, some harsh, some pleasing.
Habitat: Widespread in fairly open country, particularly among royal palms. Absent from dense rain forest. Most numerous at low elevations.
Nidification: Nest a large communal structure, composed of dead twigs, usually situated high in a palm; in a tree in the mountains where palms are not present, the nest then smaller and seldom occupied by more than two pairs. The various compartments open separately on the outside, allowing a degree of privacy to each pair. The tunnels lead to roughly-lined inner chambers in which the eggs are deposited. Eggs (2–4) heavily spotted.
Range: Hispaniola, Gonâve, and Saona Island.

STARLINGS *Sturnidae*

A familiar Old World family. Two species have been introduced into North America. One of these, the Common Starling, is now widespread on that continent, and has become well established in Jamaica since its introduction (1903–4) near Annotto Bay.

Common Starling *Sturnus vulgaris*

Description: 8.5″. Adult black with green and purple gloss, sometimes with profuse pale spotting; appears black at a distance, *has a pointed bill, pointed wings and short tail*; bill yellow in breeding season. Young are greyish brown. Gregarious, and largely terrestrial in habits.
Voice: Song a rambling series of chirruping, gurgling and clicking notes, interspersed with occasional whistles. Often mimics other birds.
Habitat: Open, farming country, chiefly in the hills of Jamaica.
Nidification: Nests in cavities in trees or buildings. Eggs very pale blue.
Range: Eurasia. Introduced resident in Jamaica; winters elsewhere in Greater Antilles (rare) and in Bahamas (Oct. 14–March 18).

VIREOS *Vireonidae*

Vireos are for the most part plainly coloured birds about the size of warblers. Many of the species have the bill conspicuously hooked. They delight in tangled shrubbery where they continually creep about in search of food, their movements more deliberate than those of warblers. They often hang upside down in order to peer under the leaves in search of insects or berries. Their songs readily betray their presence, and they sing more frequently than most West Indian birds.

The present small family is probably tropical North American in origin, and is represented in the West Indies by indigenous species of the Red-eyed and White-eyed Vireo groups, although most of the latter have brown or greyish brown irides. Some of the West Indian members of this family are poorly characterised, but are given specific rank until more is known of their relationships. Some ornithologists regard *modestus, caribaeus, crassirostris* and *gundlachii* as conspecific with the White-eyed Vireo, *magister* with the Black-whiskered Vireo. The most distinct Antillean species are the Flat-billed Vireo and Blue Mountain Vireo of Hispaniola and Jamaica respectively.

Flat-billed Vireo *Vireo nanus*   page 144

Local name: Unknown.
Description: Resembles the Jamaican White-eyed Vireo, but upperparts greyish green; outer tail feathers narrowly and *inconspicuously* tipped with whitish, not as illustrated; bill wider at base; iris white.
Voice: A chattering *wit-wit-wit-wit-wit* or a more rapid *wi-wi-wi-wi-wi*, suggestive of the song of a White-breasted Nuthatch, and indistinguishable from certain songs of the Jamaican White-eyed Vireo.
Habitat: Mainly semi-arid scrub. Not found in mountains.
Nidification: Like that of Jamaican White-eyed Vireo, but eggs (2) minutely speckled. Both species occasionally sing while incubating.
Range: Hispaniola and Gonâve Island.

Jamaican White-eyed Vireo *Vireo modestus*   page 144

Local name: Sewi-sewi.
Description: 5″. Upperparts olive-green; two white wing-bars; underparts vary from whitish to pale yellow; iris white.
Voice: Very variable; often a loud, chattering *wit-wit-wit-wit-wit*, or *sewi-sewi-sewi-sewi-sewi*; also emits songs reminiscent of the White-eyed Vireo.

Habitat: Widespread in low trees and shrubbery; found in semi-arid districts as well as in humid forest.
Nidification: Like that of Thick-billed Vireo, but nests much less bulky, in the mountains composed almost entirely of moss.
Range: Jamaica.

St. Andrew Vireo *Vireo caribaeus*

Local name: Unknown.
Description: Closely resembles the Jamaican White-eyed Vireo, but bill slightly longer, the culmen straighter; underparts whitish, faintly tinged with yellow; a pale yellow supraloral stripe (barely indicated in *modestus*); iris greyish brown, not white.
Voice: Songs like those of Jamaican White-eyed Vireo.
Habitat: Widespread on St. Andrew's Island in shrubbery and mangrove swamps.
Nidification: Like that of *V. crassirostris*, but eggs (2) lightly spotted.
Range: Island of St. Andrew.

Thick-billed Vireo *Vireo crassirostris*   page 144

Local names: Sweet-Joe-Clear; Chick-of-the-Village (Bahama Is.); Shear-bark (Cayman Is.); Oiseau Canne (Tortue).
Description: Resembles the White-eyed Vireo, but entire underparts more or less pale yellow (washed with tawny buff in individuals from Tortue); bill slightly larger; *iris dark*, brown or greyish brown. Perhaps conspecific with the Mangrove Vireo (*V. pallens*) of Mexico and Central America.
Voice: A sprightly *chik-wi-wea-chik* or *chin-chin-chi-guao*, with many variations, resembling songs of the White-eyed Vireo; but on Old Providence utters a simple chatter like that of a Mangrove Vireo.
Habitat: Shrubbery and undergrowth.
Nidification: Nest a pendant, cup-shaped structure, situated in a bush. Eggs (2–3) usually more heavily spotted than those of other vireos.
Range: Bahama Islands, Ile Tortue, Cayman Islands and Old Providence. Once recorded from Dry Tortugas, Florida.

White-eyed Vireo *Vireo griseus*

Description: 5.25″. Upperparts mainly dark olive-green, tinged with grey; lores and eye-ring yellow; two white wing-bars; underparts white, the sides and flanks yellow; *iris white*.
Range: Eastern United States, south to the Florida Keys; also eastern Mexico and the Bermuda Islands where a permanent resident. Winters

south to the Bahamas, Cuba, the Isle of Pines, Swan Island, Grand Cayman, Mona, Puerto Rico and Panama (Sept. 16–April 22).

Cuban Vireo *Vireo gundlachii*

Local names: Juan Chiví; Juan Chiví Rico; Chinchiguao; Ojón.
Description: 5.25″. Upperparts dark olive-grey; white wing-bars obsolete; a pale eye-ring; underparts dull yellow or buffy yellow; iris brown.
Voice: Songs like those of the White-eyed Vireo (see Thick-billed Vireo).
Habitat: Mainly undergrowth, and found in both humid and semi-arid areas. Like the Puerto Rican Vireo ranges higher in trees than the Thick-billed and White-eyed Vireos.
Nidification: Like that of Puerto Rican Vireo.
Range: Cuba and the Isle of Pines.

Puerto Rican Vireo *Vireo latimeri*

Fig. 137 Puerto Rican Vireo

Local name: Bien-te-veo.
Description: 5″. Pileum, hindneck, wings and tail greyish brown; remainder of upperparts olive-brown; a white eye-ring; no distinct wing-bars; chin, throat, foreneck and upper chest greyish white: remainder of underparts pale yellow; iris brown. Fig. 137.
Voice: Songs like those of White-eyed Vireo (see Thick-billed Vireo).
Habitat: Chiefly undergrowth on limestone hills; also coffee plantations. Not found in extreme eastern Puerto Rico.
Nidification: The nests resemble those of other vireos, and are situated at low elevations in trees or shrubs. Eggs (3) spotted.
Range: Puerto Rico.

Blue Mountain Vireo   *Vireo osburni*   page 144

Description: 6″. Resembles the Cuban Vireo, but larger with a heavier bill; anterior underparts with a greyish tinge; *no wing-bars* and no pale ring around eye. Jamaican White-eyed Vireo has conspicuous white wing-bars, is decidedly smaller and has white irides.
Voice: A very rapid trill, slightly descending in pitch at end.
Habitat: Chiefly mountain rain forest, but also upland woods and coffee plantations. Not uncommon near Hardwar Gap.
Nidification: Nest a pendant cup of moss at low or moderate elevations above the ground; resembles mountain nests of Jamaican White-eyed Vireo, but larger and relatively shallower. Eggs spotted.
Range: Jamaica.

Yellow-throated Vireo   *Vireo flavifrons*

Description: 5.5″. Anterior upperparts olive-green; rump and upper tail-coverts grey; wings and tail blackish with white margins to many of the feathers; two white wing-bars; eye-ring and anterior underparts bright yellow, the posterior underparts white. Arboreal in habits.
Range: Eastern North America. Winters south to northern South America. Rather rare to rare winter resident in the western Bahamas, Cuba, Isle of Pines, Jamaica and Swan Island; casual on St. Vincent and Grenada (Aug. 31–May 8).

Solitary Vireo   *Vireo solitarius*

Description: 5.5″. Pileum and sides of head dark grey, the lores and eye-ring white; entire back dull green; wings and tail with white markings like those of Yellow-throated Vireo; underparts white, marked with yellow and olive-green on sides and flanks. Arboreal.
Range: North America and northern Central America. Northern individuals winter south to Nicaragua. A rare winter resident in Cuba, the Isle of Pines and Jamaica and apparently transient in the Bahama Islands (Oct. 5–April 19).

Red-eyed Vireo   *Vireo olivaceus*

Description: 6″. Resembles the Black-whiskered Vireo, but pileum slate-grey in striking contrast with the green of the rest of the upperparts; *no dusky streak bordering throat*; bill shorter; iris red.

Range: North, Central and South America. Winters in South America. The North American race migrates chiefly through Central America. Rare transient through the Bahamas, Cuba, Isle of Pines, Jamaica and recorded from Barbados (Aug. 28–Nov. 13: March 31–April 27).

Black-whiskered Vireo   *Vireo altiloquus*   4/3/97 DR

Fig. 138 Black-whiskered Vireo

Local names: John-to-whit; John Philip; Tom Kelly; Whip-Tom-Kelly; Cheap-John-Stirrup; Lady Bird; Bastard Grive; Predicator; Bien-te-veo (Cuba); Juan Chiví; Julián Chiví; Chavos-por-el (D.R. and P.R.); Oiseau Canne; Petit Panache (Haiti); Chouèque; Piade; Père Gris (Lesser Antilles).

Description: 6.5″. Upperparts olive-green, the pileum more or less tinged with grey; *a whitish superciliary stripe* and dusky streak through eye; *sides of throat narrowly bordered with dusky*; underparts white, washed with yellowish green on sides and flanks; under tail-coverts pale yellow; iris reddish brown. The West Indian representative of the Red-eyed Vireo. Fig. 138.

Voice: Song much like that of Red-eyed Vireo, but phrases (usually three-syllabled) more abrupt. May be recalled by many of its local names. On Old Providence and St. Andrew phrases are two-syllabled.

Habitat: Woodland and mangrove swamps in both humid and arid sections.

Nidification: Nest a pendant cup situated in a tree or shrub. Eggs (2–3) rather sparsely but distinctly spotted.

Range: West Indies, excluding Grand Cayman and Swan Islands; also southern Florida and extralimital islands in the southern Caribbean Sea, including the Dutch islands. Bahaman and most Greater Antillean populations winter in northern South America, but many individuals in Hispaniola and Lesser Antilles are permanent residents.

Yucatan Vireo   *Vireo magister*   page 144

Local names: Sweet Bridget; Shear-bark.

Description: Closely resembles the Black-whiskered Vireo, but pileum concolour with back; sides of head, including superciliary stripe, whiter;

dusky streaks bordering throat absent or but faintly indicated; underparts white, more or less tinged with yellowish.

Voice: Song resembles that of Black-whiskered Vireo, the phrases consisting of two or three notes.

Habitat: Low woodland and mangrove swamps.

Nidification: Nest like that of Black-whiskered Vireo. Eggs (2) sparsely spotted to almost immaculate.

Range: Grand Cayman (permanent resident); also coast and islands of Yucatán Peninsula and British Honduras and the Bay Islands of Honduras.

WOOD WARBLERS *Parulidae*

The American warblers are small, insectivorous (sometimes frugivorous), usually brightly coloured birds, related to the tanagers and finches, but not to the thrushes as are the Old World warblers (Sylviidae). The family is well represented in the West Indies, both by native species and North American migrants. Of the seven West Indian genera, five (*Teretistris*, *Microligea*, *Xenoligea*, *Leucopeza* and *Catharopeza*) are endemic to this region.

North American wood warblers comprise an important and conspicuous element in the avifauna of the islands, but only the Black-and-white Warbler and American Redstart have specific local names. The *Seiuri* (Ovenbird and waterthrushes) are known by such names as "Betsey-kick-up", "Mary-shake-well", "Walk-and-shake", 'Señorita', "Pizpita". The remainder are called "Northern Birds", "Cold Birds", "Christmas Birds", "Chip-chips", "Bijiritas", "Siguitas", "Petits Chittes". They are more active than the resident species. They frequently "chip" but rarely sing on their wintering grounds, although a few give voice to half-hearted songs in spring, prior to their northward migrations. Adult males in nuptial plumage are readily identifiable, but females of some species and, particularly, young in first winter plumage are often difficult, if not impossible, to distinguish in the field. The term "eastern North America" as given in their breeding ranges, implies east of the Rocky Mountains.

Black-and-white Warbler *Mniotilta varia*

Local names: Ants Bird; Japanese Canary; Bijirita Trepadora; Reinita Trepadora; Mi-Deuil; Madras.

Description: 5.25″. Male: Upperparts streaked black and white; underparts white streaked with black, this streaking more restricted in winter plumage when throat is immaculate. Female: Resembles male in winter plumage, but duller, and streaks on underparts less distinct. Readily identified by its habit of *creeping* around the trunks and along branches of trees. Fig. 139.

Range: North America. Winters south to northern South America. Common winter resident in the West Indies, except in the Lesser Antilles, where rare (July 29–May 25).

Prothonotary Warbler 4/5/97
Protonotaria citrea ♂ ℞

Description: 5.5". Male: Head and underparts bright orange-yellow; mantle yellowish green; rump, upper tail-coverts and most of wings grey; *much white on tail* and under tail-coverts white. Female: Resembles male but duller; pileum yellowish green like back; much less white on tail. The *grey wings* and rump and lack of yellow on tail readily distinguish the female from Yellow Warblers. On Caribbean islands usually found in or near mangrove swamps.

Range: South-eastern North America. Winters mainly from Central America to Colombia and Venezuela. Transient virtually throughout the West Indies, and winter resident in the Greater Antilles, Lesser Antilles, Tobago and Trinidad (August 3–April 23).

Fig. 139 Black-and-white Warbler

Swainson's Warbler *Limnothlypis swainsonii*

Description: 5.25". Upperparts plain olive-brown, browner on the head; *a conspicuous white* or *whitish superciliary stripe*; a dusky stripe through eye; underparts whitish with a faint yellowish wash. Inhabits undergrowth.
Range: South-eastern North America. Winters in the Yucatan Peninsula and in Belize; also the Bahamas, Cuba, Grand Cayman, Swan Island, Jamaica and St. John (Sept. 9–April 24).

Worm-eating Warbler *Helmitheros vermivorus*

Description: 5.25". Pileum buff *boldly streaked* with black, and a black stripe through eye; rest of upperparts greyish green; underparts plain buffy. Inhabits undergrowth.
Range: Eastern United States. Winters from Mexico to Panama and in the West Indies (east to the Virgin Islands) and Florida (July 30–May 5).

Golden-winged Warbler   *Vermivora chrysoptera*

Description: 5″. Male: Forehead, crown and larger wing-coverts yellow; a narrow white superciliary stripe; rest of upperparts mostly grey; some white on outer tail feathers; gorget and a broad stripe through eye black; rest of underparts white, the sides and flanks grey. Female: Differs chiefly in having the throat-patch and streak through eye sooty grey instead of black.

Range: South-eastern North America. Winters chiefly in Central America. Rare as winter resident or transient in Bahamas, Cuba, Jamaica, Hispaniola and Puerto Rico (Sept. 2–May 7).

Blue-winged Warbler   *Vermivora pinus*

Description: 5″. Forehead, crown and underparts yellow; *a black streak through eye*; tail and wings grey; some white on outer tail feathers, and two white wing-bars; rest of upperparts green. The female has less yellow on crown than male.

Range: South-eastern North America, chiefly south of breeding range of the Golden-winged Warbler. Winters in Central America. Rare as winter resident or transient in West Indies, whence recorded from the northern Bahamas, Cuba, Jamaica, Hispaniola, St. John (Aug. 21–May 6).

Bachman's Warbler   *Vermivora bachmanii*

Description: 4.5″. Male: Forehead, eye-ring and underparts yellow; crown black to grey; hindneck and tail grey; some white on outer tail feathers, but no wing-bars; back green; *a large black patch on foreneck*, encroaching on throat and chest. Female: Differs from male in having no black on crown and underparts; yellow of forehead and underparts duller; little white on tail. The immature female is very plain, the upperparts olive-grey, the underparts whitish with a faint yellowish wash; a pale eye-ring; faintly yellowish on forehead. Frequents blossoming hibiscus trees.

Range: South-eastern United States. Winters in Cuba and the Isle of Pines and recorded from Cay Sal, Bahamas (Sept. 7–April 6).

Tennessee Warbler   *Vermivora peregrina*

Description: 4.5″. A plain little warbler. Pileum grey, grey tinged with green, or green, depending on age, sex and season; rest of upperparts green; *a conspicuous white* or *yellowish superciliary stripe*; underparts whitish, tinged with yellow in winter plumage.

Range: Canada and some border states. Winters mainly from southern Mexico to northern South America. Chiefly transient in West Indies, recorded from Bahamas, Cuba, Isle of Pines, Hispaniola, Cayman Islands, Old Providence, St. Andrew; once from Barbados (Sept. 14–May 23).

Parula Warbler *Parula americana*

Description: 4.25–4.5″. A very small arboreal warbler, the male larger than the female. In breeding plumage the upperparts are greyish blue with a patch of olive-green on the mantle; two white wing-bars and some white on outer tail feathers; anterior underparts yellow, the male with a more or less well-defined black and chestnut band across foreneck and chest; posterior underparts white. In winter plumage the entire upperparts are washed with green, and the dark chest band of the male is obsolete. Fig. 140.

Fig. 140 Parula Warbler

Range: Eastern North America. Winters chiefly in the West Indies, but rare in Lesser Antilles south of Guadeloupe; also winters from Mexico to Costa Rica (July 31–May 14).

Yellow Warbler *Dendroica petechia* 4/5/97 *DR*

Local names: Canary; Bastard Canary; Mangrove Canary; Yellow Bird; Canario; Canario de Manglar; Sucrier Mangle; Oiseau Jaune; Petit-jaune; Didine; Sucrier Barbade.

Description: 5.5″. Male: Often appears entirely yellow in the field. Upperparts greenish yellow, the crown similar or marked with rufous; underparts golden yellow, more or less streaked with chestnut. Males from Guadeloupe southward have dark chestnut (Barbados) or orange-rufous crowns, those from Martinique rufous heads; those from Jamaica vary in extent of rufous. Female: Greener above than male, and underparts with chestnut streaks absent or obsolete. Young are more or less whitish below. Figs. 141, 142, 143, 144.

Voice: Song usually a sprightly *wee-chee-wee-chee-chee-wur* with many variations, like the less energetic songs of North American races. Some songs resemble in quality those of the Magnolia Warbler.

Fig. 141 Yellow Warbler
(Grand Cayman)

Fig. 142 Yellow Warbler
(Guadeloupe)

Fig. 143 Yellow Warbler
(Martinique)

Fig. 144 Yellow Warbler
(Barbados)

Habitat: Chiefly mangrove swamps, but occurs also in scrub, particularly on the smaller islands.

Nidification: Nest a neat and compact cup situated in a bush or low tree. Eggs (2–3) spotted.

Range: West Indies, but does not breed on Saba, St. Vincent, Grenada, most of the Grenadines (inhabits Carriacou, Union and Prune Island), nor on the Swan Islands. Also North America, Central America and northern South America, Cocos and Galápagos Islands and a number of extralimital islands in the Caribbean Sea. North American individuals migrate through western Cuba and a few occur (late Sept. to March 24) on the southernmost Lesser Antilles (Barbados, St. Vincent, Grenada), their winter range Central America and northern South America, including Trinidad and Tobago.

Magnolia Warbler *Dendroica magnolia*

Description: 4.75″. Male (nuptial plumage). Most of upperparts black; pileum blue-grey bordered with white behind eye; rump yellow; *much white on tail*, appearing as a broad band across its centre when viewed from below; wing-coverts largely white; underparts yellow streaked with black, the black markings tending to form a band across foreneck. Female: Resembles the male but greyer, much less black, on upperparts; underparts less heavily marked with black. The sexes closely resemble each other in winter plumage, when the back is green, spotted with black; underparts yellow streaked with black on sides and flanks; two white wing-bars. The tail pattern is always diagnostic.

Range: Northern and eastern North America. Winters from Mexico to Colombia; rather rare in West Indies east to Virgin Islands, and very rare in Lesser Antilles south to Barbados (Sept. 10–May 20).

Cape May Warbler *Dendroica tigrina* 4/3/97 ᗝR

Description: 5.25″. Male (nuptial plumage): Pileum mostly black; *ear-coverts chestnut*; mantle greyish green mottled with black; rump yellow; a white patch on wing-coverts, and some white on tail; sides of neck yellow; underparts yellow streaked with black. Female: Dull greyish green above, the rump and *sides of neck yellowish*; less white on wing; underparts whitish or pale yellowish, streaked with blackish. In winter plumage the male more closely resembles the female, but is much yellower below and on sides of neck. Immature female nondescript, but shows whitish on sides of neck, dusky streaks on underparts.

Range: Canada and some border states. Winters in the West Indies and on Tobago and extralimital islands in western Caribbean; rare in Central America; most numerous in Bahamas and Greater Antilles (Aug. 29–May 17).

Black-throated 4/3/97 ᗝR Blue Warbler
Dendroica caerulescens

Description: 5.25″. Male: Upperparts greyish blue, the mantle

Fig. 145 Black-throated Blue Warbler

sometimes spotted with black, chin, throat, sides of head and sides of breast black; rest of underparts white; some white on tail and a white wing spot or speculum. Female: Upperparts olive; a whitish superciliary stripe extending over ear-coverts; *a conspicuous white spot on wing* when adult; underparts dull olive-yellow. Fig. 145.

Range: Eastern North America. Winters chiefly in the Bahamas and Greater Antilles; casual in Lesser Antilles; also islands in the western Caribbean and sparingly in Central and northern South America (July 29–May 15; one June record).

Yellow-rumped (Myrtle) Warbler *Dendroica coronata*

Description: 5.5″. Upperparts greyish brown (grey in nuptial plumage of male), the back streaked with black; underparts white with little (winter) or much (summer) black on breast and sides; two pale wing-bars and some white on tail; *four patches of yellow* (on rump, crown, on each side of breast), but immature females in first winter plumage have only rump distinctly yellow in contrast with black-streaked back.

Range: Northern and north-eastern North America. Winters from the United States to Colombia. Winter visitant to West Indies east to Virgin Islands; rare in Lesser Antilles (Sept. 18–May 6).

Plate 15 FINCHES

Black-throated Green Warbler *Dendroica virens*

Description: 5.25″. Upperparts green, the wings and tail blackish; two white wing-bars and some white on tail; *sides of head and neck yellow*; underparts white, the throat, chest and sides more or less black. Males in nuptial plumage have the throat, foreneck and chest solid black, whereas in females in winter plumage the black of the underparts is more or less obsolete.

Range: Northern and eastern North America. Winters from Mexico to Colombia, and in the West Indies, east to the Virgin Islands; casual in Lesser Antilles (Sept. 12–May 6).

Cerulean Warbler *Dendroica cerulea*

Description: 5″. Male: Upperparts blue or greyish blue; streaked with black; two white wing-bars and some white on tail; *a blackish band across chest* (lacking in immature) and sides streaked with blackish. Female: Differs from male in having upperparts green, inclining to blue in nuptial plumage; a whitish or yellowish superciliary stripe; underparts white, more or less tinged with yellow.

Range: Eastern United States and southern Ontario. Winters in South

Plate 16 TANAGERS

America. Rare transient in West Indies, unrecorded east of Cuba and Jamaica (Aug. 4–Oct. 18: April).

Blackburnian Warbler   *Dendroica fusca*

Description: 5.25″. Male (nuptial plumage; acquired in early winter): Upperparts black and white; a white patch on wing; crown patch, superciliary stripe and sides of neck yellow; *anterior underparts bright orange*; rest of underparts white, streaked with black on the sides. Male (winter plumage): Upperparts greyish brown, streaked with black; crown-patch obsolete and more or less whitish; a narrow superciliary stripe and anterior underparts yellow; less white on wing (two white wing-bars); sides less heavily streaked with black. Female (nuptial plumage): Resembles male in winter plumage, but brighter below and blacker above. Female (winter plumage): Resembles male in winter plumage but duller, the anterior underparts merely tinged with yellow, and streaks on sides dusky. *Range:* Southern Canada to south-eastern United States. Winters in South America. Rare transient in West Indies, casual east of Puerto Rico (Aug. 9–Dec. 8; April 11–May 24).

Yellow-throated Warbler   *Dendroica dominica*

Local name: Chip-chip (Bahaman race).
Description: 5.5″. Upperparts chiefly slate-grey; superciliary stripe, spot below eye, and sides of neck more or less white; two white wing-bars and some white on tail; *throat, foreneck and chest yellow, bordered with black*; the yellow extends to abdomen in Bahaman race, but in migrant forms the posterior underparts are white; sides streaked with black.
Voice: Song a loud clear warble. One of the better songsters of the family.
Habitat: The Bahaman race inhabits pine forest (where behaviour reminiscent of *Mniotilta*), migrant races rather open country, towns, etc.
Nidification: Nest at high or moderate elevation near top of pine against trunk. Eggs presumably spotted like those of continental forms.
Range: Resident on Grand Bahama and Abaco. Also breeds in eastern United States. Continental races winter from southern North America to Central America and the West Indies, east to the Virgin Islands; casual on Montserrat and Guadeloupe (July 11–April 29).

Adelaide's Warbler   *Dendroica adelaidae*   page 144

Local names: Christmas Bird (Barbuda); Reinita Mariposera (Puerto Rico); Petit Chitte (St. Lucia).
Description: 4.75–5.25″. Upperparts grey or, in Barbuda, brownish grey; two white or whitish wing-bars and some white on tail; a yellow streak

Fig. 146 Adelaide's Warbler
(Puerto Rico)

from bill to above eye and some yellow below eye; *underparts bright yellow*. Fig. 146.

Voice: Song a variable trill, more melodious as sung by Lesser Antillean individuals in comparison with those of Puerto Rico.

Habitat: Lowland thickets; in St. Lucia also found in mountain forest, often high in trees.

Nidification: Nest a thin cup with some feathers in lining, situated in a shrub or tree at low or moderate elevation above the ground. Eggs (2–3) spotted.

Range: Puerto Rico, Vieques, Barbuda and St. Lucia.

Olive-capped Warbler *Dendroica pityophila* page 144

Local names: Chip-chip; Bijirita del Pinar.

Description: 5″. Upperparts grey, the crown olive-green; two whitish wing-bars and some white on tail; throat, foreneck and chest yellow, the chest bordered with black streaks; posterior underparts whitish. No white on sides of head and neck and no black streaking on sides of lower breast as in the larger Yellow-throated Warbler. Fig. 147.

Voice: Song a rather shrill *wisi-wisi-wisi-wiseu-wiseu*, with variations.

Fig. 147 Olive-capped Warbler

Habitat: Pine barrens. In Cuba apparently confined to Pinar del Río Province and north-eastern Oriente Province.
Nidification: Nest cup-shaped with some feathers in lining, situated in a pine from 7 to 45 feet above ground, usually near trunk. Eggs (2) spotted.
Range: Cuba, Grand Bahama and Abaco.

Pine Warbler *Dendroica pinus* 4/3/97 ♂R

Local names: Chip-chip; Siguita del Pinar; Petit-Chitte de Bois Pin.
Description: 5.25″. Upperparts yellowish green; two white wing-bars and some white on tail; anterior underparts yellow, becoming white on lower abdomen. Young are whitish below, greyish brown above; wing-bars greyish white.
Voice: A simple, rather loud and variable trill.
Habitat: Pine woods.
Nidification: The cup-shaped nests are situated high in pines. Eggs doubtless spotted like those of continental races.
Range: North-western Bahama Islands (Grand Bahama, Abaco, Andros, New Providence; vagrant to Cay Sal) and Hispaniola. Also eastern North America; casual in Cuba (Oct. 22–Nov. 8).

Chestnut-sided Warbler *Dendroica pensylvanica*

Description: 5″. In nuptial plumage the upperparts are yellowish green, heavily streaked with black; crown yellow; two yellowish wing-bars; some white on tail; a black patch below eye; underparts white, *the sides chestnut.* Females are duller than males. In winter plumage the upperparts (pileum and back) are bright yellowish green; sides of head grey; *underparts white* with little or no chestnut on sides.
Range: Eastern North America. Winters mainly in Central America. Rare transient in West Indies, vagrant to Lesser Antilles (Antigua, Barbados); casual in winter (Sept. 3–May 11).

Bay-breasted Warbler *Dendroica castanea*

Description: 5.5″. Male (nuptial plumage): Forehead and sides of head black; crown chestnut; rest of upperparts olive-grey, streaked with black on the mantle; two white wing-bars and some white on tail; *a buff patch on side of neck: throat and foreneck chestnut,* this colour extending along sides of breast to flanks; rest of underparts white. Female (nuptial plumage): Much duller than male; lacks the solid black forehead and sides of head; much less chestnut on head and underparts. In winter plumage both sexes have the upperparts green, obscurely streaked with black; sides of head greenish yellow; underparts white, washed with buffy yellow, *the flanks buff* (in adult females and immature individuals) *or chestnut* (adult males); feet dark.

Range: Canada and some border states. Winters in Panama and northern South America. Transient through the West Indies, but rare or casual on islands east of Cuba and Jamaica (Sept. 28–Nov. 29: April 7–May 7).

Blackpoll Warbler *Dendroica striata*

Description: 5.5". Male (nuptial plumage): Pileum black; rest of upperparts olive-grey, streaked with black; two white wing-bars and some white on tail; *sides of head white*; underparts white; streaked laterally with black. Female (nuptial plumage): Differs from male by greyish green upperparts, streaked on back and pileum with black; underparts whitish, streaked laterally with black, the sides of head not white. In winter plumage both sexes are dull green above, the mantle more or less streaked with black; *underparts decidedly yellowish*, the streaking on sides obsolete; feet usually pale, the soles always yellow.

Range: Northern and north-western North America. Winters in northern South America. Migrates through the West Indies (Sept. 16–Dec. 9: March 22–June 7; one late August record).

Prairie Warbler *Dendroica discolor* 4/5/97

Description: 4.75". Upperparts green; adult male with a more or less well-defined chestnut patch on back, this less evident in winter and sometimes lacking; some white on tail; middle wing-coverts broadly tipped with yellowish; superciliary stripe yellow, bordered with black below (through eye); underparts yellow, streaked laterally with black and with a black malar stripe. Female has duller black markings and little or no rufous on back. Immature individuals have very little yellow, and no black markings, on sides of head.

Range: Eastern United States and southern Ontario. Winters mainly in the West Indies, whence recorded south to Barbados and Grenada; also in Florida and islands in western Caribbean (July 20–May 13).

Vitelline Warbler *Dendroica vitellina*

Local name: Chip-chip.
Description: 5". Resembles the Prairie Warbler, but a little larger; upperparts plain olive-green, never with any chestnut on back; *dark streaking on head and underparts obsolete*.
Voice: Song a series of wheezy notes, usually rising in pitch, much like

that of a Prairie Warbler, but sometimes more reminiscent of a Black-throated Blue Warbler (e.g. *ze-ze-zwee*).

Habitat: Scrubby thickets.

Nidification: Builds a compact, cup-shaped nest at low elevations. Eggs (2) spotted.

Range: Cayman and Swan Islands.

Kirtland's Warbler　*Dendroica kirtlandii*

Description: 5.75″. Upperparts grey (washed with brownish in winter), streaked with black, the streaks most pronounced on mantle; some white on tail; underparts pale yellow, the sides streaked with black, and the chest sometimes flecked with black. In winter plumage, when viewed from above, resembles a Myrtle Warbler, but lacks yellow rump. Frequently flirts its tail.

Range: Central Michigan. Winters in the Bahama Islands (August 27–May 5).

Palm Warbler　*Dendroica palmarum*

Fig. 148 Palm Warbler

Description: 5.5″. Upperparts greyish brown with dusky streaks, the rump and tail-coverts yellowish olive; crown chestnut (spring), bordered by yellow (spring) or whitish superciliary stripes; some white on tail; underparts whitish, more or less washed with yellow, *particularly in spring*, and streaked with brown (spring) or dusky; *under tail-coverts yellow* at all seasons. *Constantly flirts tail.* Found in open country, lawns, parks, usually on or near ground. Fig. 148.

The eastern "Yellow Palm Warbler" (*D. p. hypochrysea*) has been recorded from Grand Bahama (Oct. 30–Nov. 9). This race is much yellower on underparts.

Range: Canada and some border states. Winters from south-eastern North America and the Bahamas south to the Greater Antilles and islands in western Caribbean. Common winter resident in Bahamas and Greater

Antilles, but rare in Puerto Rico and unknown east of St. Thomas and St. Croix (Sept. 6–May 17).

Arrow-headed Warbler *Dendroica pharetra*

Local names: Ants Bird; Ant-eater; Guinea-hen Canary (see Black-and-white Warbler).

Description: 5.25". Most of upperparts *heavily streaked black and white*, the black streaks narrow on pileum and hindneck, much broader on the mantle; rump and upper tail-coverts plain greyish olive; two narrow white wing-bars and a little white on tail; underparts, except buffy under tail-coverts, white, heavily spotted with black, the markings more or less triangular or arrow-headed in shape. The immature is yellowish green above; pileum sometimes indistinctly streaked with white; two ill-defined white wing-bars; underparts yellowish, with indistinct dusky streaks. Frequently flirts tail. Fig. 149.

Fig. 149 Arrow-headed Warbler

Voice: Normal song a weak, rapidly uttered trill, suggestive of that of a Worm-eating Warbler. Rarely emits a canary-like "whisper-song". Call-note a weak *git*, quite different from the *chip* of a migrant warbler.

Habitat: Mainly mountain forest but also wooded hills at comparatively low elevations. Most numerous in Blue Mountains.

Nidification: Nest a thin, but compact, cup situated in a bush or sapling. Eggs (2–3) spotted.

Range: Jamaica.

Elfin Woods Warbler *Dendroica angelae*

Local name: Reinita.

Description: Resembles the Arrow-headed Warbler, but adults entirely black and white. Upperparts black, with conspicuous white markings on sides of head (including broken eye-ring), wings (wing-bars and alar speculum), and at tips of rectrices; underparts like *D. pharetra*.

Voice: Like that of Arrow-headed Warbler.

Habitat: Humid forest at high elevations from the Sierra de Luquillo to the Maricao National Forest.

Nidification: Apparently similar to that of *D. pharetra*.

Range: Puerto Rico.

Plumbeous Warbler *Dendroica plumbea*

Local names: Caféiette; Tic-tic; "Papia".

Description: 5.5". Upperparts plain slate-grey; a white superciliary stripe and suborbital spot; two white wing-bars and a little white on tail; median underparts white with an admixture of grey on the breast; sides grey. Immature birds are greyish green above, the tail grey; lores and interrupted superciliary stripe white or yellowish; two white wing-bars; underparts yellowish. Fig. 150.

Voice: Song a short, but rather melodious, *pa-pi-a*. Call-note a simple *chek*. Also utters rattling, wren-like notes.

Habitat: Rain forest, as well as dry, scrubby woodland.

Nidification: Like that of Arrow-headed Warbler, but nest less compact.

Range: Guadeloupe, Terre-de-haut (casual?), Marie Galante and Dominica.

Fig. 150 Plumbeous Warbler

Whistling Warbler *Catharopeza bishopi*

Local name: Whistling Bird.

Description: 5.75". Upperparts blackish; loral spot and *eye-ring white*; outer tail feathers tipped with white; throat and *a broad band across chest blackish*; rest of underparts white medially, grey laterally. Immature individuals are *brownish*, paler, less olivaceous on underparts, but with a darkish band across chest. Fig. 151.

Fig. 151 Whistling Warbler

Voice: Song a series of short, rich notes, at first soft and low, then rising rapidly with crescendo effect, terminating with two or three emphatic notes. Call-note a short *tuk*.

Habitat: Mountain forest (e.g. Bonhomme Mts.). Usually in undergrowth, but sometimes high in trees; tail often cocked.
Nidification: Said to build a cup-shaped nest in a sapling, and to lay 2 spotted eggs.
Range: St. Vincent.

Semper's Warbler *Leucopeza semperi*

Local name: Pied-blanc.
Description: 5.75″. Upperparts dark grey; underparts whitish; feet pale. The immature has the upperparts, in particular the rump and upper tail-coverts, washed with olive-brown and the underparts with brownish buff. Fig. 152.
Voice: Song unknown. Said to chatter when alarmed.
Habitat: Mountain forest, where found in undergrowth. An excessively rare warbler.
Nidification: Unknown.
Range: St. Lucia.

Fig. 152 Semper's Warbler

Ovenbird *Seiurus aurocapillus*

Description: 6″. Centre of crown brownish orange, bordered laterally with black; rest of upperparts olive-green; lores and eye-ring white; underparts white, heavily spotted and streaked on the breast and sides with black, and with blackish stripe on side of throat. Usually seen *walking on ground* beneath shrubbery.
Range: North America. Winters south to northern South America, but mainly in Central America and the West Indies; uncommon in Lesser Antilles (August 15–May 24).

Northern Waterthrush *Seiurus noveboracensis* 4/5/97 ⅅℛ

Description: 5.5″. Upperparts dark olive-brown; a yellowish superciliary stripe; underparts pale buffy yellow, heavily streaked with blackish. *Constantly flirts its tail.* Chips loudly when alarmed. *Found mostly in or near mangrove swamps.*

Range: North America. Winters from Mexico and Florida south to northern South America, and occurs as winter resident throughout the West Indies (Aug. 13–May 28; several early summer records).

Louisiana Waterthrush   *Seiurus motacilla*

Description: 6″. Closely resembles the Northern Waterthrush, but a little larger; superciliary stripe white; underparts white or whitish, with less numerous black streaks on breast, the throat usually immaculate; flanks and under tail-coverts buffy. *Found principally on freshwater streams.* Fig. 153.

Fig. 153 Louisiana Waterthrush

Range: Eastern North America, for the most part south of the range of the Northern Waterthrush. Winters from the West Indies and northern Mexico to northern South America. Less common winter resident in West Indies than the preceding species, and rare east of Puerto Rico (July 2–April 22).

Kentucky Warbler   *Oporornis formosus*

Description: 5.5″. Upperparts plain olive-green; more or less black on pileum; *superciliary stripe and incomplete eye-ring yellow*; a broad black stripe (dusky in female) from lore to side of neck; underparts yellow. The dusky facial markings in young females are undeveloped, but the yellow superciliary stripe is conspicuous.
Range: Eastern United States. Winters mainly in Central America. Rare transient in the Bahamas and Greater Antilles; casual on Guadeloupe; very rare in winter (Aug. 3–April 15).

Connecticut Warbler   *Oporornis agilis*

Description: 5.75". The adult male in nuptial plumage is olive-green above, greyish on the crown; *a white eye-ring*; sides of head and anterior underparts to chest grey; posterior underparts dull greenish yellow. Males in winter plumage and females have the crown and anterior underparts more or less brownish.

Range: Canada and some border states. Winters in South America. Transient in the West Indies. Recorded, but rarely, from the Bahamas (Grand Bahama, Andros, New Providence and several cays), and from Hispaniola to St. Martin. Frequent on Netherlands Leeward Islands in southern Caribbean (Sept. 13–Nov. 18; May 9–17).

✓Common Yellowthroat   *Geothlypis trichas*   4/5 /97 DR

Description: 5". Male varies from olive to brownish above; throat and breast yellow, fading to whitish on abdomen and becoming brownish on flanks; under tail-coverts yellow; *a broad black "mask"*, or band through eye. Female and immature individuals lack the black "mask"; abdomen varies from white to buff or pale yellow. Found in thickets near the ground.

Range: North America. Winters south to extreme north-western South America. Common winter resident in the West Indies east to Hispaniola; rare in Puerto Rico and the Virgin Islands, and casual in the Lesser Antilles and on Tobago (Aug. 13–May 24; two June records).

Bahama Yellowthroat   *Geothlypis rostrata*   page 144

Local names: Black-eyed Bird; Sage Bird.

Description: 6". Closely resembles the Common Yellowthroat, but decidedly larger with a longer and heavier bill; males often show more

or less yellow on upper border of "mask". Less active than Common Yellowthroat. Fig. 154.

Voice; Song a loud *wi-chí-tu, wi-chí-tu, wi-chí-tu, wich*, the phrases sometimes *wi-che-tee* or *wicher-wichu*; very like songs of yellowthroats of south-eastern North America. Call-note less harsh than that of the Common Yellowthroat.

Habitat: Shrubbery and bracken.

Nidification: The cup-shaped nests are situated near the ground. Eggs (2) spotted.

Fig. 154 Bahama
       Yellowthroat

Range: Grand Bahama and Abaco (including many offshore cays), Andros, New Providence, Eleuthera, Cat Island.

Ground Warbler *Microligea palustris* page 144

Local names: Siguita; Petit Chitte.

Description: 5.75″. Pileum, hindneck, sides of head and extreme upper back slate-grey; rest of upperparts green; underparts pale greyish to whitish; a broken white eye-ring; iris red. Immature individuals have the anterior upperparts suffused with green, the underparts with olive; iris brown. Fig. 155.

Fig. 155 Ground Warbler

Voice: Utters curious rasping notes like a small bird in distress.

Habitat: Near ground in thickets. In Haiti known from high elevations in the Massif de la Selle and xeric areas of extreme north-west: primarily mountains of the Dominican Republic; local in lowlands.

Nidification: The cup-shaped nest is situated in a shrub or blackberry thicket. Eggs (2) pale greenish, spotted.

Range: Hispaniola and Beata Island.

White-winged Warbler *Xenoligea montana* page 144

Local names: Siguita; Petit Chitte; Petit Quatre-yeux.

Description: Resembles the preceding species, but tail slate-grey, the outer rectrices blackish, tipped with white; *a prominent white streak on wing* (outer margins of primaries); a white stripe from bill to above eye and a white spot below eye; underparts white, greyish on sides and flanks; bill thicker than that of *M. palustris*, and appears more robust and active than that species, and ranges higher in the undergrowth. Fig. 156.

Fig. 156 White-winged Warbler

Voice: A low chattering; also a thin *tseep*.

Habitat: Found in low trees and thickets in the mountains (e.g. Cordillera Central and Sierra de Bahoruco in the Dominican Republic; Massif de la Selle and Massif de la Hotte, Haiti).

Nidification: Unknown.

Range: Hispaniola.

Yellow-headed Warbler *Teretistris fernandinae* page 144

Local names: Bijirita; Chillina; Chillona; Chillina Vuelta-abajo; Chinchilita.

Description: 5.25″. Pileum and hindneck yellowish green; sides of head

Fig. 157 Yellow-headed Warbler

greenish yellow, the lores, eye-ring, chin, throat and foreneck yellow; rest of upperparts grey; rest of underparts greyish white, darker on the sides. *Appears yellow-headed* in the field. Fig. 157.

Voice: Utters peculiar rasping sounds, somewhat like those of Ground Warblers.

Habitat: Forest undergrowth; scrubby thickets.

Nidification: The cup-shaped nest is situated in a bush or sapling. Eggs (2–3) spotted.

Range: Western Cuba, including the Isle of Pines, ranging east to Matanzas (Punta de Hicacos) and south-western Las Villas provinces.

Oriente Warbler   *Teretistris fornsi*

Fig. 158 Oriente Warbler

Local names: Bijirita; Pechero; Chillina Vuelta-arriba.

Description: Differs from the Yellow-headed Warbler in having the pileum and hindneck grey like the back; underparts yellow, becoming greyish on the flanks and under tail-coverts. Fig. 158.

Voice, habitat and *nidification:* Like Yellow-headed Warbler. Found from semi-arid coastal districts to humid forest on higher mountains.

Range: Eastern Cuba, west near north coast to eastern Matanzas Province.

Hooded Warbler   *Wilsonia citrina*

Description: 5.5″. Male: Chiefly green above, yellow below; forehead and sides of head yellow, the posterior portion of pileum, sides of neck and anterior underparts black, forming a *black "hood"*; outer rectrices largely white. Female: Differs from male in having the black "hood" obsolete or lacking; often entirely green above, yellow below, with or without a yellow forehead; sides of head yellow. White on tail present in all plumages.

Range: Eastern United States and southern Ontario. Winters chiefly from Mexico to Panama. Transient and rare winter resident in the West Indies; casual in Lesser Antilles (Aug. 3–April 28).

American Redstart   *Setophaga ruticilla*

Local names: Butterfly Bird; Bijirita; Mariposera; Candelita; Officier; Carougette; Carte; Petit du Feu; Gabriel du Feu.

Description: 5". Male: Largely black, with *bright orange patches on sides, wings and tail*; posterior underparts white medially. Female: Chiefly olive-brown above, whitish below; *orange patches of the male are replaced by yellow.* A very active warbler that *constantly spreads its tail*, displaying the orange or yellow bases to the outer rectrices. Fig. 159.

Range: North America. Winters south to Brazil and Peru. Winter resident through-

Fig. 159 American Redstart

out the West Indies, but most numerous in the Greater Antilles (throughout the year).

HONEYCREEPERS *Coerebidae*

The honeycreepers comprise a heterogeneous assemblage of New World birds that feed on fruit, nectar and small insects. They are often encountered while probing blossoms of shrubs or trees, their tongues being adapted for this method of feeding. Of the three West Indian species, the Bananaquit and Red-legged Honeycreeper are now considered tanagers, whereas the Orangequit of the monotypic genus *Euneornis* is placed tentatively with the emberizine finches.

Bananaquit *Coereba flaveola*   4/2/97   DR   page 176

Fig. 160 Bananaquit (Bahamas)

Local names: Banana Bird; Banana Quit; Yellow-breast; Paw-paw Bird; Marley Quit; Sugar Bird; Bessie Coban; Honey-sucker; Yellow See-see; Black See-see (melanic phase); Siguita; Reinita; Gusanero; Sucrier.

Description: 4–5". Exhibits much geographical variation. Upperparts sooty grey to sooty black; rump yellow or greenish yellow; a *conspicuous white superciliary stripe* (yellow in immature); on most islands, a conspicuous white spot on wing; throat greyish white to sooty black; breast yellow; bill decidedly curved. Most individuals on St. Vincent and Grenada are black (melanic phase) with a slightly greenish yellow wash on the breast and upper tail-coverts not apparent in the field. Fig. 160.

Voice: Song sibilant or wheezy, such as *zee-e-e-swees-te*, but sometimes (on Jamaica and Cayman Islands) a simple trill.

Habitat: Widespread, but most numerous in settled districts and secondary growth.

Nidification: Nest usually at moderate elevation above the ground near the extremity of a branch of a tree or shrub, globular in shape with the entrance at the side. Eggs (usually 2–3) heavily spotted. Empty nests often used for roosting.

Range: West Indies, except the Republic of Cuba (apart from vagrants from the Bahamas) and Swan Islands. Widespread in Central and South America, including many extralimital islands in Caribbean Sea.

Red-legged Honeycreeper   *Cyanerpes cyaneus*   page 176

Local names: Azulito; Aparecido de San Diego.

Description: 5″. Male: Stripe through eye, mantle, wings and tail black; crown light turquoise-blue; inner webs of remiges and under surface of wing largely yellow; *rest of plumage bright violet-blue*; feet red. Female: Upperparts green; underparts pale olive-green, streaked with yellowish white; feet purple. Immature male and adult male in eclipse plumage may resemble female but wings and tail black.

Voice: Song (in Central America) a simple, deliberate and protracted *tsip-tsip-chaa-tsip-tsip-tsip-chaa*, etc. More frequently utters a weak, nasal note, such as *chaa*, delivered in various keys, at times suggestive of a gnatcatcher.

Habitat: Woodlands and copses, particularly among blossoming hibiscus and other flowering trees or shrubs. Numerous only in Oriente province.

Nidification: Nest a thinly constructed cup situated in a tree or bush. Eggs (2) spotted.

Range: Cuba and Isle of Pines (introduced?). Also Mexico, Central America and South America, including Trinidad and Tobago.

Orangequit   *Euneornis campestris*   page 176

Local names: Orange Quit; Long-mouthed Quit; Blue Baize; Blue Gay; Swee.

Description: 5.5″. Male: Mainly greyish blue, appearing brighter blue in sunlight; throat chestnut; lores black. Female: Pileum and hindneck olive-grey; rest of upperparts dark olivaceous, slightly browner on wings and tail, underparts greyish white with indistinct pale buffy streaks on throat and abdomen.

Voice: A faint, high-pitched *swee*.

Habitat: Rather open woodland and borders of clearings, chiefly in the hills; rare in lowlands. Comes readily to feeding stations, where tame and aggressive in behaviour.

Nidification: Nest a deep, roughly-built cup, situated in a bush or tree. Eggs (2–4) spotted.

Range: Jamaica.

TANAGERS *Thraupidae*

Of the six indigenous West Indian genera of this large and, for the most part, beautiful family of New World birds, three (*Nesospingus, Phaenicophilus* and *Calyptophilus*) are endemic to the West Indies, while one other (*Spindalis*) occurs elsewhere only on the island of Cozumel, off the Yucatán Peninsula. The remainder are widespread in tropical parts of continental America.

Tanagers, unlike their relatives the finches and wood warblers, subsist almost entirely on a diet of fruit. Euphonias, in particular the Blue-hooded Euphonia, thrive on mistletoe berries. The Jamaican Euphonia also feeds on a variety of ripe fruits and occasionally on tender shoots of the cho-cho and other vegetable matter.

Blue-hooded Euphonia *Euphonia musica* page 193

Fig. 161 Blue-hooded Euphonia (Puerto Rico)

Local names: Mistletoe Bird; Blue-head Parakeet; Canario del País; Canario Criollo; Perruche; Louis d'Or.

Description: 4.75″. Male: Forehead yellow, narrowly bordered posteriorly with black; rest of pileum and hindneck violet-blue; rest of upperparts, except rump and sides of head, *dark* violet-blue, appearing black in the field; rump and underparts yellow (Puerto Rico); ochraceous yellow (Hispaniola); the chin and throat dark violet (Hispaniola). *Lesser Antillean males resemble females.* Female: Mostly green above, becoming more or less yellowish on rump; forehead yellow or yellowish, the rest of the pileum blue; underparts yellowish green. A chunky little tanager with short tail and bill. Fig. 161.

Voice: Song a soft *tuk-tuk*, etc., varied occasionally by a plaintive *ee-oo*; also a soft warbling.

Habitat: Woodland. Most numerous in hills and mountains where there is mistletoe.

Nidification: The globular nest with a side entrance is situated in a tree or among vines on a forest palm. Eggs (4) spotted.

Range: Hispaniola, La Gonâve, Puerto Rico, Saba, St. Barts (casual), Barbuda, Antigua, Montserrat, Guadeloupe, Dominica, Martinique, St. Lucia, St. Vincent, Bequia (casual), and Grenada (formerly). Also Mexico, Central and South America, including Trinidad.

Jamaican Euphonia *Euphonia jamaica* page 193

Local names: Blue Quit; Chocho Quit; Short-mouthed Quit.

Description: 4.75″. Male: Upperparts greyish blue, sometimes appearing bright blue in sunlight; underparts bluish grey; abdomen and lower flanks yellow; under tail-coverts buff. Female: Upperparts green becoming decidedly bluish on head; underparts mostly grey; flanks washed with olive-green. A chunky little tanager, with a short, parrot-like bill. Sometimes associates in flocks, particularly when roosting.

Voice: Song a chuckling warble.

Habitat: Widespread, but most numerous in rather open country. Mainly arboreal.

Nidification: Nest globular with entrance at the side, situated in a tree, often in "Spanish moss". Eggs (3–4) heavily spotted.

Range: Jamaica.

Hooded Tanager *Tangara cucullata* page 193

Local names: Prince Bird (St. Vincent); Soursop Bird; Ci-ci Corossol; Dos-bleu (Grenada).

Description: 6″. Male: Plumage highly iridescent. Upperparts pale metallic golden, greenish in certain lights, the wings and tail bluish green; pileum a rich reddish chestnut (St. Vincent) or dark chestnut (Grenada); sides of head blackish; underparts buffy with a violet-blue wash. Female: Reresembles male but duller; upperparts except for brown pileum, green. Fig. 162.

Voice: A weak *weet-weet-weet-witwitwitwit.*

Habitat: Secondary growth and forest.

Fig. 162 Hooded Tanager
(Grenada)

Nidification: The cup-shaped nest is situated in a bush or low tree. Eggs
(2) spotted.
Range: St. Vincent and Grenada.

Stripe-headed Tanager *Spindalis zena* page 193

Local names: Orange Bird; Cashew Bird; Spanish Quail; Markhead;
Goldfinch; Silver-head (Jamaica); Gold Bird; Bastard Cock (Grand
Cayman); Robin; Red Robin; Hen Robin (female); Rooster Robin;
Tom James' Bird (Bahamas); Cabrero (Cuba); Sigua Amarilla (Dom. Rep.);
Reina Mora (Puerto Rico); Moundélé.
Description: 6–8″. Exceedingly variable, showing much geographical
variation in colour and size, the Jamaican race largest. Male: May readily
be identified on all islands by mainly black head, with broad white superciliary and malar stripes; underparts always brightly coloured and more or
less yellow; wing feathers margined with white. Female: Most races
mainly plain olive-grey, darker on upperparts; in Puerto Rico and
Hispaniola the rump and upper tail-coverts are yellowish and the underparts are streaked with dusky: in Jamaica head greyish in contrast with
olive-yellow breast and abdomen and small orange patch on chest; back
dull green, becoming yellowish posteriorly. Females of all forms have
white, or at least pale, margins to wing feathers.
Voice: Song a prolonged but weak warble, seldom heard. Call-note a
drawn-out *seep*.
Habitat: Forest and shrubbery; most numerous in the hills and mountains
on the larger islands.
Nidification: Nest a loosely constructed and often remarkably small cup,
situated in a bush or tree. Eggs (2–3) spotted or marbled.
Range: Bahama Islands and Greater Antilles (Cuba, Isle of Pines, Grand
Cayman, Jamaica, Hispaniola, Gonâve Island, and Puerto Rico); also

Cozumel Island off the Peninsula of Yucatán; vagrant to Florida from the Bahamas.

Scarlet Tanager *Piranga olivacea*

Description: 7″. Male (nuptial plumage): Scarlet, with black wings and tail. Female: Plain greyish green above, greenish yellow below. Male in winter plumage resembles female, but wings and tail black.

Range: North America, east of the Rockies. Winters in South America from Colombia to Bolivia. Rare transient in West Indies, most frequent in western Cuba (Aug. 23–Nov. 6: March 19–May 31).

Summer Tanager *Piranga rubra*

Description: Male: Plumage red, both in summer and winter, the underparts bright vermilion. Female: Resembles female Scarlet Tanager, but upperparts olive or yellowish green, not greyish green; underparts dull golden yellow, not greenish yellow. The young male in first autumn resembles the female but is more richly coloured.

Range: The southern United States south into northern Mexico. Winters from Mexico, Cuba and Jamaica south to Bolivia; one January record from New Providence. Rare transient and winter resident in Bahamas (e.g. Grand Bahama, New Providence and Andros), Cuba, Isle of Pines, Jamaica, Grand Cayman, and Swan Island; casual in the Lesser Antilles (e.g. Barbados and Mustique) (Sept. 1–May 4).

Black-crowned Palm Tanager 4/2/97 DR page 193
Phaenicophilus palmarum

Local names: Cuatro-ojos; Sigua de Cabeza Prieta; Quatre-yeux (pron. "ka-jé").

Description: 7″. Pileum and sides of head black with white spots above lores and above and below eyes; hindneck grey; back, wings and tail yellowish green; chin, throat and median portion of breast and abdomen white; rest of underparts grey. Immature individuals are duller than adults.

Voice: A nasal *pe-u*.

Habitat: Widespread in woodland and thickets, both in semi-arid and humid localities, but most numerous in lowlands.

Nidification: The deep, cup-shaped nest is situated in a bush or tree. Eggs (2–3) whitish to pale greenish, spotted.

Range: Hispaniola including Saona Island; not found west of the Trouin Valley (a short distance west of Port-au-Prince), which separates the Massif de la Selle from the Massif de la Hotte.

Grey-crowned Palm Tanager
page 193
Phaenicophilus poliocephalus

Local name: Quatre-yeux.
Description: Resembles the Black-crowned Palm Tanager, but posterior portion of pileum grey like hindneck; breast, foreneck and lower throat grey in striking contrast with the white of the chin, upper throat and malar region. Hybrids occur east of Jacmel.
Voice: Utters a short *peu*, much like that of a North American Song Sparrow; also a canary-like "whisper song" heard occasionally during breeding season.
Habitat: Similar to that of preceding species.
Nidification: Nest and eggs (2–4) resemble those of Black-crowned Palm Tanager.
Range: Southern peninsula of Haiti; also Ile-à-Vache, Grande Cayemite and Gonâve Island.

Puerto Rican Tanager *Nesospingus speculiferus*
page 193

Local names: Llorosa; Pájaro Llorón.
Description: 7″. Upperparts greyish olive-brown, the sides of head darker: a *conspicuous white wing-spot* or speculum; underparts mostly white, the breast flecked with dusky. Young are brownish and lack the white wing-spots.
Voice: Call-note a loud, sharp *chewp*, repeated vigorously; less frequently *tsweep*. Occasionally emits a soft, melodious warbling during nesting season.
Habitat: Mountain and upland forest. Numerous in the Sierra de Luquillo and in the National Forest near Maricao.
Nidification: Nest cup-shaped, situated in trees from seven to thirty feet above the ground. Eggs (2–3) spotted, often heavily.
Range: Puerto Rico.

Chat Tanager *Calyptophilus frugivorus*
page 193

Local names: Chirrí; Cornichon.
Description: 7–8″. Upperparts greyish olive to olive-brown; a yellow loral spot and some yellow on bend of wing; underparts chiefly white, but sides and flanks washed with greyish or greyish brown. Individuals from south-western Hispaniola are darker than those from elsewhere, those from Gonâve Island paler. Largely terrestrial in habits.

Voice: Song a loud, *chip-chip-swerp-swerp-swerp*, or as a variation *swerp-sweep-chip-chip-chip*. Call-note a dry *tic*.

Habitat: Dense thickets in mountains of southern Haiti and western Dominican Republic, occurring locally at lower elevations in eastern Hispaniola. Inhabits semi-arid scrub in the lower, hotter parts of Gonâve Island.

Nidification: A cup-shaped, horsehair-lined nest, believed to pertain to this species, was situated in a fern thicket about two feet above the ground. It contained one spotted egg.

Range: Hispaniola and Gonâve Island.

AMERICAN ORIOLES OR TROUPIALS *Icteridae*

This New World family, which includes such remarkable birds as the oropendolas, is quite distinct from the Oriolidae, the Old World orioles. Of the numerous West Indian species, the Jamaican *Nesopsar* constitutes a genus endemic to this region.

The majority of icterids have black in the plumage, and yellow is the dominant colour of many species. Males are usually decidedly larger than females.

Glossy Cowbird   *Molothrus bonariensis*

Fig. 163 Glossy Cowbird

Local names: Blackbird's Cousin; Corn Bird; Tordo; Pájaro Vaquero; Merle de Barbade (St. Lucia); Merle de Sainte Lucie (Martinique).

Description: 7–8″. Male: Black with a strong violet gloss. Female: Greyish brown above, the wings and tail dusky brown; underparts light brownish grey. Immature individuals resemble the adult female, but are more or less buffy on underparts, streaked with dusky in males. Often associated in flocks. Fig. 163.

Voice: Song a melodious warble, suggestive of an oriole. Also utters a variety of short call-notes.

Habitat: Rather open country in lowlands, particularly semi-arid areas.

Nidification: Parasitic, depositing its eggs in nests of other birds, usually those of smaller species, but sometimes those of grackles and mocking-birds. Eggs spotted or immaculate.

Range: South America; a rather recent arrival in the West Indies, perhaps introduced; now well established in Lesser Antilles north to Martinique; also from western Virgin Islands to Cuba. Has been undergoing a population explosion on Caribbean islands.

Greater Antillean Grackle *Quiscalus niger* 4/4/97 *DR*

Local names: Tinkling; Cling-cling; Ting-ting (Jamaica); Ching-ching (Cayman Is.); Chichinguaco; Hachuela; Quiebra (Cuba); Chinchilín (Dom. Rep.); Mozambique; Chango; Pichón Prieto (Puerto Rico); Merle (Haiti).

Description: 10–12″. Male: Black with a violet or steel-blue gloss; iris light yellow, appearing white. Female: Smaller and duller than male. Immature individuals have light brown irides. Grackles have *V-shaped tails*, most evident in males. They are highly gregarious.

Voice: Utters various harsh or rasping sounds, such as *chak-chak* or *chin-chin-chi-lin*; occasionally a high-pitched *whee-see-ee* or a ringing bell-like note.

Habitat: More or less open, settled districts. Great numbers roost in some towns (e.g. Havana and Santa Clara).

Nidification: Usually in colonies, cup-shaped nests, high above the ground in trees or palms; rarely in cat-tails. Eggs (3–5) pale bluish or putty coloured, spotted and scrawled.

Range: Cuba (including many coastal cays), Isle of Pines, Cayman Islands, Jamaica, Hispaniola (including adjacent islands), Puerto Rico and Vieques Island.

Carib Grackle *Quiscalus lugubris*

Local names: Blackbird; Bequia-sweet; Merle.

Description: 9.5–11″. Male: Closely resembles males of Q. *niger*. Female: Females on Barbados are rather dull black; those from Grenada to St. Lucia are paler; those from Martinique to Montserrat much paler, the underparts inclining to white, particularly on throat. Fig. 164.

Voice: Somewhat louder and harsher than that of preceding species and differs on various islands. A common rendering is *wee-tsi-ke-tsi-ke-tsi-ke*, another a squeaky *etsywee*; also "chucks" and whistles.

Habitat: Settled districts.

Nidification: For the most part colonial, the nests in trees or palms. Eggs (2–4) like those of other grackles.

Range: Lesser Antilles from Montserrat, Guadeloupe and Désirade south to Barbados and Grenada. Introduced on St. Martin, Barbuda and Antigua. Also northern South America, including Trinidad and Tobago, and some Venezuelan islands.

Fig. 164 Carib Grackle

Fig. 165 Cuban Blackbird

Cuban Blackbird   *Dives atroviolacea*

Local names: Totí; Choncholí.

Description: 10–11″. Black with a slight purple and greenish gloss; iris brown. Resembles a grackle except for its tail, which is normal in shape, and dark irides. An arboreal species that often associates with grackles. Fig. 165.

Voice: A harsh *toti* or *choncholi*; also a loud, clear *ti-o*, repeated several times and reminiscent of the North American Tufted Titmouse.

Habitat: Mainly settled districts.

Nidification: Nest usually situated at base of palm frond; occasionally in cavity of tree or building. Eggs (3–4) spotted.

Range: Cuba; of doubtful occurrence on Isle of Pines.

Orchard Oriole   *Icterus spurius*

Description: 6.5–7″. Male: Plumage mainly dark chestnut, the head, neck, mantle, tail and most of wings black. Female: Upperparts yellowish olive, the mantle greyish olive; wings chiefly dusky, with two white wing-bars; underparts yellow. The immature male resembles the adult female, but has a black throat-patch.

Range: Eastern half of United States and south-eastern Ontario; an allied race in north-eastern Mexico. Winters from Mexico to north-western South America. Rare transient in the Bahamas, Cuba, Jamaica and Swan Island ("October": April 6–May 13).

Black-cowled Oriole *Icterus dominicensis* page 177

Local names: Coconut Bird (Andros); Banana Bird (Abaco); Solibio (Cuba); Sigua Canaria (Dom. Rep.); Calandria (Puerto Rico); Banane Mûre (Haiti).

Description: 7.75–8.5″. Chiefly black, the rump, smaller upper wing-coverts, bend of wing and under wing-coverts bright yellow; posterior underparts more or less yellow, Bahaman birds having the most yellow, the colour reaching the lower breast. Immature individuals are mostly greenish, the throat and foreneck sometimes black or rufescent.

Voice: Song a series of loud and melodious whistles. Also utters a harsh *chur-r-r*, or sharp *chic*.

Habitat: Widespread, occurring from mangrove swamps and coconut plantations in lowlands to mountain forest. Apparently shuns pine woods and the highest mountains.

Nidification: Nest a basket-shaped, neatly woven structure suspended from and sewn to leaves of a tree or palm frond. Eggs (3–4) spotted.

Range: Bahama Islands (Abaco and Andros), Cuba, the Isle of Pines, Hispaniola, Gonâve, Tortue, Ile-à-Vache, Saona and Puerto Rico. Also southern Mexico and Central America.

Montserrat Oriole *Icterus oberi*

Local names: Tannia Bird; Blantyre Bird.

Description: 8–8.5″. Male: Plumage mostly black; rump yellow, the upper tail-coverts ochraceous; lower breast to under tail-coverts yellow, washed with ochraceous; bend of wing and under wing-coverts yellow, the wing otherwise black. Female: Upperparts chiefly yellowish olive-green; underparts golden yellow. Fig. 166.

Voice: Like that of Black-cowled Oriole.

Habitat: Forested mountain slopes, occurring at an elevation as low as 750 feet.

Nidification: Nests, constructed like those of Black-cowled Oriole, are attached to fronds of forest palms or banana plants. Eggs (2) spotted.

Range: Montserrat.

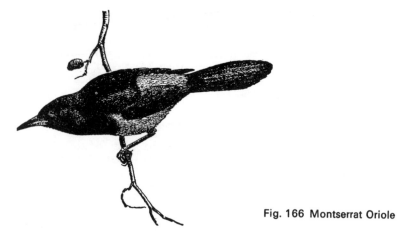

Fig. 166 Montserrat Oriole

St. Lucia Oriole *Icterus laudabilis* page 177

Local name: Carouge.
Description: 8–8.5″. Plumage mostly black; smaller upper wing-coverts, bend of wing, under wing-coverts, rump, abdomen, flanks and under tail-coverts a rich orange or orange-yellow. The female has the orange parts of the plumage a trifle paler and yellower. Immature birds resemble the young of the Black-cowled Oriole.
Voice: Like that of Black-cowled Oriole but song more protracted and melodious. Resembles the song of an Orchard Oriole.
Habitat: Widespread from coastal lowlands to mountain rain forest, and occurs in semi-arid districts.
Nidification: Nest like that of a Black-cowled Oriole but more strongly built. Eggs (3) spotted.
Range: St. Lucia.

Martinique Oriole *Icterus bonana* page 177

Local name: Carouge.
Description: 7.75–8.25″. Head, neck and upper breast dark chestnut; mantle, tail and most of wings black; smaller upper wing-coverts, rump and posterior underparts orange-rufous or tawny, palest on rump.
Voice: Like that of Black-cowled Oriole.
Habitat: Most numerous in semi-arid hills in southern half of Martinique.
Nidification: Nest like that of St. Lucia Oriole. Eggs (2–3) spotted.
Range: Martinique.

Jamaican Oriole *Icterus leucopteryx*

page 177

Fig. 167 Jamaican Oriole (Jamaica)

Local names: Banana Bird (all islands); Ma-Katie; Auntie Katie; Auntie Essie.
Description: 8–8.5″. Upperparts yellowish green; wings black and white, the wing-coverts mostly white; tail black (yellowish green in immature); "face" and anterior underparts ("bib") to chest black; rest of underparts greenish yellow. Birds from St. Andrew's Island are brighter than those from Jamaica, those from Grand Cayman much brighter, the greenish yellow of the plumage replaced by clear yellow. Fig. 167.

Voice: Song a series of two to five whistling notes, reminiscent of the Baltimore Oriole, but softer.
Habitat: Copses, gardens, plantations, mountain rain forest. Rare, if not extinct, on Grand Cayman.
Nidification: Nest a pendant, hammock-shaped structure attached to a branch of a tree or palm frond, but not sewn to the leaves as those of preceding species. Eggs (3–5) scrawled and spotted.
Range: Jamaica, St. Andrew's Island and Grand Cayman.

Northern (Baltimore) Oriole *Icterus galbula*

Description: 8–8.5″. Male: Head, hindneck and mantle black; wings mostly black and white, the smaller wing-coverts orange; tail orange-yellow and black; *underparts bright orange*, apart from black "bib" that extends to centre of upper breast. Female: Upperparts mostly golden olive, mottled more or less with black, the mantle greyish in winter plumage; wing and underparts duller than male; black throat-patch more restricted and sometimes absent.
Range: North America. Winters south to northern South America. Rare winter resident in the Greater Antilles, and transient in the Bahamas; casual on Barbados (Sept. 14–May 16).

Troupial *Icterus icterus*

page 177

Local names: Bugler Bird; Turpial.

Description: 10–11″. Resembles adult male Baltimore Oriole, but decidedly larger, a broad orange-yellow "collar" across hindneck; black "bib" more extensive; much more white on wings; tail black without any yellow; bare skin about eye blue or bluish; iris yellowish white. Sexes similar.

Voice: A variety of loud whistles.

Habitat: Semi-arid woodland and mangrove swamps, chiefly in south-western Puerto Rico (e.g. Guánica State Forest) and east and south coasts of St. Thomas.

Nidification: Nests variable in shape, placed in thick scrub or cacti, or attached to palm fronds. Eggs spotted and scrawled.

Range: Northern South America, including the islands of Aruba and Curaçao. Introduced (apparently) and established in Puerto Rico and St. Thomas, including Water Island; also reported from Jamaica, St. John, Antigua, Dominica and Grenada (escaped cage birds?). In Puerto Rico numerous near Guánica. Recently ineroduced on Mona.

Red-winged Blackbird *Agelaius phoeniceus*

Local names: Blackbird; Rice Bird; Mayito de la Ciénaga; Totí de la Ciénaga; Chirriador.

Description: 7.5–9″. Male: Black, with *scarlet lesser wing-coverts*, the feathers of the back with rusty margins in winter plumage. Female: Above brownish with an admixture of black; a whitish superciliary stripe; underparts buffy or whitish, heavily streaked with black. *Females from Cuba and the Isle of Pines are entirely black*.

Voice: Song a loud *o-kra-lee* or *o-kra-lee-o*, uttered more rapidly by Cuban individuals. Call-note a short *chek*.

Habitat: Swamps, marshes and borders of lagoons.

Nidification: The cup-shaped nest is situated near the ground or water in a mangrove, shrub, or among rushes. Eggs (3–4) spotted.

Range: North-western Bahamas (Grand Bahama and Abaco, including off-shore cays, Bimini [occasional] and Berry Islands, Andros, New Providence, Eleuthera and Cay Sal), Cuba (western half) and Isle of Pines. Also North and Central America.

Tawny-shouldered Blackbird *Agelaius humeralis*

Local names: Mayito; Conguito; Merle.

Description: 7.5–8.5″. Black, with *tawny shoulder-patches* margined with buff, these patches more restricted in females and often inconspicuous. Associates in flocks and sometimes roosts in towns with grackles and Cuban Blackbirds.

Voice: Utters strange, wheezy notes. Call-note a short *chic* or *chuc.*

Habitat: Edges of woods, groves, farm lands, mangrove swamps and elsewhere in rather open country in lowlands. In Haiti known from the lower Artibonite River and from the vicinity of Port-de-Paix.

Nidification: The cup-shaped nest is situated in a tree or palm. Eggs (4) spotted.

Range: Cuba (including Cayo Cantiles), and Hispaniola (Haiti).

Fig. 168 Yellow-shouldered
Blackbird

Fig. 169 Jamaican Blackbird

Yellow-shouldered Blackbird *Agelaius xanthomus*

Local names: Mariquita; Capitán.

Description: 8–9″. A blackbird with *yellow* shoulder-patches. The middle wing-coverts are sometimes whitish at the tips. Associates in flocks. Fig. 168.

Voice: Like that of Tawny-shouldered Blackbird.

Habitat: Lowlands of Puerto Rico, most numerous in vicinity of lagoons and swamps near the coast, but found in many localities in rather open country; rare in woodland, and does not occur at high elevations. On Mona restricted to the limestone plateau.

Nidification: Often colonial, the cup-shaped nests built in trees, palms and cacti, occasionally in a tree cavity. Eggs (3–4) spotted.

Range: Puerto Rico and Mona Island.

Jamaican Blackbird *Nesopsar nigerrimus*

Local names: Black Banana Bird; Corporal Bird; Wild Pine Sergeant.

Description: 7–8″. Plumage entirely black, the upperparts quite glossy.

Smaller, with a much shorter tail than a grackle. The sharp, pointed bill readily distinguishes it from a bullfinch or male becard. Unlike species of *Agelaius*, exclusively arboreal. Fig. 169.

Voice: A rather loud note, followed by a rattling sound (*kep-chur-r-r-r*).

Habitat: Mainly humid, mountain forest; rarely observed in lowland woods. Most readily found near Hardwar Gap.

Nidification: Nest a cup-shaped structure, situated in a tree. Eggs (2) sparsely spotted and scrawled.

Range: Jamaica.

Common Meadowlark   *Sturnella magna*

Fig. 170 Common Meadowlark

Local name: Sabanero.

Description: 9″. A chunky, terrestrial species, with a flat head and short tail. Upperparts variegated-black, brown and buff; underparts mostly yellow, with a large black patch on chest and black streaks on sides and flanks; outer tail feathers largely white, conspicuous in flight. Fig. 170.

Voice: A series of shrill notes, not nearly as melodious as songs of North American races, although the call-note is similar.

Habitat: Fields and savannas; also open stretches of the Zapata Swamp. Apt to be seen at airports.

Nidification: Nest dome-shaped with the entrance at the side, situated on the ground. Eggs (4–5) spotted.

Range: Cuba and the Isle of Pines. Also North, Central and northern South America.

Bobolink   *Dolichonyx oryzivorus*

Local names: Rice Bird; Butter Bird; October Pink; Chambergo.
Description: 6.5–8″. Male (nuptial plumage): Black with some white or whitish on upperparts and a broad buffy band across hindneck. Female: Buffy or buffy-yellow, the upperparts with an admixture of black; pileum striped black and buff; sides and flanks streaked with black. Males in winter plumage resemble females. Associates in large flocks during migration.
Voice: A sharp *ping*. Does not sing in the West Indies.
Habitat: Fields, in particular rice plantations.
Range: Southern Canada and northern United States. Winters in South America. Transient in West Indies (Aug. 13–Dec. 12: March 5–May 28).

WEAVER FINCHES, WAXBILLS and ALLIES   *Ploceidae*

Many of these Old World birds have recently been introduced in Puerto Rico, the Spice Finch in the Dominican Republic as well. Only those established as residents fifty or more years ago are described in this book (see p. 240).

House Sparrow   *Passer domesticus*

Local names: English Sparrow; Gorrión; Gorrión Doméstico.
Description: 6″. Male: Pileum grey, rest of upperparts mostly brown, the mantle streaked with black; a chestnut streak behind eye; a white wing-bar; underparts mostly whitish except for a black "bib" that extends from chin to chest. Female: Differs from male chiefly in having a brown pileum and by having the underparts brownish grey, without a trace of black.
Voice: A persistent *chirrup*.
Habitat: Primarily in or near large towns.
Nidification: Usually nests in a crevice of a building or other man-made structure, such as a bridge, but sometimes builds in a tree a large globular nest with a side entrance. Eggs spotted.
Range: Native to Eurasia. Introduced with variable success on Grand Bahama (Freeport), New Providence (Nassau), Cuba (widespread), Jamaica (formerly in and near Port Antonio), Hispaniola (north coast of Dominican Republic), Puerto Rico (Playa de Ponce to Yauco), St. Thomas (extirpated?).

Village Weaver   *Ploceus cucullatus*   4/5/97   page 177

DR

Fig. 171 Village Weaver

Local name: Madam Sagá; Madame Sara.

Description: 6.5″. Male: Head black; rest of plumage chiefly bright yellow with considerable black on upperparts; tail olive-green; hindneck chestnut and underparts washed with this colour. Female: Pileum and hindneck yellowish green; back olive-grey; wings blackish, some feathers with yellow margins; tail olive-green; underparts yellow, becoming white on abdomen. A stockily built weaver with large bill and short, square tail. Gregarious in habits. Fig. 171.

Voice: A continuous wheezy chatter.

Habitat: Chiefly fairly open lowland country in Haiti, in particular the Cul-de-Sac plain, including Port-au-Prince. Has in recent years become widespread in Hispaniola.

Nidification: In colonies. Nest, built by male and either accepted or rejected by female, a strongly built globular structure with a spout-like entrance, suspended from the limb of a tree or palm frond; over seventy nests have been counted in a single tree. Eggs white, sometimes lightly spotted.

Range: Hispaniola and Saona Island (introduced). Native to Africa.

Orange-cheeked Waxbill   *Estrilda melpoda*

Local name: Veterano.

Description: 4.25″. Pileum grey; back and wings brown; upper tail-coverts red, the tail dusky; sides of head and bill orange-red; underparts greyish white, the abdomen sometimes with a reddish wash. Immature individuals have the sides of the head cinnamon, and the underparts tinged with this colour. An active little weaver, somewhat tit-like in appearance. Associates in flocks.

Voice: A weak *tsee-tsee-tsee* or a low chattering; also a sharp metallic chirp.

Habitat: Western Puerto Rico. Frequents marshes, acacia thickets, cane-fields, pastures and gardens.

Nidification: Nest roughly globular, the spouted entrance directed downwards; one found in Puerto Rico was about 10 feet up in a trumpet vine Eggs white.

Range: Puerto Rico (introduced). Native to West Africa.

Hooded Mannikin *Lonchura cucullata*

Local name: Diablito.

Description: 4″. Head, foreneck and chest black with a green gloss, particularly on pileum; rest of upperparts mainly brownish grey, barred with dusky and whitish posteriorly; scapular patch glossy green; tail black; posterior underparts white, mottled with black on sides. Immature individuals are greyish brown, darker above than below; many show traces of adult plumage. A tiny weaver, usually in flocks.

Voice: Utters low churring notes when flushed.

Habitat: Chiefly open, lowland country. Often encountered along streams, and in or on the borders of grassy fields and lawns. Common in San Juan.

Nidification: Builds a decidedly slovenly nest in a tree or palm, the structure globular in shape with a side entrance. Eggs white.

Range: Puerto Rico and Vieques Island (introduced). Native to Africa.

GROSBEAKS, FINCHES, SPARROWS & BUNTINGS *Fringillidae*

Finches comprise a large and heterogeneous group of birds, readily recognised by the shape of their bills that are more or less conical, adapted to seed-eating, although many species also feed on fruit and insects. In the case of crossbills the tips of the mandibles cross each other to enable the birds to extract seeds from cones. Of the West Indian species some ornithologists include only those of the genera *Carduelis* and *Loxia* in the Fringillidae, referring the remainder to the "Emberizidae".

Most of the species that occur in the Antilles inhabit shrubbery and are easily identified in the field. As many as five of the genera (*Melanospiza*, *Loxipasser*, *Loxigilla*, *Melopyrrha* and *Torreornis*) are endemic to these islands.

P

B.W.I.

Lesser Goldfinch   *Carduelis psaltria*

Description: 4″. Male: Upperparts glossy black, with some white on wing; underparts bright yellow. Female: Upperparts greenish; two pale wing-bars, and whitish margins to inner remiges; underparts dull yellow.
Voice: Song suggestive of that of a canary. Also utters a plaintive *tee-wee* or *tweea*.
Habitat: An active, arboreal species of rather open country. Recorded from Habana Province and once from Santiago de Cuba. Extirpated?
Nidification: The cup-shaped nest is situated in a tree. Eggs bluish white.
Range: Cuba. Probably introduced from Yucatán. Also western North America south to north-western South America.

Antillean Siskin   *Carduelis dominicensis*   page 192

Local names: Canario; Siguita Amarilla; Petit Serin.
Description: 4.5″. Male: Head black; dorsal surface yellowish green, becoming yellower on rump; wings black with greenish yellow margins to the feathers; tail yellow and black; underparts and sides of neck yellow. Female: Upperparts olive-green; underparts whitish with a yellowish wash and with faint dusky streaks. An active little finch, frequently in flocks. Fig. 172.
Voice: A soft *chut-chut* and a wiry siskin-like *e-see-ip*, often emitted in flight; also a low chattering trill in breeding season.

Fig. 172 Antillean Siskin

Habitat: Chiefly mountain pine forest and seldom found far from this environment, though breeds near Kenscoff. In Haiti, apparently confined to the Massif de la Selle and Massif de la Hotte. Often flushed from patches of weeds.
Nidification: Nest a compact cup of moss, situated in a shrub or pine. Eggs (2–3) usually pale greenish, spotted.
Range: Hispaniola.

White-winged Crossbill *Loxia leucoptera*

Fig. 173 White-winged Crossbill

Local names: Turquesa; Periquito; Bec-croisé.

Description: 6″. Male: General colour rosy red; wings and tail blackish; two white wing-bars; mandibles crossed. Female: Differs from male in being chiefly dusky, the rump and underparts washed with greenish yellow; white on wing as in male. The immature is blackish above, streaked with whitish; wings and tail as in adults; underparts whitish with blackish streaks. Apt to be seen in flocks. Fig. 173.

Voice: An impatient high-pitched *shik-shik*, repeated indefinitely. Also a subdued warbling during breeding season as northern races.

Habitat: Mountain pine forest. In Haiti known from the Massif de la Selle and Massif de la Hotte.

Nidification: The cup-shaped nest is built high up on a branch of a pine in Hispaniola. Eggs presumably spotted like those of northern races.

Range: Hispaniola. Also northern Eurasia and northern North America; several seen in Jamaica (Antillean race?) from Dec. 1970 to April 1971.

Saffron Finch *Sicalis flaveola* page 192

Local names: Canary; Wild Canary.

Description: 5.5″. Upperparts greenish yellow, the forehead orange, the back with indistinct dusky streaks; *sides of head and underparts yellow.* Female slightly duller than male. Immature birds are greyish to brownish above, more or less washed with olive and streaked with blackish; underparts mostly whitish with yellow under tail-coverts and thighs and, in older individuals, a well-developed yellow band across foreneck and chest.

Voice: A melodious warble of four or five notes uttered rather deliberately.

Habitat: Open country and gardens. May be seen in Kingston, Mandeville and Moneague. Often in flocks on ground.

Nidification: Nest bulky, cup-shaped; in tree, cavity of tree, at base of palm frond or under eaves of a house. Eggs (2–3) spotted.

Range: Jamaica (introduced). Native to South America.

Yellow Grass Finch   *Sicalis luteola*   page 192

Local names: Grass Sparrow; Grass Canary; Petit Serin.

Description: 4.75″. Upperparts yellowish green to brownish, heavily streaked with blackish, the rump and upper tail-coverts immaculate yellowish green; *underparts yellow.* Male brighter than female. Immature birds have blackish streaks on anterior underparts. An active species, sometimes encountered in small flocks.

Voice: Utters shrill but melodious notes, often when in flight.

Habitat: Chiefly open fields.

Nidification: Nest a cup-shaped structure, situated on the ground. Eggs (2–3) spotted.

Range: Lesser Antilles (Antigua, Guadeloupe, Martinique, St. Lucia, St. Vincent and Barbados); casual on Mustique. Also Mexico, Central America, and South America. Apparently introduced (about 1900) on Barbados, whence it has spread to other islands.

Blue-black Seedeater
Volatinia jacarina

Local names: Blue-black See-see; Johnny-jump-up; Prézite; Ci-ci des Herbes Noir.

Description: 4.25″. Male: Entirely glossy blue-black. Female: Upperparts olive-brown; underparts brownish buff, paler on abdomen; *chest and sides of breast conspicuously streaked with dusky.* The immature male resembles the female, but shows more or less black. Fig. 174.

Voice: Song a characteristic *ee-slick,* much like that of a Henslow's Sparrow. When singing the male

Fig. 174 Blue-black Seedeater

usually leaps about a foot in the air, sometimes turning completely around in the process.

Habitat: Borders of fields and shrubbery in settled districts at low elevations.

Nidification: Nest cup-shaped, situated on the ground or in a bush. Eggs (2) greenish white to pale greenish blue, spotted.

Range: Grenada. Also Tobago and Trinidad, Mexico, Central America and South America.

Yellow-bellied Seedeater   *Sporophila nigricollis*

Fig. 175 Yellow-bellied Seedeater

Local names: White-beak See-see.

Description: 4.5″. Male: Head and foreneck black; rest of upperparts olive-green; rest of underparts mostly pale yellow or yellowish white; *bill whitish* or yellowish white. Female: Upperparts plain brownish olive; underparts buffy brown, becoming yellowish buff or buffy white on abdomen; bill dusky. Fig. 175.

Voice: Song a short, melodious warble.

Habitat: Borders of fields and thickets in settled districts. At times associates with Black-faced Grassquits.

Nidification: Nest cup-shaped, situated in a bush or low tree. Eggs (2–3) spotted.

Range: Grenada and Carriacou; vagrant to St. Vincent. Also Tobago and Trinidad, southern Central America, South America.

Cuban Bullfinch *Melopyrrha nigra*   page 192

Local names: Black Sparrow; Negrito.
Description: 5.5–5.75″. Plumage black, with *conspicuous white patch on wing.* Grand Cayman females and immature males are greyish olive instead of black, darker on the head. Fig. 176.

Voice: A pleasant, melodious warbling.
Habitat: Scrub-covered country and woodland.

Fig. 176 Cuban Bullfinch

Nidification: Nest more or less globular in shape with the entrance at the side, situated in a bush or low tree. Eggs (3–4) spotted.
Range: Cuba, the Isle of Pines and some cays; also Grand Cayman.

Puerto Rican Bullfinch *Loxigilla portoricensis*   page 192

Local names: Mountain Blacksmith (St. Kitts); Come-Ñame; Come-Gandul; Capacho; Gallito.
Description: 6.75–8″. Plumage mostly black; crown (except posterior part), chin, throat, foreneck, upper chest and under tail-coverts rufous. The immature is brownish olive, darker above than below; under tail-coverts rufous. The St. Kitts form was larger than that of Puerto Rico with a much heavier bill.
Voice: A loud cardinal-like whistling usually of six or seven notes; also wheezy sounds. Call-note a soft *tseet.*
Habitat: Woodland, including rain forest, coffee plantations, arid wasteland and mangrove swamps. Inhabited the forested slopes of Mt. Misery, St. Kitts, until at least 1929; apparently exterminated on that island by introduced monkeys, which presumably destroyed the nests.
Nidification: The bulky nest is either cup-shaped or globular with a side entrance, and is situated in a bush or tree from five to thirty feet above the ground. Eggs (usually 3) spotted.
Range: Puerto Rico; formerly St. Kitts.

Greater Antillean Bullfinch *Loxigilla violacea*   page 192

4/2/97 DR

Local names: Black Sparrow; Jack Sparrow; Jack Spaniard; Black Bill; Black Charles; Cotton-Tree Sparrow; Coffee Bird; Cocoa Bird; Spanish Parakeet; Hard-mouthed Parakeet; Red-breast; Gallito; Gallito Prieto; Petit-Coq.

Description: 6–7″. Superciliary stripe, chin, throat and under tail-coverts rufous; *rest of plumage black*. Immature birds are dark olive-grey above, paler below; patch above eye and under tail-coverts rufous and usually more or less rufous on throat. Fig. 177.

Voice: A harsh *wichi-wichi-wichi*, followed by a buzzing, cicada-like *scree*.

Fig. 177 Greater Antillean Bullfinch

Habitat: Shrubbery, including undergrowth of mountain rain forest and semi-arid scrub. Most numerous in dense secondary growth.

Nidification: Nest usually globular with the entrance at the side, but sometimes a cup-shaped structure. It is usually situated in a shrub or low tree, but occasionally (Hispaniola) among grass on the ground, or (Jamaica) in a cavity of a tree. Eggs (usually 3) spotted.

Range: Bahama Islands, Hispaniola (including surrounding islands), and Jamaica.

Lesser Antillean Bullfinch *Loxigilla noctis* Page 192

Local names: Red-breast; Red-throat See-See; Robin; Sparrow; Brown Sparrow; Rouge-gorge; Père Noir (male); Moisson (female).

Description: 5.5–6″. Male: An inconspicuous spot above lores, *chin and throat rufous*; under tail-coverts black, partly rufous or entirely rufous; *rest of plumage black*. Female: Upperparts dark olive-grey; some brown on wings; underparts greyish, *the under tail-coverts tawny. Adult males from Barbados resemble females*, as do the young.

Voice: A simple twittering, with an occasional harsh petulant note or a shrill *tseep-tseep*; also a sharp trill.

Habitat: Widespread in shrubbery and forest undergrowth; common and remarkably tame in gardens of Barbados.

Nidification: Nest globular in shape with the entrance at the side, situated in a bush or tree. Eggs (2–3) spotted.

Range: Lesser Antilles, apart from the Grenadines; St. John (introduced?).

St. Lucia Black Finch *Melanospiza richardsoni*

Local name: Moisson Pied-blanc.

Description: 5.25–5.5″. Male: Plumage black; feet pale pink. Female: Resembles females of the Lesser Antillean Bullfinch, but pileum grey,

Fig. 178 St. Lucia Black Finch

the back brown in striking contrast if seen under favourable conditions; underparts mainly buffy, not greyish; bill larger; feet pale pink. The immature male resembles the female but is darker. Has a characteristic habit of twitching its tail, and flight is more direct than that of a *Loxigilla*. Fig. 178.

Voice: Song a wheezy *tic-zwee-swizewiz-you*, a little like that of a Bananaquit.

Habitat: Borders of forest and shrubbery, chiefly in mountains; also in semi-arid scrub in lowlands. Most numerous in mountains behind Soufrière.

Nidification: Nest like that of Lesser Antillean Bullfinch, but bulkier and more loosely constructed; situated in a sapling or bamboo near the ground. Eggs (2) spotted.

Range: St. Lucia.

Yellow-faced Grassquit *Tiaris olivacea* page 129

Local names: Grass Bird; Yellow-faced Grass Bird; Grass Quit; Gorrión Barba-Amarilla; Viudo; Viudito; Viudita; Chamorro; Tomeguín; Tomeguín de la Tierra; Chinchilita; Pechito; Petit des Herbes (pron. "ti-zeb").
Description: 4.5″. Male: Upperparts greyish green; superciliary stripe, lower eyelid chin and upper throat yellow; a large black patch on foreneck and chest; rest of underparts greyish. Female: Lacks the black on the underparts; yellow head markings but faintly indicated (lacking in young),

Fig. 179 Yellow-faced Grassquit

most apparent above lores. A tiny finch abundant in most parts of its range. Fig. 179.

Voice: Song a weak, rapidly uttered trill, like that of the Worm-eating Warbler.

Habitat: Borders of fields, roadsides, gardens and thickets in fairly open country. Does not inhabit forested areas.

Nidification: Nest globular, with the entrance at the side, situated on or near the ground. Eggs (usually 3) spotted.

Range: Greater Antilles, including the Cayman Islands, east to Vieques and Culebra. Also Mexico to north-western South America. Introduced (1963) on New Providence.

Black-faced Grassquit   *Tiaris bicolor*   page 129

Fig. 180 Black-faced Grassquit
(Jamaica and Hispaniola)

Local names: Parson Bird; Parson Sparrow; Sin Bird; Chitty Bird; Black Sparrow; White See-see (female); Grass Sparrow; Ground Sparrow; Grass Bird; Straw Bird; Cane Sparrow; Tobacco Seed; Parakeet; Grass Quit; Chamorro Negro; Gorrión Negro; Juana Maruca; Barbito (Cuba); Tomeguín Prieto (Cuba); Petit des Herbes (pron. "ti-zeb"); Ci-ci des Herbes (pron. "si-si-zeb").

Description: 4.5″. Male: Differs from male Yellow-faced Grassquit by darker and duller green upperparts and more extensively black underparts; *no yellow markings on head*. Female: Often indistinguishable in the field from the female Yellow-faced Grassquit; no yellowish markings on head. Fig. 180.

Voice: Song a buzzing *tik-zeeëë* or *tik-tik-zeeëë*.

Habitat: Like that of Yellow-faced Grassquit.

Nidification: Like that of Yellow-faced Grassquit, but nest rarely on ground, occasionally as high as twenty feet above ground.

Range: Virtually throughout the West Indies, with the notable exceptions of Cuba (but inhabits cays off northern Las Villas), the Isle of Pines, Cayman and Swan Islands. Also Tobago, islands in the southern Caribbean Sea and northern South America.

Cuban Grassquit   *Tiaris canora*   page 129

Fig. 181 Cuban Grassquit

Local names: Tomeguín del Pinar (western Cuba); Senserenico (eastern Cuba).

Description: 4.5″. Male: Resembles the Black-faced Grassquit but with a ruff of yellow feathers on each side of neck. Female: Yellow ruff less developed than in male, and black of "face" replaced for most part by chestnut. Fig. 181.

Voice: Song a soft, not unpleasant *chibiri-wichii*, subject to considerable variation.

Habitat: Mainly shrubbery bordering fields; also woodland, including pine woods in western Cuba.

Nidification: Nest like that of other grassquits, situated at low or moderate elevations in a bush or tree. Eggs (2–3) spotted.

Range: Cuba, and (?) Isle of Pines. Introduced (1963) on New Providence.

Yellow-shouldered Grassquit   *Loxipasser anoxanthus*   page 129

Local names: Yellow-back; Yellow-backed Grass bird.

Description: 5″. Male: Head and most of underparts black; back and wings yellowish green; yellow on lesser wing-coverts and bend of wing; under tail-coverts chestnut. Female: Upperparts yellowish green, greener on the crown and yellower on bend of wing; underparts plain olive-grey,

the under tail-coverts pale cinnamon. The immature male more or less resembles the female. Behaviour like that of Greater Antillean Bullfinch. "Yellow-backed Finch" is a more appropriate English name. Fig. 182.
Voice: Song a rapidly uttered insect-like *zwee-ze-ze-ze-ze*; resembles that of a Golden-winged Warbler.
Habitat: Shrubbery in the hills and mountains, but not present in dense rain forest. Rare at low elevations.
Nidification: Nest globular in shape with the entrance at the side, decidedly larger than that of other grassquits; situated low in a bush or tree. Eggs (3–4) spotted.
Range: Jamaica.

Fig. 182 Yellow-shouldered
Grassquit

Fig. 183 Streaked Saltator

Streaked Saltator *Saltator albicollis* page 177

Local names: Gros-bec; Grive Gros-bec.
Description: 8.5". Upperparts dull green becoming grey posteriorly; a white superciliary stripe; throat white, bordered with blackish; rest of underparts white, washed with olive-green on breast and with narrow and obscure dusky streaks; under tail-coverts buffy. A rather sluggish and plainly coloured "grosbeak", larger than other finch-like birds of the Lesser Antilles. Fig. 183.
Voice: A series of rather loud, deliberately uttered notes of inferior quality.
Habitat: Secondary growth thickets; semi-arid scrub.
Nidification: Nest cup-shaped, situated in a bush or low tree. Eggs (2–3) light greenish blue, scrawled with black at large ends.
Range: Guadeloupe, Dominica, Martinique, St. Lucia; accidental on Nevis. Also Central and South America, including Trinidad.

Rose-breasted Grosbeak *Pheucticus ludovicianus*

Local name: Degollado.

Description: 7″. Male (nuptial plumage): Upperparts black, the rump white and some white on wings and tail; head and neck entirely black; *chest and middle of lower breast red*, as are under wing-coverts; remainder of underparts white; bill short and thick. Female: Upperparts greyish brown, streaked with dusky; a white superciliary stripe and another through centre of pileum; underparts white, streaked on the breast, sides and flanks with blackish. Males in winter plumage resemble females but under wing-coverts and axillars red (yellow in female), and usually a little red on anterior underparts.

Range: North America east of the Rocky Mountains. Winters from Mexico and western Cuba (rarely) south to northern South America. More numerous as transient in West Indies, whence recorded from the Bahama Islands, Greater Antilles, Swan Island, Barbuda, Dominica, Barbados and Grenada (Sept. 23–May 7).

Blue Grosbeak *Guiraca caerulea*

Local names: Azulejón; Azulejo Real.

Description: 7″. Male: Chiefly deep violet-blue, the feathers with rusty or whitish tips in winter plumage; *two chestnut wing-bars*. Female: Resembles female Indigo Bunting, but larger and with a heavier and paler bill; *two rufous or buffy wing-bars*. Young in first winter plumage resemble adult female.

Range: Southern North America and Central America. Rare transient and winter resident in West Indies, whence recorded from the Bahama Islands, Cuba, Grand Cayman, Swan Island, Jamaica, Hispaniola, Mona Island and St. John (September 1–May 2).

Indigo Bunting *Passerina cyanea*

Local name: Azulejo.

Description: 5.5″. Male (nuptial plumage): Violet-blue, darker on head. Female: Upperparts plain greyish brown; underparts white, more or less washed with light greyish brown; sometimes with indistinct dusky streaking on breast. Males in winter plumage resemble females, but always show some blue on wings and tail.

Range: Chiefly eastern North America. Winters for the most part in Mexico and Central America; also on islands in the western Caribbean, Bahamas and virtually throughout the Greater Antilles; in Lesser Antilles recorded only from Saba (Sept. 21–May 19).

Painted Bunting *Passerina ciris*

Local names: Arco-iris (male); Verderón (female).
Description: 5.5″. Male: Pileum, hindneck and sides of head and neck violet-blue; mantle yellowish green; rump, upper tail-coverts and underparts red. Female: Upperparts plain green; underparts yellowish green, becoming yellow or yellowish on abdomen. Young resemble the adult female.
Range: Southern and south-eastern North America. Winters chiefly in Middle America, but also in southern Florida, Cuba, Jamaica (casual), and in the Bahamas whence recorded from the north-western islands of this group (July 22–April 29).

Dickcissel *Spiza americana*

Description: 6–6.5″. Upperparts much as female House Sparrow, but underparts white with a patch of yellow on the breast (more restricted in female); a conspicuous yellow or yellowish superciliary stripe; male with a black patch anterior to yellow of breast. Usually in flocks on ground among shore vegetation or in coconut groves.
Range: North America east of the Rocky Mountains. Winters in Central America and northern South America. Transient through western islands of West Indies; recorded from the Bahamas, Cuba, Jamaica, Swan Island, Old Providence, St. Andrew's, Albuquerque; accidental in Puerto Rico (Sept. 3–Dec. 15; March 18–May 2).

Zapata Sparrow *Torreornis inexpectata*   page 192

Local names: Cabrero de la Ciénaga; Cabrerito de la Ciénaga.
Description: 6.5″. Upperparts chiefly greyish olive (greyish in eastern races); mantle indistinctly streaked with blackish (western race); pileum chestnut (obsolete in eastern races) with an admixture of grey; throat and supraloral spot white; a black submalar stripe; *breast and abdomen primrose-yellow*, greyish olive on sides and flanks. Juvenile individuals have entire upperparts dark greyish olive; secondaries margined with

Fig. 184 Zapata Sparrow

rufous; underparts yellow, olivaceous laterally and anteriorly. Flight like that of a fledgling sparrow, due to short wings. Fig. 184.

Voice: Pairs emit "buzz" and "chatter" duets. Call-note a thin *tseep*, like that of many other small birds.

Habitat: Open shrubbery in Zapata Swamp from Santo Tomás westward; coastal grassy areas east of Santiago de Cuba; Cayo Coco.

Nidification: The cup-shaped nest is well concealed in a hummock of saw-grass in the Zapata Swamp. Eggs spotted.

Range: Cuba.

Savannah Sparrow *Passerculus sandwichensis*

Description: 5.5–6″. Resembles the Grasshopper Sparrow but underparts white, *heavily streaked with black*; a yellowish superciliary stripe, most apparent on lores; no chestnut on upperparts and no yellow on bend of wing; bill slender. Like the Grasshopper Sparrow, a bird of open fields, but less secretive.

Range: North America and northern Central America. Northern individuals winter in West Indies, whence recorded from the Bahamas (south to Rum Cay), Cuba, Isle of Pines, Grand Cayman and Swan Island (October 11–April 25).

Grasshopper Sparrow *Ammodramus savannarum*

Local names: Savanna Bird; Grass-dodger; Grass Pink; "Tichicro"; Chamberguito (Cuba); Tumbarrocío (Dom. Rep.); Gorrión de Chicharra (P.R.); Oiseau Canne.

Description: 5″. Upperparts a mixture of black, grey, buff and chestnut; lesser wing-coverts and bend of wing yellow or yellowish in adults; *underparts buffy*, becoming white on lower breast and abdomen; tail feathers narrow and pointed. Young are white below, the chest

Fig. 185 Grasshopper Sparrow

streaked with blackish, but much less so than in Savannah Sparrow. The short tail and relatively thick bill are diagnostic. Secretive in habits, and flies but a short distance when flushed. Fig. 185.

Voice: An insect-like *tsik-zeee*, varied at times by rapid twittering.

Habitat: Open fields and savannas.

Nidification: The more or less arched nest is situated on the ground. Eggs (3) spotted.

List of Vagrants

Swift (*Apus melba*). Barbados (Sept. 22, 1955).
ecked Jacobin (*Florisuga mellivora*). Tobago race recorded from Carriacou
9, 1904).
az Hummingbird (*Chrysolampis mosquitus*). Grenada (Sept. 8–9, 1962).
Kingbird (*Tyrannus verticalis*). Northern Bahamas and Swan Island (Oct.
rch 16).
led Flycatcher (*Muscivora forficata*). Grand Bahama, San Salvador, western
d Puerto Rico (Oct. 31–Dec. 13).
oebe (*Sayornis phoebe*). Grand Bahama, Bimini and Cuba (Sept. 11–
).
ed Flycatcher (*Empidonax flaviventris*). Western Cuba (Sept. 8–Oct. 4).
atcher (*Empidonax traillii*). Western Cuba, Isle of Pines and Jamaica
Oct. 7).
her (*Empidonax minimus*). Grand Cayman (March 10).
her (*Toxostoma rufum*). Grand Bahama, Harbour Island and western
29–Nov. 28); "almost certainly seen" on New Providence (Jan. 8).
h (*Catharus guttatus*). Winter resident in northern Bahamas; recorded
Bahama, New Providence, Eleuthera and Cat Island (Oct. 21–April

tear (*Oenanthe oenanthe*). Santiago de Cuba (Oct. 16), Puerto Rico
n, Sept. 22), and a December record from Barbados.
Kinglet (*Regulus calendula*). Grand Bahama, Bimini, New Provi-
Island, western Cuba and Jamaica (Oct. 18–March 13).
Anthus rubescens). Grand Bahama, Andros, New Providence, Cat
ador, Green Cay, Swan Island, Old Providence and St. Andrew
ecords of Sprague's Pipit (*Anthus spragueii*) are questionable.
(*Lanius ludovicianus*). Grand Bahama (Oct. 10), Great Exuma
ros.
(*Vireo philadelphicus*). New Providence, Eleuthera, Cuba and
ov. 1; Feb. 1–27).
gilvus). Cuba (Sept. 22) and Jamaica (Oct. 8).
rbler (*Vermivora celata*). Grand Bahama, Andros, New Provi-
arbour Island and San Salvador (Oct. 14–Jan. 2).
Vermivora ruficapilla). Bahamas and Greater Antilles (Sept.

porornis philadelphia). New Providence, Puerto Rico and
ember; March 21).
(*Icteria virens*). Grand Bahama, Abaco, Bimini, Andros
an (Aug. 16–May 5).
onia pusilla). Grand Bahama, New Providence, Cuba
ept. 7–April 11).
ia canadensis). Bahama Islands, Cuba, Jamaica, Puert
ix and Guadeloupe (Sept. 2–Oct. 27; Feb. 17–April 3)
udoviciana). New Providence (Sept. 11, 26) and Cul

Xanthocephalus xanthocephalus). Grand Bahama, S
dos (autumn).
othrus ater). New Providence, Great Inagua and Cu

s tristis). Grand Bahama, Abaco, Bimini and Cu

nineus). Grand Bahama (Aug. 12–late Dec.).
ammacus). Northern Bahama Islands and C

Finches 239

Range: Breeds in Jamaica, Hispaniola, Puerto Rico and Vieques Island. Also North America, Central America and north-western South America, including Curaçao and Bonaire. Individuals from eastern North America winter in the Bahamas, Cuba, the Isle of Pines, Cayman Islands and Swan Island (October 12–May 1).

Rufous-collared Sparrow *Zonotrichia capensis* page 192

Fig. 186 Rufous-collared Sparrow

Local names: Sigua de Constanza; Siguita de Constanza; Pincha.
Description: 6–6.5". Pileum and sides of head grey, *boldly streaked with black*; a chestnut collar around hindneck; mantle olive-brown, streaked with black, the rump plain olive-brown; brownish margins to wing feathers and two narrow white or whitish wing-bars; underparts mostly white, the sides and flanks olive-brown; *a conspicuous black band across foreneck.* Feathers of crown often elevated. Young have underparts spotted with dusky; no distinct black or rufous markings, but traces of adult plumage evident in older birds. Fig. 186.
Voice: A simple, clear trill (*wis-wis-wis-wis-wiswiswis*): resembles song of Swamp Sparrow but terminated rapidly; variable. Extralimital races utter melodious, meadowlark-like whistles.
Habitat: Mountains of the Dominican Republic (Cordillera Central west to Sierra de Neiba and doubtless the Montagnes du Trou d'Eau). Found in thickets along streams and on borders of deciduous forest; less numerous among growths of bracken in pine forest.
Nidification: In the Dominican Republic the cup-shaped nest is situated in a shrub. Eggs (2) pale bluish, thickly spotted.
Range: Hispaniola. Also Central and South America, including Curaçao and Aruba.

ADDENDA: List of Vagrants

Much information on West Indian birds has been forthcoming in recent years, and the more important is included in this revised edition. A high proportion pertains to North American migrants, many of which (listed below with asterisks) should no longer be considered vagrants, since they are now known to occur more or less regularly in the region. Unique records of North American landbirds far from their normal winter ranges are omitted because they probably had been transported by ships.

Almost all of the indigenous birds of Old Providence and St. Andrew inhabit the Antilles, but some transients there and on the Swan Islands migrate primarily through Central America. Dates of occurrence of such species in this guide apply to the Bahamas and Antilles.

Puerto Ricans have permitted wholesale introductions of exotic species, at least 30 of which are established residents. Herbert Raffaele is the only person with a comprehensive knowledge of these, so a visitor to that island is advised to obtain a copy of his *A Guide to the Birds of Puerto Rico and the Virgin Islands* (1983) distributed by the Addison-Wesley Publishing Co. of Reading, Massachusetts 01867.

Scientific nomenclature in *Birds of the West Indies* follows closely that of the mid century rather than the latest (1983) edition of the A.O.U. Check-list, which would not have been feasible. This will not detract from the usefulness of the volume.

Common Loon (*Gavia immer*). Havana, Cuba (Nov. 30, May 13).
Black-browed Albatross (*Diomedea melanophris*). Off Vauclin, Martinique (Nov. 12, 1956).
*Cory's Shearwater (*Puffinus diomedea*). At sea in Caribbean, Gulf of Mexico and among Bahamas (Feb.–Nov.).
*Greater Shearwater (*Puffinus gravis*). At sea in Caribbean and Bahaman waters chiefly spring and summer).
*Sooty Shearwater (*Puffinus griseus*). Off north coast of Cuba, Exuma Sound, St. Lucia (June–Nov.).
Manx Shearwater (*Puffinus puffinus*). At sea in Caribbean (Nov.–March).
Harcourt's Petrel (*Oceanodroma castro*). Cuba (July 25, Dec. 6).
Northern Gannet (*Sula bassanus*). Berry Islands, Bahamas (Jan. 5–6, 1984).
Grey Heron (*Ardea cinerea*). Montserrat (Sept. 20, 1959; banded in France in May 1959) and Barbados (sight record, Aug. 1963).
Little Egret (*Egretta garzetta*). Martinique (Oct. 6, 1962; banded in Spain in June 1962), and Barbados (April), St. Lucia (Jan.); also Trinidad.
Western Reef Heron (*Demiegretta gularis*). Barbados (Feb. 20–April 13, 1984), St. Lucia (Feb. 18, 1984; Jan. 31, 1985).
Scarlet Ibis (*Eudocimus ruber*). Grenada (January–June).
Whistling Swan (*Cygnus columbianus*). Cuba (Dec. 17, 1944). Puerto Rico (Dec. 16, 1944), St. Thomas (Dec. 21, 1983).
Canada Goose (*Branta canadensis*). Cuba (Dec. 11, 1966; April 7, 1972).
White-fronted Goose (*Anser albifrons*). Cuba; last reported in 1916.
*Snow Goose (*Anser caerulescens*). Bahamas, Cuba, Puerto Rico (inclusive dates of occurrence unknown; rather frequently shot in Cuba).
White-faced Tree Duck (*Dendrocygna viduata*). Cuba, Hispaniola and Barbados; latest record from the Dominican Republic in May 1926.
Black Duck (*Anas rubripes*). Puerto Rico (early winter records).
Cinnamon Teal (*Anas cyanoptera*). Grand Bahama, Cuba and Jamaica (Dec. 5–March 24).
Garganey Teal (*Anas querquedula*). Barbados (Aug. 29).
European Widgeon (*Anas penelope*). Hispaniola, Puerto Rico, Barbuda (individual banded in Iceland), and Barbados (Oct. 9–Feb. 22).

Greater Scaup (*Aythya marila*). New Providence (Jan. 31): o
San Salvador, Rum Cay and Cuba.
Bufflehead (*Bucephala albeola*). Cuba, Jamaica and Puert
European Kestrel (*Falco tinnunculus*). Martinique (Dec.
Virginia Rail (*Rallus limicola*). Cuba (Oct. 16, etc.).
Spotted Crake (*Porzana porzana*). St. Martin (Oct. 8,
Yellow Rail (*Coturnicops noveboracensis*). Grand Ba
Ringed Plover (*Charadrius hiaticula*). Barbados (Se
European Lapwing (*Vanellus vanellus*). Hog Islar
Barbados (July; Nov.–Dec.).
*American Avocet (*Recurvirostra americana*).
Cuba, Jamaica, Puerto Rico, St. Croix and B
Jack Snipe (*Lymnocryptes minimus*). Barbados
Eskimo Curlew (*Numenius borealis*). Forme
Latest Antillean record from Barbados (Se
Spotted Redshank (*Tringa erythropus*). Bark
Wood Sandpiper (*Tringa glareola*). Barbad
Baird's Sandpiper (*Calidris bairdii*). Barba
Curlew Sandpiper (*Calidris ferruginea*). Barbados (Sept.–Oct.).
*Dunlin (*Calidris alpina*). Barbados (
Providence, Great Inagua, Jamaica
St. Lucia (Aug. 10–April 22).
Red Phalarope (*Phalaropus fulicaria*
*Wilson's Phalarope (*Steganopus tr
Hispaniola, Puerto Rico, Guade
April 1–May 11).
Northern Phalarope (*Lobipes lo
Dec. 10) and Jamaica (Jan. 7
*Pomarine Jaeger (*Stercorariu
(Oct. 23–April 21).
*Long-tailed Jaeger (*Sterc
April).
Skua (*Catharacta* sp.). O
individual banded on I
*Great Black-backed G
Puerto Rico, St. Bar
*Lesser Black-backed
April 20).
*Black-headed Gul
Antilles (Nov. 2
Franklin's Gull (
Black-legged Ki
(December–N
Sabine's Gull (
Arctic Tern (
Large-billed
White-wing
Barbad
Dovekie
Passeng
Europe
Dark-
Long-ear

Green-tailed Towhee (*Chlorura chlorura*). Casilda, Cuba (Jan. 8).

Slate-coloured Junco (*Junco hyemalis*). Grand Bahama, New Providence, Jamaica (Nov. 8–April 17); one carried by ship to St. Thomas.

*Chipping Sparrow (*Spizella passerina*). Grand Bahama, Abaco, New Providence and Cuba (Oct. 28–April 14).

*Clay-coloured Sparrow (*Spizella pallida*). Grand Bahama, New Providence and Cuba (Oct. 15–Feb. 13).

*White-crowned Sparrow (*Zonotrichia leucophrys*). Bahama Islands, Cuba and Jamaica (Oct. 4–April 25).

*Lincoln's Sparrow (*Zonotrichia lincolnii*). Bahamas, Cuba, Jamaica, Hispaniola and Puerto Rico (Oct. 22–April 20).

Swamp Sparrow (*Zonotrichia georgiana*). New Providence (Nov. 10, 18) and Mayaguana (April 10).

Snow Bunting (*Plectrophenax nivalis*). Cat Island (Dec. 1).

Note. The Black or Lesser Noddy (*Anous tenuirostris*) is still unknown from the West Indies, although it breeds on islands of the southern and western Caribbean and has occurred in summer on the Dry Tortugas, outermost of the Florida Keys, since 1962.

Index

246

Range: Breeds in Jamaica, Hispaniola, Puerto Rico and Vieques Island. Also North America, Central America and north-western South America, including Curaçao and Bonaire. Individuals from eastern North America winter in the Bahamas, Cuba, the Isle of Pines, Cayman Islands and Swan Island (October 12–May 1).

Rufous-collared Sparrow *Zonotrichia capensis*   page 192

Local names: Sigua de Constanza; Siguita de Constanza; Pincha.

Fig. 186 Rufous-collared Sparrow

Description: 6–6.5″. Pileum and sides of head grey, *boldly streaked with black*; a chestnut collar around hindneck; mantle olive-brown, streaked with black, the rump plain olive-brown; brownish margins to wing feathers and two narrow white or whitish wing-bars; underparts mostly white, the sides and flanks olive-brown; *a conspicuous black band across foreneck.* Feathers of crown often elevated. Young have underparts spotted with dusky; no distinct black or rufous markings, but traces of adult plumage evident in older birds. Fig. 186.

Voice: A simple, clear trill (*wis-wis-wis-wis-wiswiswis*): resembles song of Swamp Sparrow but terminated rapidly; variable. Extralimital races utter melodious, meadowlark-like whistles.

Habitat: Mountains of the Dominican Republic (Cordillera Central west to Sierra de Neiba and doubtless the Montagnes du Trou d'Eau). Found in thickets along streams and on borders of deciduous forest; less numerous among growths of bracken in pine forest.

Nidification: In the Dominican Republic the cup-shaped nest is situated in a shrub. Eggs (2) pale bluish, thickly spotted.

Range: Hispaniola. Also Central and South America, including Curaçao and Aruba.

ADDENDA: List of Vagrants

Much information on West Indian birds has been forthcoming in recent years, and the more important is included in this revised edition. A high proportion pertains to North American migrants, many of which (listed below with asterisks) should no longer be considered vagrants, since they are now known to occur more or less regularly in the region. Unique records of North American landbirds far from their normal winter ranges are omitted because they probably had been transported by ships.

Almost all of the indigenous birds of Old Providence and St. Andrew inhabit the Antilles, but some transients there and on the Swan Islands migrate primarily through Central America. Dates of occurrence of such species in this guide apply to the Bahamas and Antilles.

Puerto Ricans have permitted wholesale introductions of exotic species, at least 30 of which are established residents. Herbert Raffaele is the only person with a comprehensive knowledge of these, so a visitor to that island is advised to obtain a copy of his *A Guide to the Birds of Puerto Rico and the Virgin Islands* (1983) distributed by the Addison-Wesley Publishing Co. of Reading, Massachusetts 01867.

Scientific nomenclature in *Birds of the West Indies* follows closely that of the mid century rather than the latest (1983) edition of the A.O.U. Check-list, which would not have been feasible. This will not detract from the usefulness of the volume.

Common Loon (*Gavia immer*). Havana, Cuba (Nov. 30, May 13).

Black-browed Albatross (*Diomedea melanophris*). Off Vauclin, Martinique (Nov. 12, 1956).

*Cory's Shearwater (*Puffinus diomedea*). At sea in Caribbean, Gulf of Mexico and among Bahamas (Feb.–Nov.).

*Greater Shearwater (*Puffinus gravis*). At sea in Caribbean and Bahaman waters chiefly spring and summer).

*Sooty Shearwater (*Puffinus griseus*). Off north coast of Cuba, Exuma Sound, St. Lucia (June–Nov.).

Manx Shearwater (*Puffinus puffinus*). At sea in Caribbean (Nov.–March).

Harcourt's Petrel (*Oceanodroma castro*). Cuba (July 25, Dec. 6).

Northern Gannet (*Sula bassanus*). Berry Islands, Bahamas (Jan. 5–6, 1984).

Grey Heron (*Ardea cinerea*). Montserrat (Sept. 20, 1959; banded in France in May 1959) and Barbados (sight record, Aug. 1963).

Little Egret (*Egretta garzetta*). Martinique (Oct. 6, 1962; banded in Spain in June 1962), and Barbados (April), St. Lucia (Jan.); also Trinidad.

Western Reef Heron (*Demiegretta gularis*). Barbados (Feb. 20–April 13, 1984), St. Lucia (Feb. 18, 1984; Jan. 31, 1985).

Scarlet Ibis (*Eudocimus ruber*). Grenada (January–June).

Whistling Swan (*Cygnus columbianus*). Cuba (Dec. 17, 1944). Puerto Rico (Dec. 16, 1944), St. Thomas (Dec. 21, 1983).

Canada Goose (*Branta canadensis*). Cuba (Dec. 11, 1966; April 7, 1972).

White-fronted Goose (*Anser albifrons*). Cuba; last reported in 1916.

*Snow Goose (*Anser caerulescens*). Bahamas, Cuba, Puerto Rico (inclusive dates of occurrence unknown; rather frequently shot in Cuba).

White-faced Tree Duck (*Dendrocygna viduata*). Cuba, Hispaniola and Barbados; latest record from the Dominican Republic in May 1926.

Black Duck (*Anas rubripes*). Puerto Rico (early winter records).

Cinnamon Teal (*Anas cyanoptera*). Grand Bahama, Cuba and Jamaica (Dec. 5–March 24).

Garganey Teal (*Anas querquedula*). Barbados (Aug. 29).

European Widgeon (*Anas penelope*). Hispaniola, Puerto Rico, Barbuda (individual banded in Iceland), and Barbados (Oct. 9–Feb. 22).

Greater Scaup (*Aythya marila*). New Providence (Jan. 31): questionable records from San Salvador, Rum Cay and Cuba.

Bufflehead (*Bucephala albeola*). Cuba, Jamaica and Puerto Rico (Nov. 3–Feb. 24).

European Kestrel (*Falco tinnunculus*). Martinique (Dec. 9).

Virginia Rail (*Rallus limicola*). Cuba (Oct. 16, etc.).

Spotted Crake (*Porzana porzana*). St. Martin (Oct. 8, 1956).

Yellow Rail (*Coturnicops noveboracensis*). Grand Bahama (Sept. 15).

Ringed Plover (*Charadrius hiaticula*). Barbados (Sept. 10, 1888).

European Lapwing (*Vanellus vanellus*). Hog Island (Bahamas), Puerto Rico and Barbados (July; Nov.–Dec.).

*American Avocet (*Recurvirostra americana*). Andros, Eleuthera, San Salvador, Cuba, Jamaica, Puerto Rico, St. Croix and Barbados (June 30–Jan. 4; April 30).

Jack Snipe (*Lymnocryptes minimus*). Barbados (Nov. 12).

Eskimo Curlew (*Numenius borealis*). Formerly Puerto Rico and Lesser Antilles. Latest Antillean record from Barbados (Sept. 4, 1963).

Spotted Redshank (*Tringa erythropus*). Barbados (March 12; Oct. 1).

Wood Sandpiper (*Tringa glareola*). Barbados (Oct. 16).

Baird's Sandpiper (*Calidris bairdii*). Barbados (Aug. 26–Nov. 5).

Curlew Sandpiper (*Calidris ferruginea*). Antigua (June), Carriacou, Grenada and Barbados (Sept.–Oct.).

*Dunlin (*Calidris alpina*). Barbados (Aug. 31, Nov. 12). Sight records from New Providence, Great Inagua, Jamaica, Puerto Rico, Virgin Islands, Dominica and St. Lucia (Aug. 10–April 22).

Red Phalarope (*Phalaropus fulicaria*). Cuba (Dec. 10, Jan. 30), and Antigua (Oct. 6).

*Wilson's Phalarope (*Steganopus tricolor*). Grand Cayman, Jamaica, Old Providence, Hispaniola, Puerto Rico, Guadeloupe, Martinique and Barbados (Sept. 8–Oct. 10; April 1–May 11).

Northern Phalarope (*Lobipes lobatus*). New Providence (Oct. 11–12), Cuba (May 20, Dec. 10) and Jamaica (Jan. 21).

*Pomarine Jaeger (*Stercorarius pomarinus*). At sea among Bahamas and in Caribbean (Oct. 23–April 21).

*Long-tailed Jaeger (*Stercorarius longicaudus*). At sea in Caribbean (November; April).

Skua (*Catharacta* sp.). Off Puerto Rico (Nov. 26), off Iles des Saintes (May 17; individual banded on Deception Island, South Shetlands) and Barbados (Nov. 2).

*Great Black-backed Gull (*Larus marinus*). San Salvador, Cuba, Hispaniola, Mona, Puerto Rico, St. Bartholomew and Barbados (October–March).

*Lesser Black-backed Gull (*Larus fuscus*). Puerto Rico and St. Martin (Nov. 8–April 20).

*Black-headed Gull (*Larus ridibundus*). Puerto Rico, Virgin Islands and Lesser Antilles (Nov. 27–April 20; June 9 record from Grenadines).

Franklin's Gull (*Larus pipixcan*). Puerto Rico and St. Bartholomew (January).

Black-legged Kittiwake (*Rissa tridactyla*). Andros, Cuba, off east coast of Jamaica (December–March).

Sabine's Gull (*Xema sabini*). Gibara Bay, Cuba (Dec. 1954).

Arctic Tern (*Sterna paradisaea*). Matanzas Bay, Cuba (June 20, 1950).

Large-billed Tern (*Phaetusa simplex*). Nipe Bay, Cuba (May 28, 1910).

White-winged Black Tern (*Chlidonias leucopterus*). Great Inagua (June 26) and Barbados (Oct. 24).

Dovekie (*Alle alle*). Grand Bahama and Cuba (Oct. 19–Dec. 21).

Passenger Pigeon (*Ectopistes migratorius*). Two old records from Cuba. Extinct.

European Cuckoo (*Cuculus canorus*). Barbados (Nov. 5, 1958).

Dark-headed Cuckoo (*Coccyzus melacoryphus*). Grenada (May 26, 1963).

Long-eared Owl (*Asio otus*). One record from Havana, Cuba.

Alpine Swift (*Apus melba*). Barbados (Sept. 22, 1955).

White-necked Jacobin (*Florisuga mellivora*). Tobago race recorded from Carriacou (Aug. 9, 1904).

Ruby-topaz Hummingbird (*Chrysolampis mosquitus*). Grenada (Sept. 8–9, 1962).

*Western Kingbird (*Tyrannus verticalis*). Northern Bahamas and Swan Island (Oct. 15–March 16).

Scissor-tailed Flycatcher (*Muscivora forficata*). Grand Bahama, San Salvador, western Cuba and Puerto Rico (Oct. 31–Dec. 13).

Eastern Phoebe (*Sayornis phoebe*). Grand Bahama, Bimini and Cuba (Sept. 11–February).

Yellow-bellied Flycatcher (*Empidonax flaviventris*). Western Cuba (Sept. 8–Oct. 4).

Traill's Flycatcher (*Empidonax traillii*). Western Cuba, Isle of Pines and Jamaica (Sept. 12–Oct. 7).

Least Flycatcher (*Empidonax minimus*). Grand Cayman (March 10).

Brown Thrasher (*Toxostoma rufum*). Grand Bahama, Harbour Island and western Cuba (Sept. 29–Nov. 28); "almost certainly seen" on New Providence (Jan. 8).

*Hermit Thrush (*Catharus guttatus*). Winter resident in northern Bahamas; recorded from Grand Bahama, New Providence, Eleuthera and Cat Island (Oct. 21–April 28).

Northern Wheatear (*Oenanthe oenanthe*). Santiago de Cuba (Oct. 16), Puerto Rico (2 reported seen, Sept. 22), and a December record from Barbados.

*Ruby-crowned Kinglet (*Regulus calendula*). Grand Bahama, Bimini, New Providence, Harbour Island, western Cuba and Jamaica (Oct. 18–March 13).

*American Pipit (*Anthus rubescens*). Grand Bahama, Andros, New Providence, Cat Island, San Salvador, Green Cay, Swan Island, Old Providence and St. Andrew (Oct.–March). Records of Sprague's Pipit (*Anthus spragueii*) are questionable.

Loggerhead Shrike (*Lanius ludovicianus*). Grand Bahama (Oct. 10), Great Exuma (Oct. 22) and Andros.

*Philadelphia Vireo (*Vireo philadelphicus*). New Providence, Eleuthera, Cuba and Jamaica (Oct. 6–Nov. 1; Feb. 1–27).

Warbling Vireo (*Vireo gilvus*). Cuba (Sept. 22) and Jamaica (Oct. 8).

*Orange-crowned Warbler (*Vermivora celata*). Grand Bahama, Andros, New Providence, Eleuthera, Harbour Island and San Salvador (Oct. 14–Jan. 2).

*Nashville Warbler (*Vermivora ruficapilla*). Bahamas and Greater Antilles (Sept. 11–April 14).

Mourning Warbler (*Oporornis philadelphia*). New Providence, Puerto Rico and Vieques (Sept. 23–December; March 21).

*Yellow-breasted Chat (*Icteria virens*). Grand Bahama, Abaco, Bimini, Andros, Cuba and Grand Cayman (Aug. 16–May 5).

*Wilson's Warbler (*Wilsonia pusilla*). Grand Bahama, New Providence, Cuba, Jamaica, Puerto Rico (Sept. 7–April 11).

*Canada Warbler (*Wilsonia canadensis*). Bahama Islands, Cuba, Jamaica, Puerto Rico, St. Thomas, St. Croix and Guadeloupe (Sept. 2–Oct. 27; Feb. 17–April 3).

Western Tanager (*Piranga ludoviciana*). New Providence (Sept. 11, 26) and Cuba (Jan. 2).

Yellow-headed Blackbird (*Xanthocephalus xanthocephalus*). Grand Bahama, San Salvador, Cuba and Barbados (autumn).

Brown-headed Cowbird (*Molothrus ater*). New Providence, Great Inagua and Cuba (Aug. 16–Feb. 12).

American Goldfinch (*Carduelis tristis*). Grand Bahama, Abaco, Bimini and Cuba (mid-October–Jan. 1; April).

Vesper Sparrow (*Pooecetes gramineus*). Grand Bahama (Aug. 12–late Dec.).

*Lark Sparrow (*Chondestes grammacus*). Northern Bahama Islands and Cuba (Aug. 12–March 25).

Green-tailed Towhee (*Chlorura chlorura*). Casilda, Cuba (Jan. 8).

Slate-coloured Junco (*Junco hyemalis*). Grand Bahama, New Providence, Jamaica (Nov. 8–April 17); one carried by ship to St. Thomas.

*Chipping Sparrow (*Spizella passerina*). Grand Bahama, Abaco, New Providence and Cuba (Oct. 28–April 14).

*Clay-coloured Sparrow (*Spizella pallida*). Grand Bahama, New Providence and Cuba (Oct. 15–Feb. 13).

*White-crowned Sparrow (*Zonotrichia leucophrys*). Bahama Islands, Cuba and Jamaica (Oct. 4–April 25).

*Lincoln's Sparrow (*Zonotrichia lincolnii*). Bahamas, Cuba, Jamaica, Hispaniola and Puerto Rico (Oct. 22–April 20).

Swamp Sparrow (*Zonotrichia georgiana*). New Providence (Nov. 10, 18) and Mayaguana (April 10).

Snow Bunting (*Plectrophenax nivalis*). Cat Island (Dec. 1).

Note. The Black or Lesser Noddy (*Anous tenuirostris*) is still unknown from the West Indies, although it breeds on islands of the southern and western Caribbean and has occurred in summer on the Dry Tortugas, outermost of the Florida Keys, since 1962.

Index

THE WEST INDIES

*Area enclosed by dotted line comprises
the West Indies as a faunal region*

Scale of Miles

0 50 100   200   300   400

25°

20°

15°

10°

70°

60°

dor I.
ng)

Mayaguana I.

Caicos Is.

Turks Is.

reat Inagua

Tortue I.

ANTILLES

HAITI

DOMINICAN
REPUBLIC

au
ince

Santo Domingo

Mona

HISPANIOLA

SEA

Aruba

Curaçao

Bonaire

St. Thomas

San Juan

PUERTO
RICO

St Croix

Anegada

Anguilla

St Martin I.

St Bartholomew

Saba

St Eustatius

St Christopher
(St Kitts)

Nevis

Barbuda

Antigua

Montserrat

Désirade

Guadeloupe

Marie Galante

LESSER
ANTILLES

Dominica

Martinique

St Lucia

Barbados

St Vincent

Grenadines

Grenada I.

Carriacou

Isla
Margarita

Tobago

Trinidad

VENEZUELA

70°

60°